S0-CXV-913

Foundations of Music

A STEP-BY-STEP APPROACH TO MUSIC THEORY

Fourth Edition

Victor J. Soto
Mountain View College

2014

Soto, Victor.
Foundations of Music: A Step-by-Step Approach to Music Theory
Fourth Edition

Published by VJS eLearning Designs, LLC.
P.O. BOX 1922
Frisco, TX 75034
http://www.elearningdesigns.com

ISBN-10: 0692210911
ISBN-13: 978-0-692-21091-8

Printed in the United States of America

CONTENTS

PREFACE

TO THE STUDENT

Foundations of Music is an intensive course in the fundamentals of music. You may have purchased this textbook as part of a music theory course, to work on your own in preparation for college music theory, or perhaps to brush up your skills after a numbers of years away from musical study.

As you begin to think about how music is structured, you should consider one very important aspect of your musical education: music theory. Your understanding of music theory is an essential element in your training, whether you specialize as a performing artist, a music technician, a music teacher, a music composer or in any other music-related field. Whatever your interest, a grasp of the fundamental concepts as they relate to harmony, melody, rhythm, form and structure is necessary.

This textbook has been designed to help you prepare for a successful experience in college as music major or minor. It is a self-help tool for learning the fundamentals of music formatted as an interactive course that requires a great bit of reading and reasoning. The chapters are presented in a logical sequence to ensure a significant progress toward the following goals:

1. Be able to write, identify and recognize musical notation symbols of traditional western music.
2. Learn to read and/or improve your skills in music reading.
3. Gain an understanding of the language used by musicians to describe and perform musical scores.
4. Be able to recognize and notate pitch, write major and minor scales and write and identify the quality of triads.
5. Determine the key of a melody, identify chords in the context of a key and be familiar with major and minor keys.

TO THE INSTRUCTOR

Foundations of Music is intended for advanced high school or college students or adult learners taking courses such as "Fundamentals of Music," "Intro to Music Theory," "Music Theory 101," "Foundations of Music," Elements of Music," or "Basics of Music." It begins at the very beginning, assuming no previous experience with musical notation or music theory. It starts with an introduction to the piano keyboard followed by notating pitch and rhythm, scales, intervals, triads, and seventh chords. It leaves off where courses in basic harmony usually begin.

FOUNDATIONS OF MUSIC is also intended to serve a variety of learning models:

- The traditional face-to-face Fundamentals of Music course, which may include non music majors who are interested in better understanding the music they hear and perform in daily life.
- The distance learning (online or hybrid) course, where the student may be required to work independently and rely on the instructor only for occasional questions.
- The prospective music student wishing to prepare for freshman placement exams, perhaps during the spring or summer semester prior to enrollment in a music theory course.

ORGANIZATION

This textbook is organized as a series of lessons focusing on specific steps in the learning process. This are some distinguishing features of the lessons:

- Early lessons are oriented around the piano keyboard.
- Each lesson includes a list of study questions, practice exercises and self-tests designed to reinforce concepts from that lesson and build on previous lessons and exercises.
- In addition to lessons in pitch notation and tonal materials, the book includes two lessons in various aspects of rhythm and meter, which are accompanied by performance exercises for practicing rhythm reading.
- Throughout the each lesson, important concepts are highlighted in bold and defined in the Glossary section of the book.
- Some of these terms, plus other common musical symbols and markings, are also summarized within the eight appendixes of this book.

NEW TO THIS EDITION

All chapters have been carefully reviewed and revised, and many new examples have been added. In comparison to earlier editions, this new fourth edition contains more rhythm drills, enhanced graphics, extra chapters, and eight new appendixes.

CHAPTER 1

PROPERTIES OF SOUND AND MUSIC NOTATION

Lesson 1: Music Notation and Musical Alphabet

Our world is filled with sounds. Through them we learn what is happening around us; we need them to communicate with each other. We may perceive sounds as pleasant or unpleasant to our ear, such as the honks of traffic, the bark of a dog or the sound of a musical instrument or an orchestra. Musical instruments are designed to produce certain sounds that composers use to create musical compositions, but in order to understand how music is created we first need to answer the following questions: what is sound, what causes it, and how do we hear it?

Sound is audible through waves-- transmissions of energy by a series of vibrations. In other words, sound is produced with the vibration of an object, such as a table that is pounded or a string that is plucked. **Vibration** is the recurrent motion of a substance. Whenever you play an instrument, parts of the instrument and the air inside and around the instrument vibrate.

Sound

Vibration

These series of vibrations are transmitted to our ears by a medium which is usually air. When our eardrums perceive these vibrations they start vibrating and signals are transmitted to our brain. There these signals are selected, organized and interpreted. **Music**, then, is an art based on the organization of sounds in time. Therefore, we can identify music from other sounds by recognizing the four properties of sound: pitch, dynamics, timbre (tone color), and duration.

Music

Pitch indicates how high or low the sound is perceived. It is determined by the frequency of the sound wave per second or cycle per second. **Dynamics** indicates the volume of the sound (how loud or soft a sound is). It is also expressed as sound intensity or amplitude. In music we have different symbols to express the intensity values, from very soft or extremely loud. The most commonly used symbols will be explained in chapter three. **Timbre** or **tone color** refers to the tone quality of a sound and is the property that helps us distinguish between different instruments or sound sources. The

Pitch
Dynamics
Timbre

Duration

timbre of a sound can be bright, mellow, dark, etc. **Duration** is the property of sound that describes the temporal aspect of music. The time elements in music include concepts such as how long a piece or musical phrase may last, the length of time a pitch may be sustained or how much time elapses between sounds. It may also refer to rhythm or the patterns of sounds as they are related to a time frame.

MUSIC NOTATION

Music Notation

Over the course of hundreds of years a system of symbols has developed so that we can share and remember music by writing it down. **Music notation,** then, is the visual representation of music. The system is imperfect and in constant change ("contemporary" music utilizes symbols which are not presented here). However, it is a system of notation which is used to represent a large body of literature and so should be understood fully.

Staff

A **staff** is used in music to indicate the precise pitch desired. It is a system that consists of five lines and four spaces which are numbered from low to high to aid in showing the particular location of each pitch.

Music is written on a five-line **staff**: five parallel lines separated by four spaces.

Five-line staff 1 2 3 4 5 1 2 3 4

Notes Noteheads

We indicate exact pitches by the upward or downward placement of symbols-- called **notes** – on a staff. A note is a symbol that indicates duration by color, black or white, or has a stem and flags, as will be explained later. As a first step on writing pitches, ovals shape called notes or **noteheads** are drawn on the lines or in the spaces of the staff. High pitches are notated toward the top of the staff, lower pitches toward the bottom.

Open Noteheads in a space | Filled-in noteheads on a line

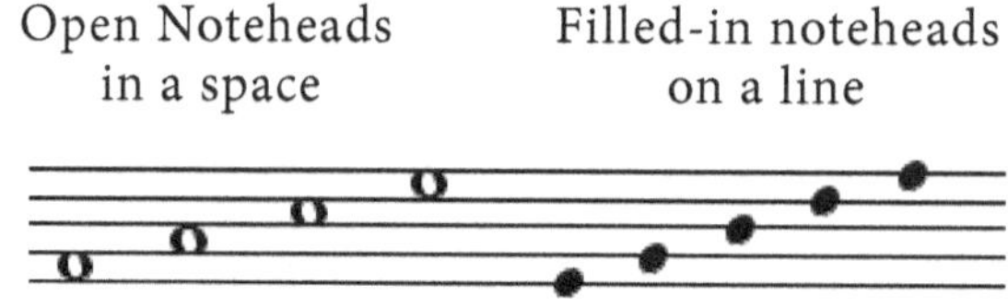

Noteheads on a staff

Activity #1:

Write seven filled-in noteheads on the lines and spaces of this staff.

Write seven open noteheads on the lines and spaces of this staff.

MUSICAL ALPHABET: LETTER NAMES

Seven of the twelve pitches (tones) found in Western music are named after the first seven letters of the alphabet: A, B, C, D, E, F and G. This sequence is repeated over and over as the tones successively ascend or descend.

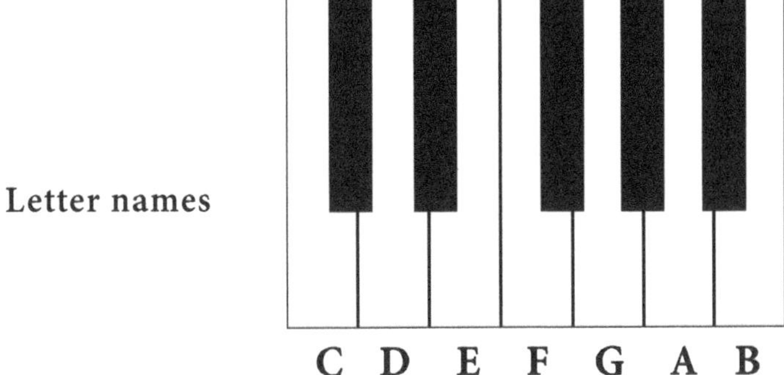

The lower the note on the staff, the lower the pitch of the note; therefore, the higher the note on the staff, the higher the pitch of the note. The position of each note on the staff corresponds to a letter name which corresponds to a white key of the piano. Because different instruments produce higher or lower ranges of pitch, the staff can be made to represent different ranges of pitch by the use of a clef sign.

In this seven-name system, each letter name reappears every eighth position (eight above or below D is another D).

Activity #2:

Find the letter name requested.

a. 7	**above**	**D:**	**C**		h. 8	above	C:	______
b. 5	above	A:	______		i. 4	below	B:	______
c. 3	below	B:	______		j. 3	above	F:	______
d. 2	below	E:	______		k. 2	above	G:	______
e. 4	above	C:	______		l. 4	below	C:	______
f. 6	below	G:	______		m. 6	below	F:	______
g. 7	above	F:	______		n. 5	below	A:	______

LESSON 2: THE PIANO KEYBOARD

When you first begin to learn the fundamentals of music theory, it is highly recommended to learn your way around the keyboard. The keyboard will be one of your best guidance tools to both hear and see concepts of musical sound such as intervals, scales, and chords. These concepts will be learned later in this book and even though it is possible to learn these concepts with other instruments such as the fingerboard or the guitar, it is far easiest to work with these concepts at the keyboard.

Although, there are many keyboard instruments that you can use, the most common are the organ, the digital piano, the electronic keyboard, and the standard acoustic piano. For the purpose of learning the keyboard an acoustic or digital piano will do equally well. A standard piano keyboard has 88 keys: 52 white ones and 36 black ones. Moving from right to left on all keyboards produces successively lower pitches, while moving from left to right the keyboard will produce successively higher pitches.

This section will help you begin to understand the keyboard. It is important for you to master the keyboard because future chapters of this book will frequently refer to the keyboard when clarifying certain concepts. The following are different exercises that will help you become familiar with the keyboard geography and pitch recognition.

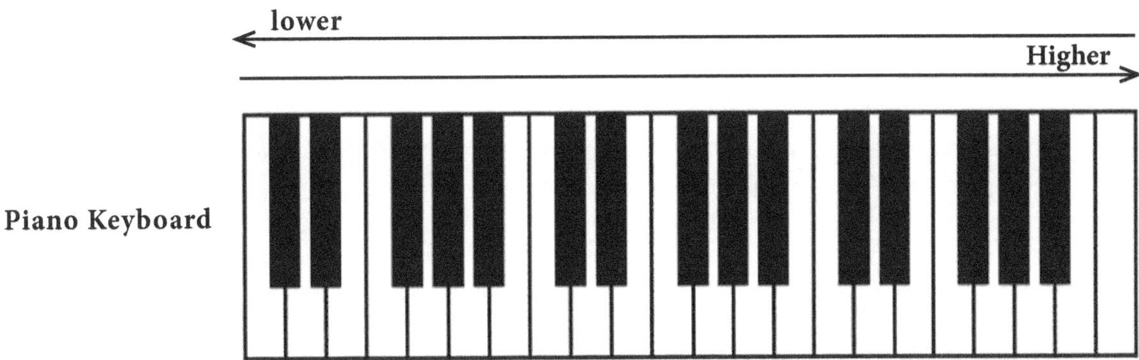

As mentioned above a standard piano keyboard has 88 keys: 52 white ones and 36 black ones. Therefore, we can say that the keyboard is divided into two sections one with white keys and the other with black keys. The function of these two sections is to represent all of the twelve tones found in our western music system.

As explained earlier, only the first seven letters of the alphabet are used to represent pitches. These seven letters name the white keys of the keyboard, beginning at the left end of the keyboard with A and successively repeating the sequences A through G up to the other end of the keyboard.

Complete representation of the piano keyboard (88 keys)

A Middle C C

Memorizing the keyboard is easier when you locate and remember certain patterns. Let's start with middle C. In the following figure, notice that the highlighted note is called middle C because is the one approximately in the middle of the keyboard. You can find any C notes on the keyboard because it always occurs immediately to the left of a group of two black keys. *(For more information about the piano keyboard see* ***APPENDIX*** *H)*

THE WHITE KEYS

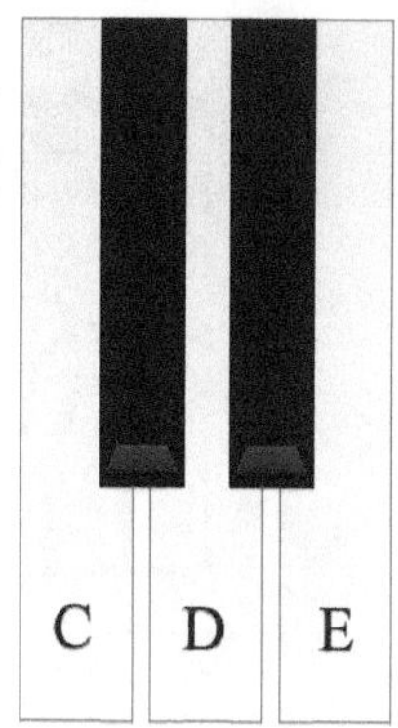

From this example, we can realize that immediately to the left of a group of two black keys there is a **C** pitch.

However, the following note immediately to the right of this group of black note there is an **E** pitch.

The note in the middle of the two black keys is a **D**.

If we take the group of three black keys we find out that immediately to the left of the group we find the **F** pitch and immediately to the right of this group is **B**.

The two notes in between **F** and **B** are **A** and **G**.

Remember, the alphabetical sequence runs from left to right.

After you have memorized the location of each pitch within the group of two and three black keys you must test yourself by putting together the two major groups as shown in the figure below.

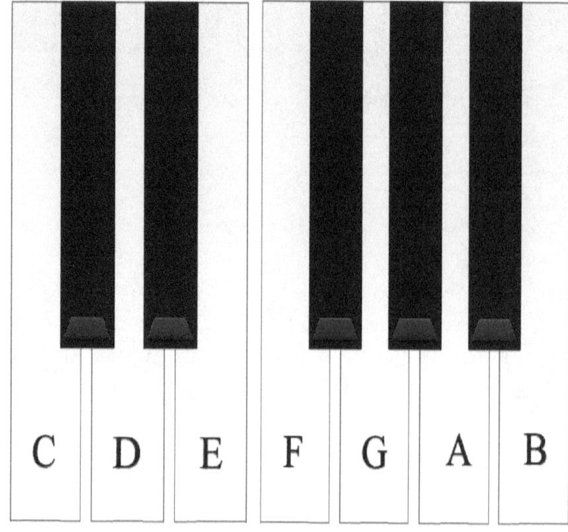

The Black Keys

The black keys of the piano are named in relation to the white keys that stand between them. If this is the case then each black key will be identified by two different names. For instance, the black key between D and E is called either D sharp (D#) or E flat (Eb). At first, it may be confusing that one black key can have two names, but once you understand the pattern it will make sense.

It is important to remember that each of the white keys has its own letter name from A through G while the black keys is related to, and takes its name from the white key on either side of it. In order to understand how the names of the black keys are assigned we must study the keyboard's musical distances and how they relate with certain symbols called accidental.

In playing the piano , it is customary to refer to your fingers by number, the thumb is the first finger; the index is the second finger, and so on.

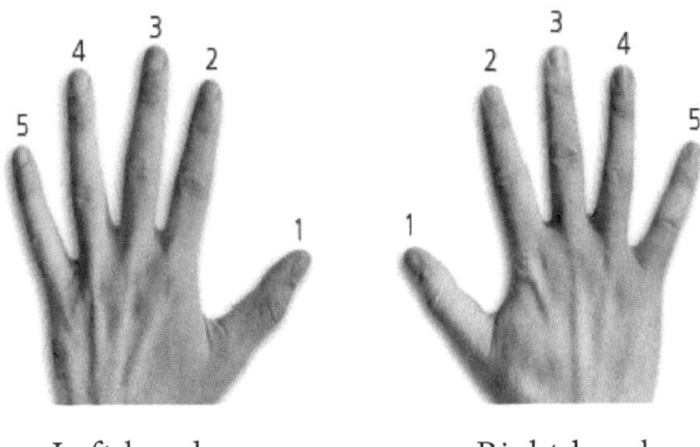

Left hand Right hand

Name:____________________

Date:__________________

Lesson 2: Practice Exercises

I. Locate and write each given pitch on the keyboard. When you have written all the pitches, practice finding and playing them on the piano.

1. C, D, G, E, A

2. F, B, G, C, E

3. B, D, F, A, G

II. Identify the name of the marked keys on the keyboard.

1.

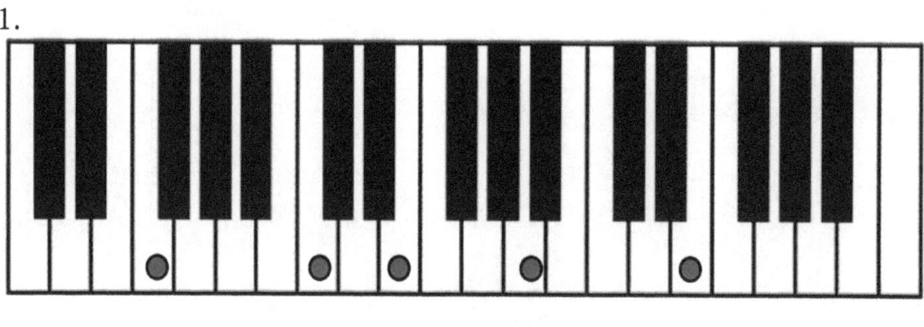

2.

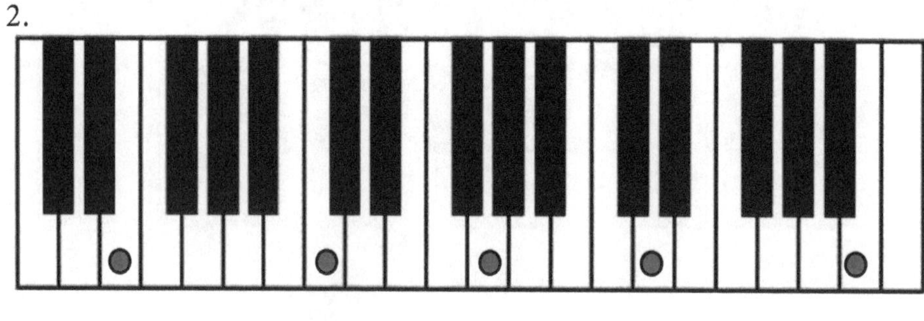

3.

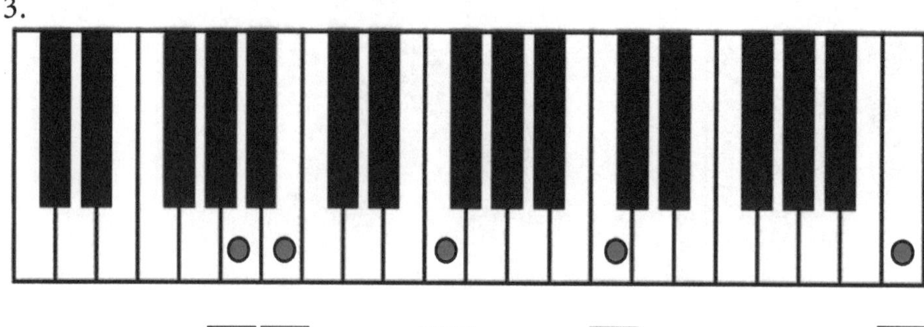

Lesson 3: Treble Clef

Clef

A **clef** must appear at the beginning of the staff in order to indicate which pitches are to be associated with which lines and spaces. The two most common clefs are the treble clef, used for relatively high pitches (such as those played by a pianist's right hand), and the bass clef, used for relatively low pitches (played by the pianist's left hand).

Treble clef or "G" clef

The **treble clef** is also called the **G clef** because the inner curve of the clef symbol marks the horizontal line associated with the note G above middle C. The treble clef is actually a stylized letter G.

Practice drawing the treble clef sign by tracing over the guidelines. Draw five more in the remaining space.

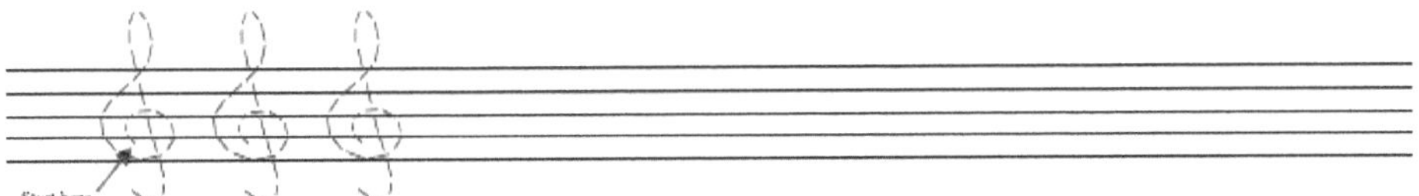

As soon as possible, memorize the note names for each line and space. Learn the "line notes" together and the "space note" together, as shown in the example below. To remember note names of the lines (**E G B D F**), you might make up a sentence whose words begin with these letters, like "**Every Good Bird Does Fly.**" The spaces simply spell the word **F A C E**.

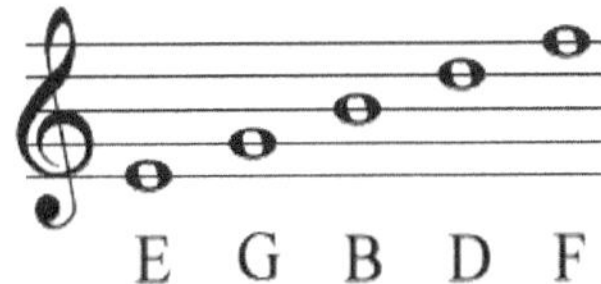

Treble clef lines

F A C E

Treble clef spaces

Activity #3:

Write the letter name of each pitch in the blanks below.

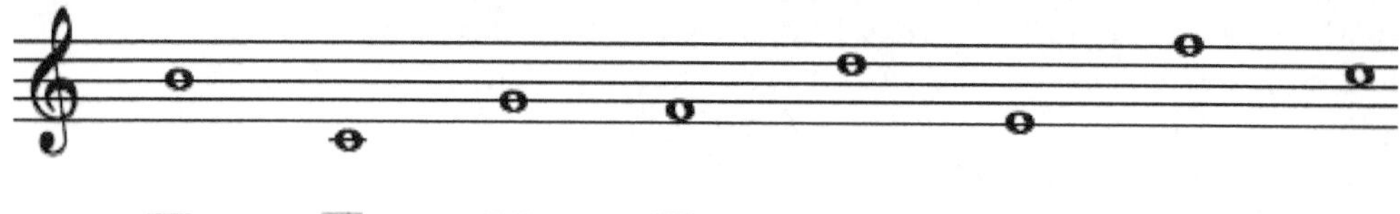

Draw a treble clef at the beginning of the staff and write the letter name of each note.

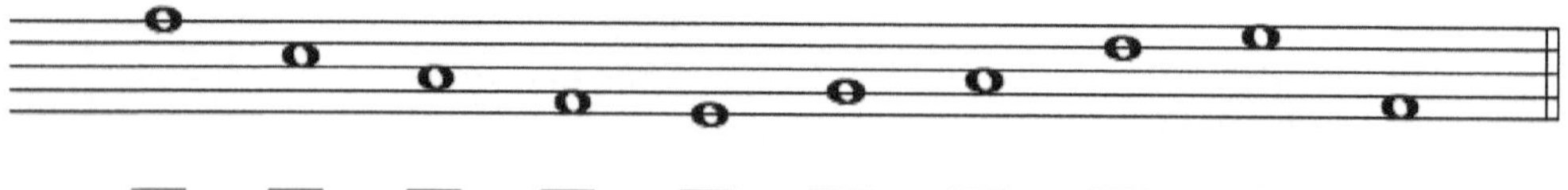

When notes extend beyond the range of the staff, ledger lines are employed. A **ledger line** is a small line which is added above or below the staff, and is only long enough to write one note upon, below or above. The lines and spaces are named in the same way as those on the staff itself. The first ledger line below the treble staff is middle C on the piano. Ledger lines, which parallel the staff, accommodate only one note.

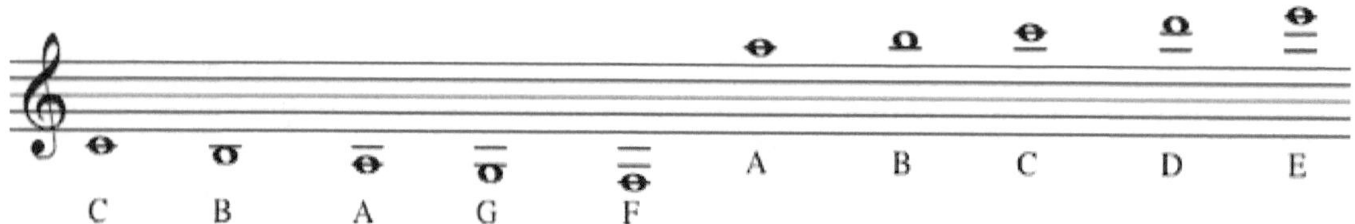

Treble Clef Ledger Lines

Name:____________________

Date:__________________

Lesson 3: Practice Exercises

Practice writing your treble clef symbol on this staff. Write at least eight clef symbols.

Write the letter names of the treble clef lines and spaces in this staff:

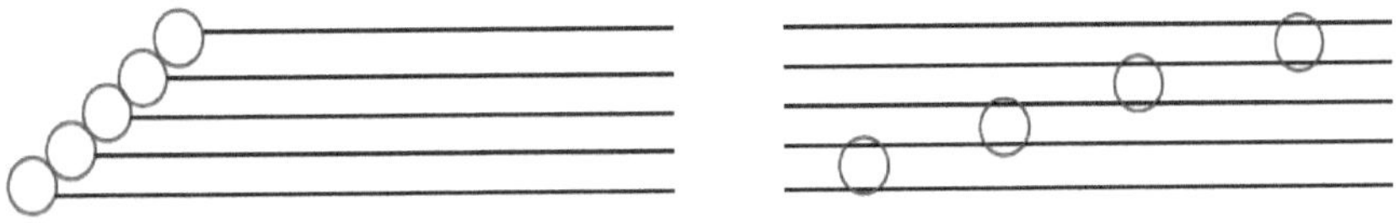

Write the clef and letter names of the three ledger lines below and the three ledger lines above your treble clef staff.

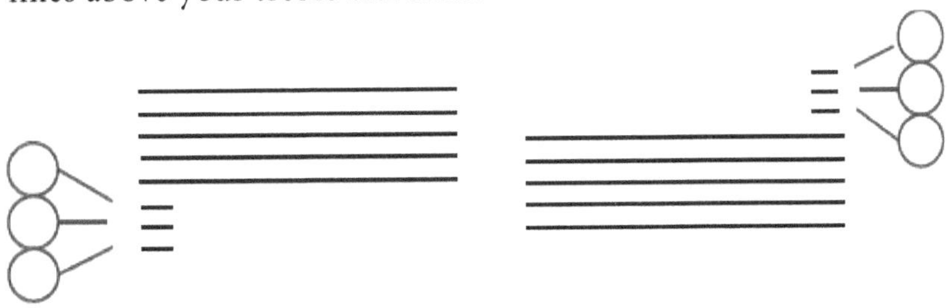

Draw the treble clef at the beginning of the staff and the draw the notes indicated. If a note can be drawn in more than one place on the staff, choose which one you want to draw.

A C E F D B A F D G

Draw the treble clef at the beginning of the staff. Write the letter name for each note.

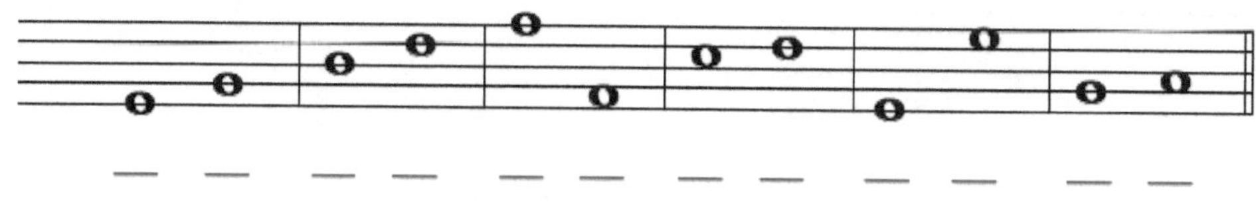

Draw a treble clef at the beginning of the staff and write the letter name of each note.

Lesson 4: Bass Clef

Bass clef or "F" clef

The **bass clef** is also called the F clef because the two dots in the clef symbol lie above and below the horizontal line associated with the note F below middle C. The bass clef symbol is actually a stylized letter F in which the two horizontal lines of the letter have been reduced to two dots.

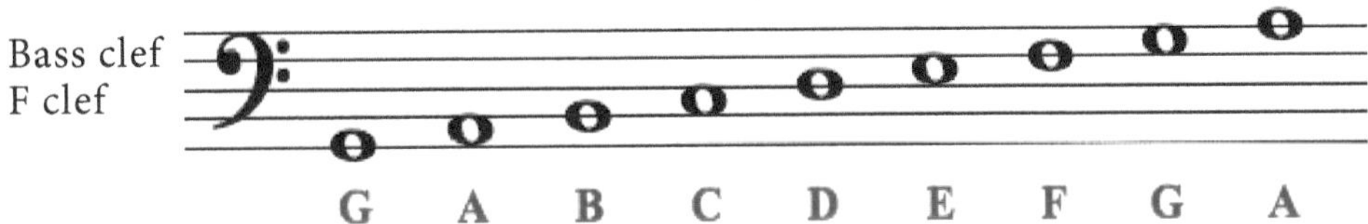

Practice drawing the treble clef sign by tracing over the guidelines. Draw five more in the remaining space.

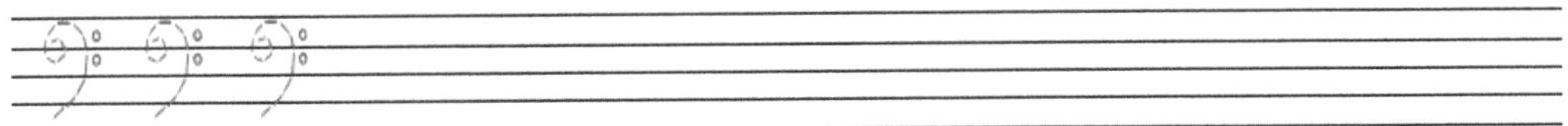

The bass clef also represents the lower notes on the keyboard. Other pitches may be counted from F, or memorized according to their position on the staff,. two was to remember the bass-clef spaces (A C E G) are "All Cows Eat Grass." The bass-clef lines (G B D F A) might be "Great Big Doves Fly Away."

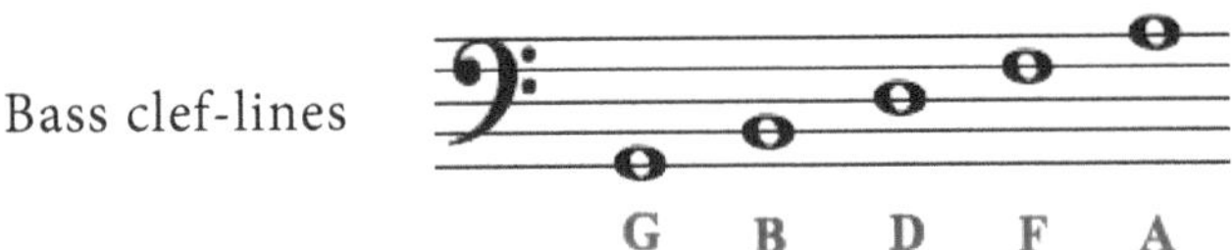

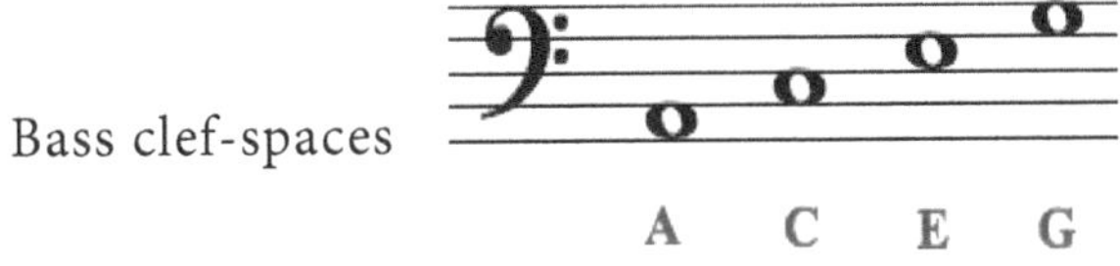

Activity #4:

Draw a bass clef and write the letter name of each pitch in the blanks below.

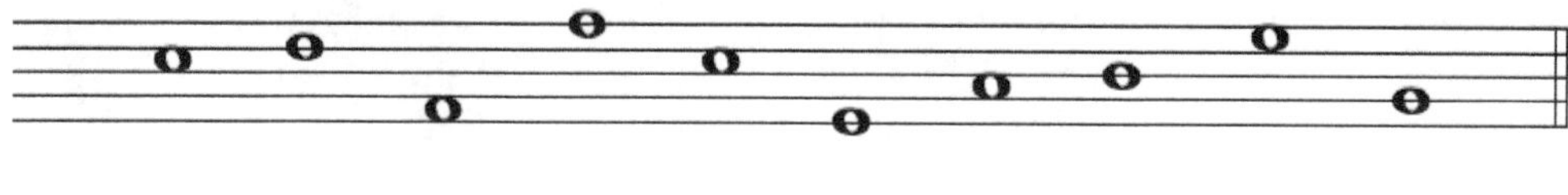

Draw a bass clef at the beginning of the staff and write the letter name of each note.

As well as in the treble clef when notes extend beyond the range of the staff, ledger lines are employed. The lines and spaces are named in the same way as those on the staff itself. The first ledger line below the bass staff is middle E on the piano. Ledger lines, which parallel the staff, accommodate only one note.

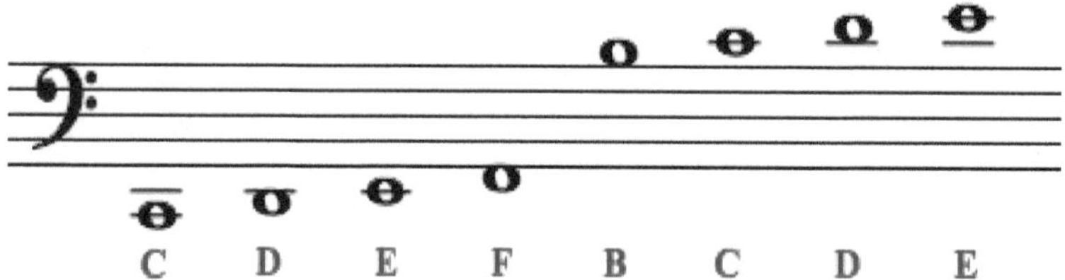

Name:____________________

Date:___________________

Lesson 4: Practice Exercises

Practice writing your bass clef symbol on this staff. Write at least eight clef symbols.

Write the letter names of the bass clef lines and spaces in this staff:

Write the clef and letter names of the three ledger lines below and the three ledger lines above your treble clef staff.

Draw the treble clef at the beginning of the staff and the draw the notes indicated. If a note can be drawn in more than one place on the staff, choose which one you want to draw.

C A E D F G B C D G

Draw a bass clef at the beginning of the staff. Write the letter name for each note.

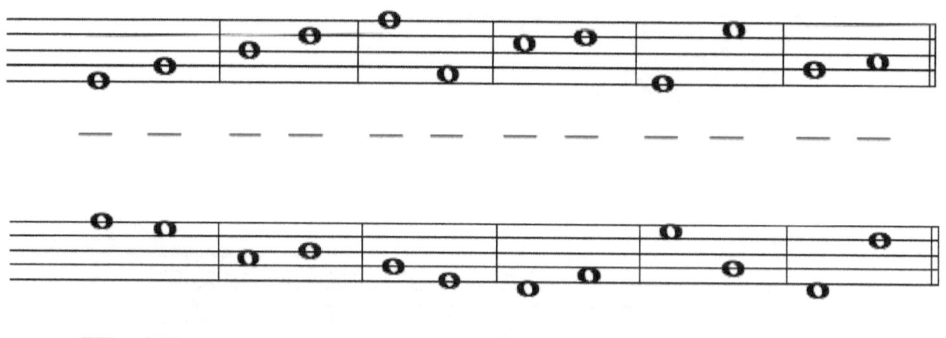

Draw a bass clef at the beginning of the staff and write the letter name of each note.

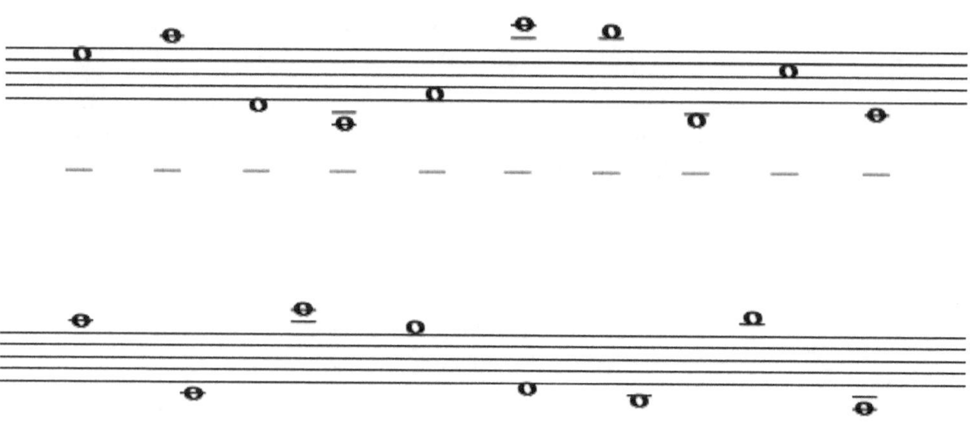

LESSON 5: THE GRAND STAFF, ACCIDENTALS, HALF AND WHOLE STEPS

Grand Staff

When the treble and bass clefs are joined together with a brace, consisting of a straight line and a curved line, the two clefs are called the **grand staff**. Keyboard music is written on a grand staff; this allows both the highest and the lowest pitches to be seen and played together.

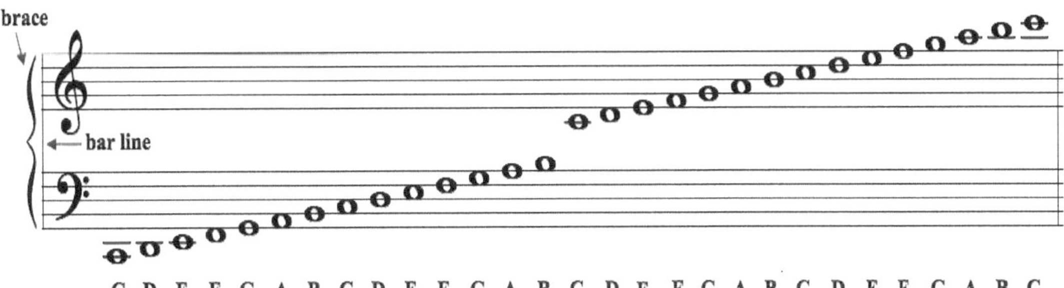

The Grand Staff

Middle C

The note located between the two clefs is called middle C; as it belongs to neither clef, it is drawn with a short line of its own. The figure below shows the relationship between the grand staff, the standard piano keyboard, and **middle C.**

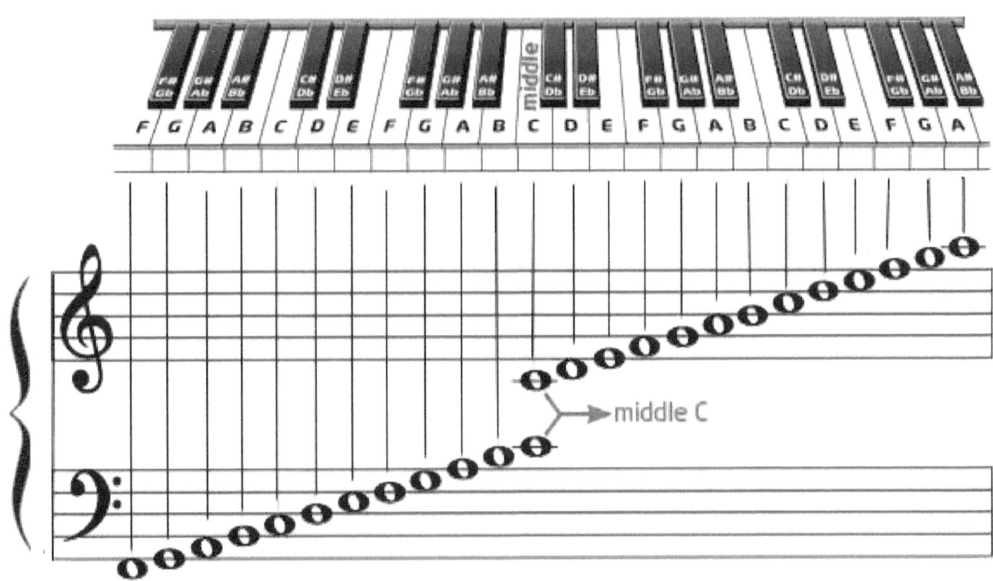

Accidentals

Accidental

Accidental are symbols that are placed to the left of the note to indicate the raising or lowering of a pitch.

Accidental Symbols

Sharp ♯ raises the pitch a half step.

Flat ♭ lowers the pitch a half step.

Natural ♮ cancels any previous sharp or flat and returns to the natural, or unaltered pitch.

Double Sharp 𝄪 raises the pitch a whole step

Double Flat 𝄫 lowers the pitch a whole step.

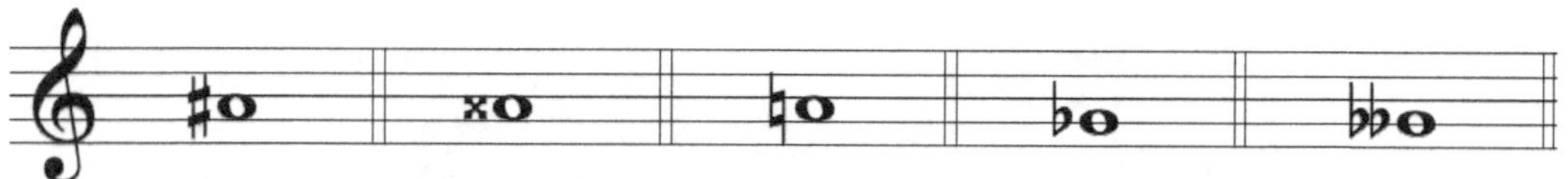

Accidentals are always written to the left of a note symbol

In most cases, a sharp raises the pitch of a note one semitone while a flat lowers it a half step. A natural is used to cancel the effect of a flat or sharp, whether from a key signature or a previous accidental.

Since about 1700, accidentals have been understood to continue for the remainder of the measure in which they occur, so that a subsequent note on the same staff position is still affected by that accidental, unless replaced by an accidental of its own. Notes on other staff positions, including those an octave away, are unaffected. Once a bar line is passed, the effect of the accidental ends, except when a note affected by an accidental (either explicit or implied from earlier in the measure) is tied to the same note across a bar line. Though this tradition is still in use particularly in tonal music, it may be cumbersome in music that features frequent accidentals, as is often the case in non-tonal

music. As a result, an alternate system of note-for-note accidentals has been adopted with the aim of reducing the number of accidentals required to notate a measure.
The system is as follows:

1. Accidentals affect only those notes which they immediately precede.

2. Accidentals are not repeated on tied notes unless the tie goes from line to line or page to page.

3. Accidentals are not repeated for repeated notes unless one or more different pitches (or rests) intervene.

4. If a sharp or flat pitch is followed directly by its natural form, a natural is used.

5. Cautionary accidentals or naturals (in parentheses) may be used to clarify ambiguities, but should be held to a minimum.

Because seven of the twelve notes of the chromatic equal-tempered scale are naturals, this system can significantly reduce the number of naturals required in a notated passage. Note that in a few cases the accidental might change the note by more than a semitone: for example, if a G sharp is followed in the same measure by a G flat, the flat sign on the latter note means it will be two semitones lower than if no accidental were present. Thus, the effect of the accidental has to be understood in relation to the "natural" meaning of the note's staff position.

Double accidentals raise or lower the pitch of a note a whole step. An F with a double sharp applied raises it a whole step so it is enharmonically equivalent to a G. Usage varies on how to notate the situation in which a note with a double sharp is followed in the same measure by a note with a single sharp: some publications simply use the single accidental for the latter note, whereas others use a combination of a natural and a sharp, with the natural understood to apply to only the second sharp.

Activity #5:

In a flat sign, the vertical line is about two spaces long. The curved portion extends to the right and is aligned horizontally with the note it modifies.

Write flats in front of these notes.

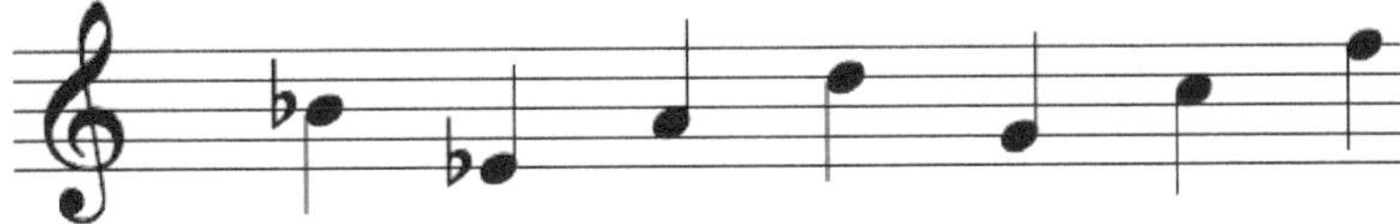

In a sharp sign, the two vertical lines are about three spaces long and the two horizontal lines are angled slightly upward. Like the flat sign, the sharp sign is aligned with the note it modifies.

Write sharps in front of these notes.

In the natural sign, the vertical lines are about two spaces long and the two horizontal lines angled slightly upward. Like all accidentas, the natural sign is aligned with the note it modifies.

Write natural signs in front of these notes.

Half Steps and Whole Steps

Half step

In the equal temperament tuning system the octave is divided exactly in twelve notes. The distance between each note is known as a **half step**. Half steps are either diatonic or chromatic. A diatonic half step consists of two pitches with adjacent letter names and staff locations. A chromatic half step employs two pitches of the same name and staff locations. On the keyboard any key is at the distance of a half step from the next and previous key:

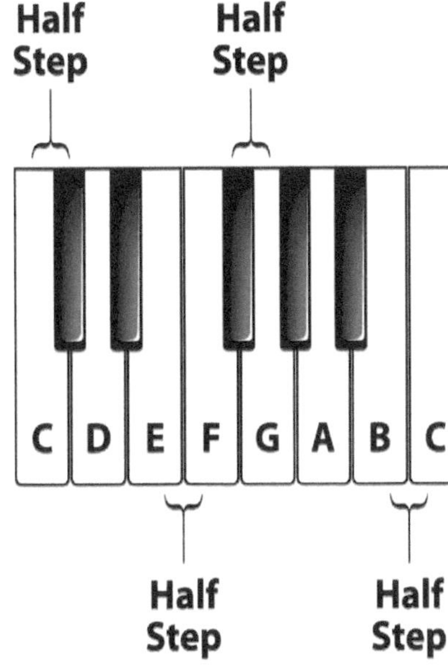

Whole step

A **whole step** contains two half steps. All the white keys on the keyboard separated by a black key are at a distance of a whole step. The keys that are not separated by a black key are at a distance of a half step:

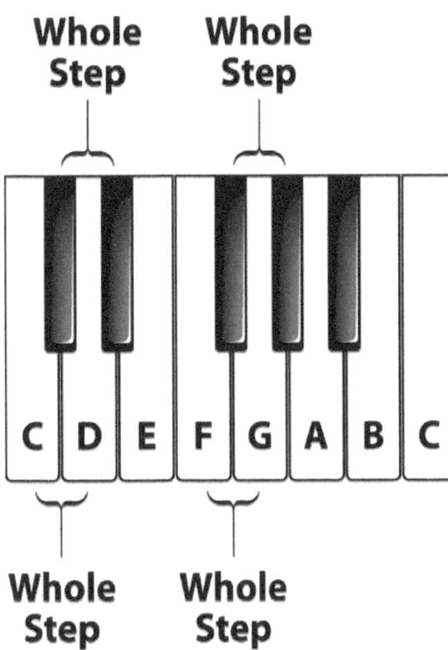

Notes corresponding to the white keys on the keyboard are called C, D, E, F, G, A and B. These notes are considered natural notes. They can be raised a half step with a sharp or lowered with a flat. A black key, for example the one between C and D, can be considered a C sharp or a D flat:

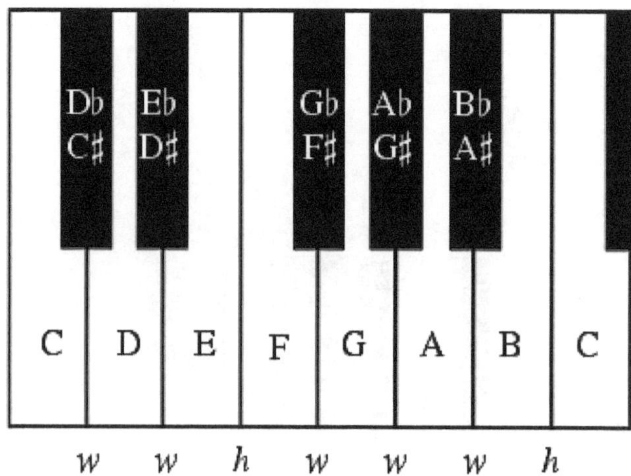

Activity #6:

Complete the following exercises.

1. Draw the indicated notes. Use half notes.

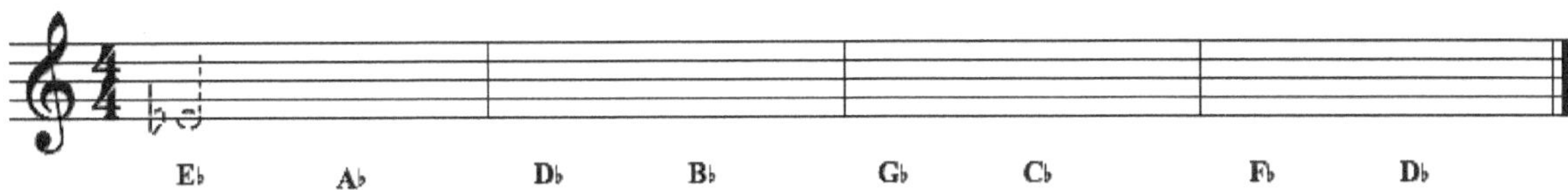

2. Draw the indicated notes. Use half notes.

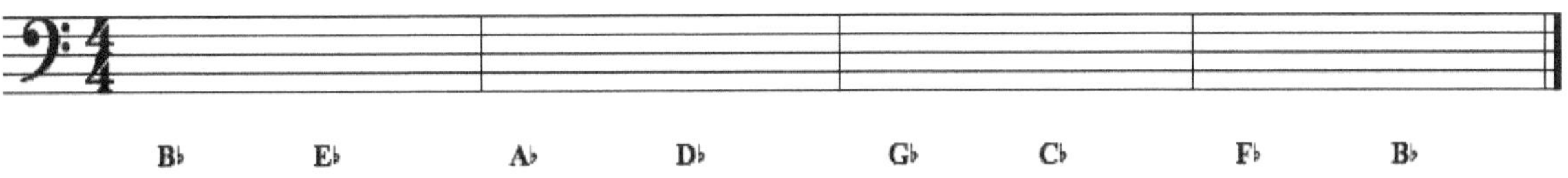

3. Draw the indicated notes. Use half notes.

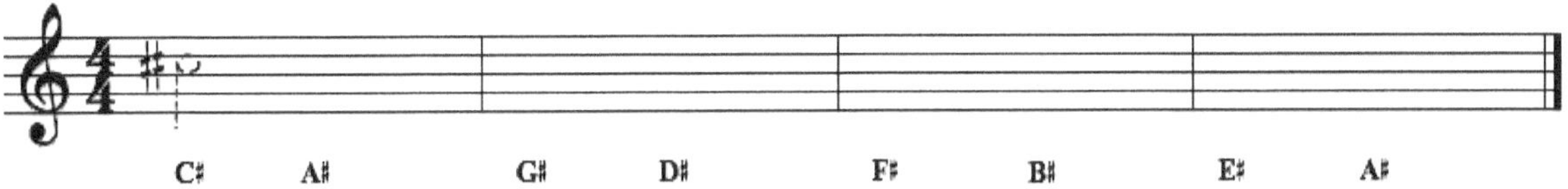

4. Draw the indicated notes. Use half notes.

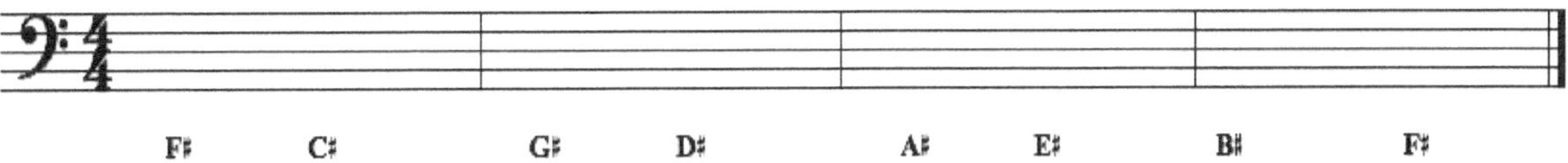

5. Name each note.

6. Name each note.

STUDY QUESTIONS FOR CHAPTER 1

1. Define the following terms:

   Treble clef

   Grand Staff

   Ledger Line

   Staff

   Whole Step

   Bass Clef

   G Clef

   Half Step

2. What are the names of the lines and spaces in treble and bass clefs?
3. Which note is in the center of the 88 keys of a piano?
4. What is an accidental?

Name:____________________ Date: ___________

Chapter 1: Self-Test

Identify these notes in the treble clef.

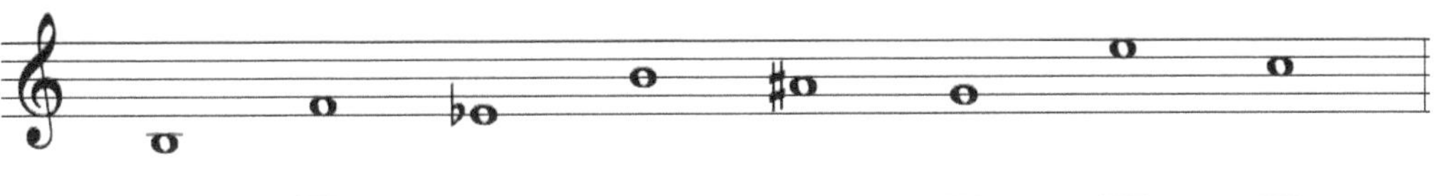

Write these notes in the treble clef:
(There will be more than one correct answer)

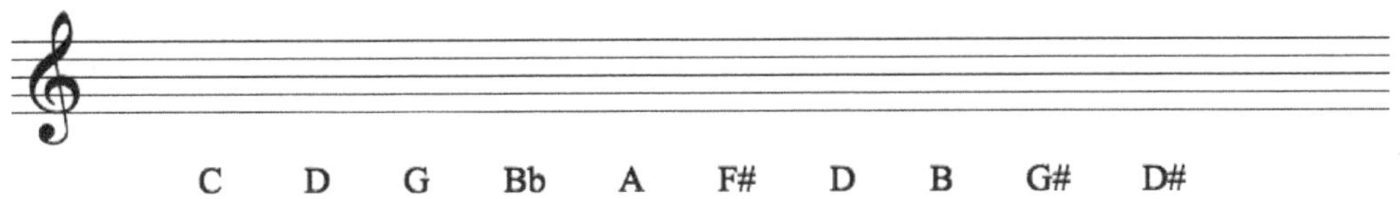

Identify these notes in the bass clef.

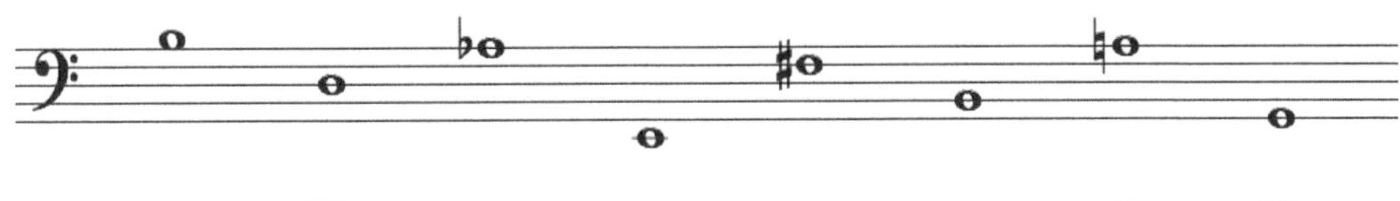

Write these notes in the bass clef:
(There will be more than one correct answer)

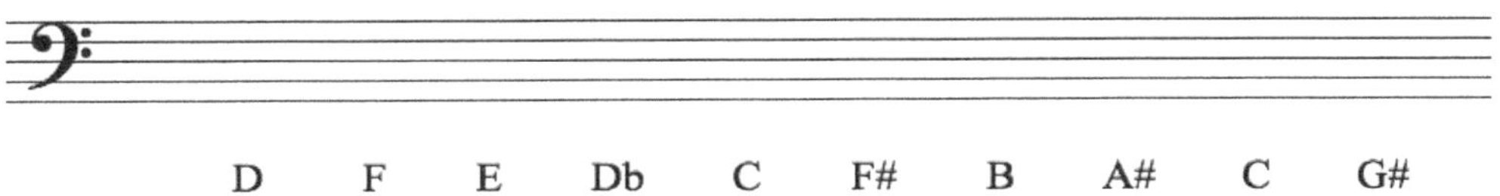

Write the letter name for each note.

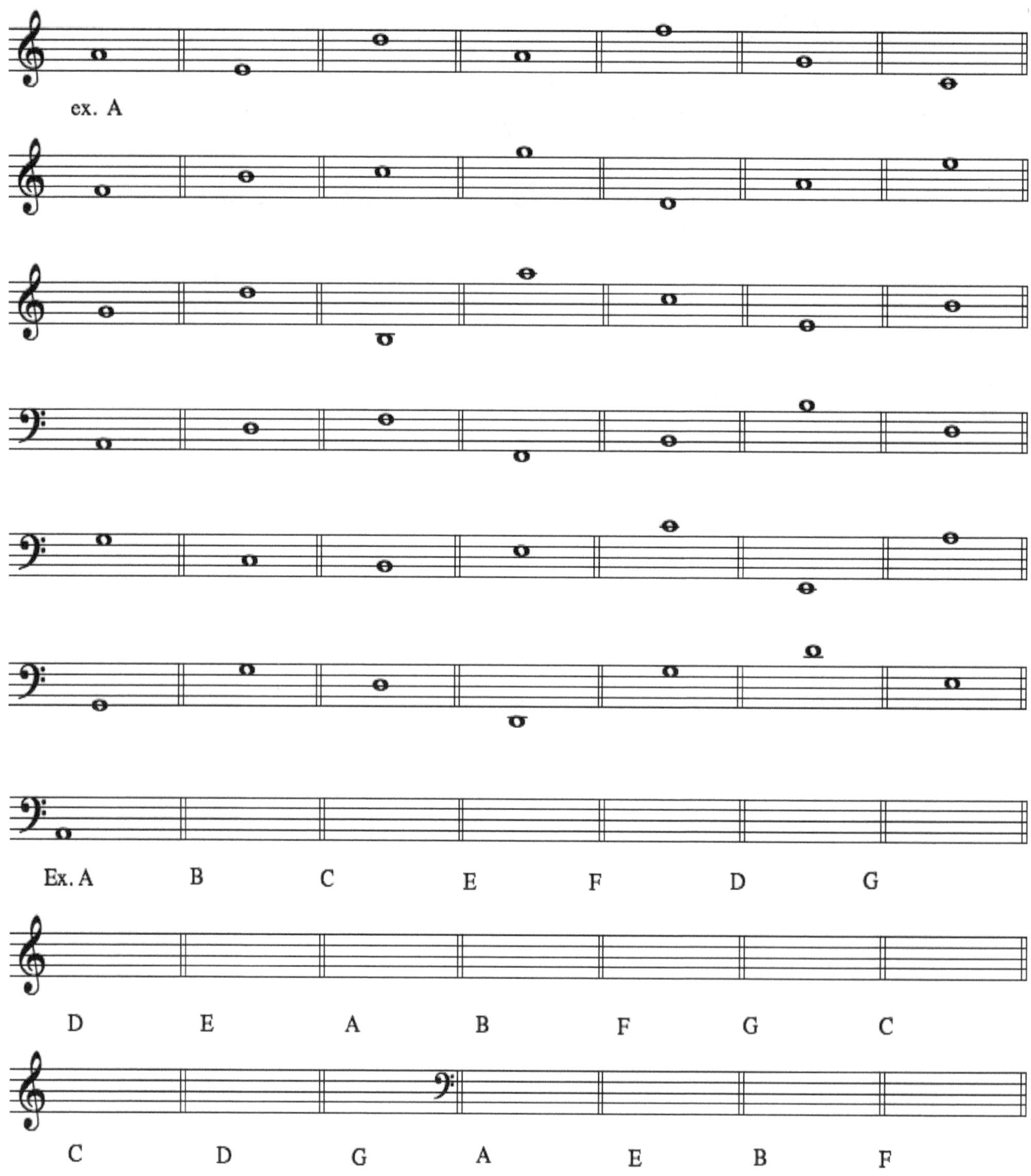

Name:______________________________

Date:____________________

Write the letter name for each note.

(ex.)

C

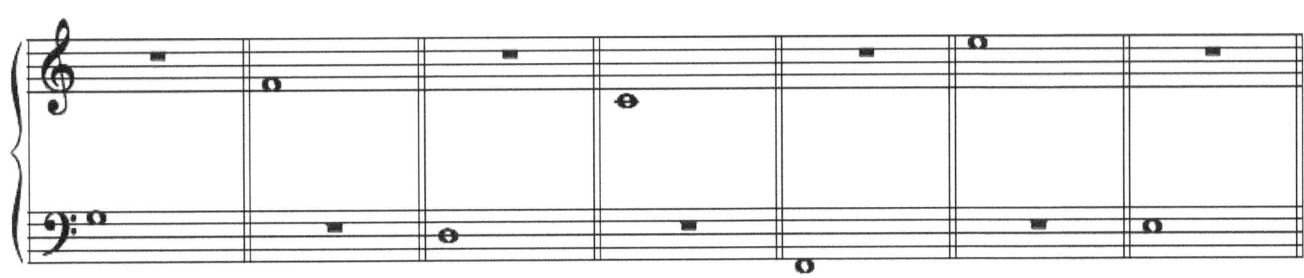

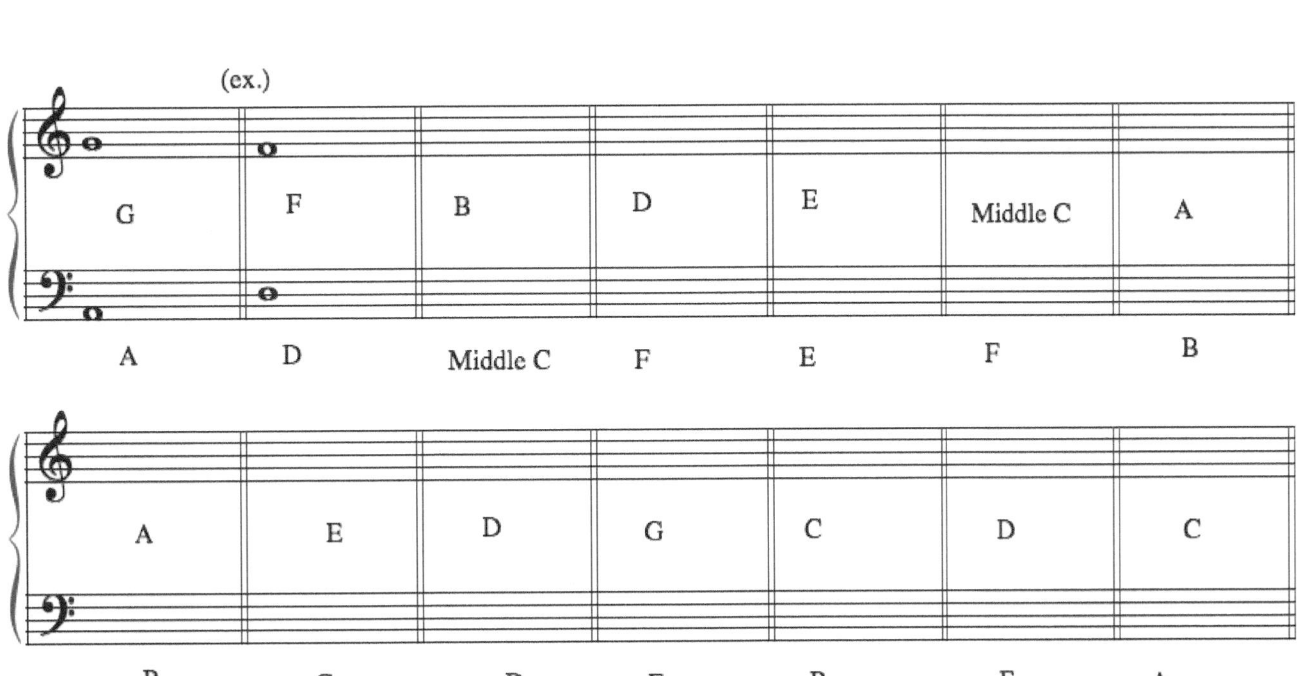

CHAPTER 2

RHYTHM AND METER

LESSON 6: RHYTHM NOTATION

Rhythm is a term we use to describe how music and sounds are organized in time. As we will learn in this section, rhythm can be expressed by notes with a pitch, like in the piano, or notes without pitches, like a snare drum. Rhythm is a concept that cannot be defined in a simple way. It is a term that we use to represent the "time" element in music. The specific terms of reference are beat, meter, and tempo, which are the basic elements of rhythm.

Rhythm

In chapter one, the pitch function of a note was discussed. Each note representing a pitch has a secondary function-- to express the duration of that pitch, relative to the pulse of the music. In order to understand the lengths of the notes it is necessary to learn about the function of the pulse in music.

We often call this pulse the **beat** (note: if musicians play a passage very fast or very slow, it may sound like there are several pulses per beat or several beats per pulse. It is important to realize that the pulse is what you hear, the beat is what is notated.) The pulse or beat provides the basic structure around which the rhythm of the music is built.

Beat

In music notation the beat is represented by a note. You will find illustrated below the different parts to notes: the stem, the note head, a beam and flags. Be sure you can draw them accurately.

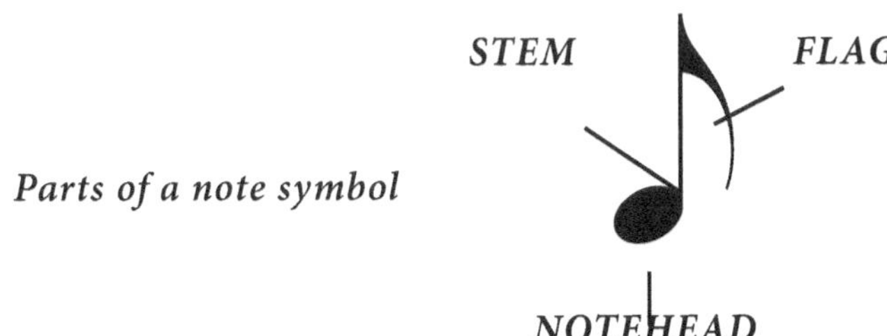

Parts of a note symbol

Meter
Accented
Unaccented

Most music has a consistent grouping of beats, and within these groupings of beats we find that some receive more emphasis than others. This organization of beats into structured groupings is called ***meter***. In other words, meter is a regular pattern of **accented** (strong) and **unaccented** (weak) beats. Let's practice accented and unaccented beats:

Establish a steady beat by clapping.

CLAP! CLAP! CLAP! CLAP! CLAP! CLAP!

Sounds that are stressed (louder claps) are said to be **accented**. The musical symbol for an accent is (>). Most music has these regular patterns of stress.

Now clap louder on every other beat (notice the accent symbols on top of the words (>):

>		>		>		>	
CLAP	CLAP	**CLAP**	CLAP	**CLAP**	CLAP	**CLAP**	CLAP
1	2	1	2	1	2	1	2

Duple
Meter

Meter can be classified by the number of beats in the pattern. In the example above you were clapping groups of two beats (one accented and one unaccented); this type of meter is called **duple meter.**

Triple
Meter

Triple meter is grouped by three beats. The first beat is strong (S) and the other two weak (w).

>			>			>		
CLAP	CLAP	CLAP	**CLAP**	CLAP	CLAP	**CLAP**	CLAP	CLAP
S	w	w	**S**	w	w	**S**	w	w
1	2	3	1	2	3	1	2	3

Quadruple
Meter

This type of meter is called **quadruple meter**. The first and thrid beat are strong the second and the fourth are weak.

>		>		>		>	
CLAP	CLAP	**CLAP**	CLAP	**CLAP**	CLAP	**CLAP**	CLAP
S	w	**S**	w	**S**	w	**S**	w
1	2	3	4	1	2	3	4

Bar Lines
Measures

In music notation each of these groups of beats are separated by a bar line; the musical content between two **bars lines** is called a **measure**. Therefore, we can say that measures divide music into equal parts. Music is organized in time in such a way that each measure has a group of beats and the bar lines separate each group.

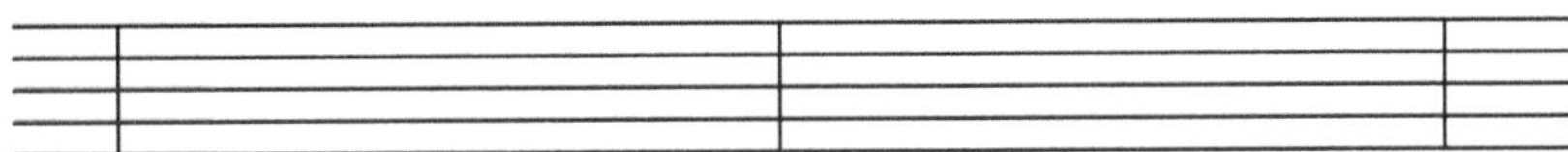

The content within each vertical bar is called a measure.
The vertical lines are call bar lines.

Music is divided into equal parts thanks to the measures. Bar lines indicate the beginning and end of measures.

Tempo

The speed of the beat varies from one piece of music to another; **tempo** is the term used to describe the various speeds. As has been mentioned, notes only represent relative duration. The precise length of a note is impossible to determine without other information. Exact duration of a note can be determined by establishing the speed "tempo" of the unit. The tempo of the unit can be established with the following indication:

M.M. ♩ = 120

Metronome

M.M. stands for Mazel **Metronome** (named after the inventor and the device for establishing tempo). The indication above is for 120 quarter notes per minute. With that indication, the exact duration of the quarter note (and all other note values) is known.

Another method of determining tempo is the use of terms that provide a vague sense of whether the music is fast or slow. Many common terms found in this literature are in German, French and Italian.

NOTE VALUES

Notes
Note Values

Notes may lie on a line (the line passes through the note-head), in the space between two lines (the notehead lies between two adjacent lines) or in the space above the top line or on the space below the bottom line. Notes can represent pitch (high and low) as we have seen by their placement on the staff in chapter one. Notes and rests can also represent duration (various lengths). Duration, then, represents the relative length of notes and rests. (Duration, a property of sound, see ch. 1)

Music is notated almost always for the sake of someone else. We write music down so that we may pass it on to another person. For that reason, notation must be clear and legible and the symbols must be understood so that little explanation is necessary. A few notational principles should be presented at this point.

Stem Direction: If the note head is below the third line of the staff, the stem is on the right side of the note head and extended upward. Stems are usually about four lines or spaces in length. If the note head is above the third line of the staff, the stem is of the left side of the note head and extended downward. If the note head is on the middle line, the stem may extend either upward or downward, whichever looks best in the context of the music.

Flags: Eighth-notes and sixteenth-notes have flags associated with them. The flag always appears on the right side of the stem whether the stem extends upward or downward.

Beams: When a group of notes with flags occur within one beat (or in vocal music within one word or syllable) they are beamed together to make the grouping more apparent to the performer. The number of beams is equal to the number of flags normally found on the note, so a group of eighth notes has a single beam, a grouping of sixteenth notes has two beams, etc. Beaming does not affect how the music sounds; it is only a notational means of making music easier to read and perform.

NOTE SYMBOLS

The symbols used to represent relative duration of notes are shown below. As you study these symbols, be sure to practice drawing them with pencil and paper.

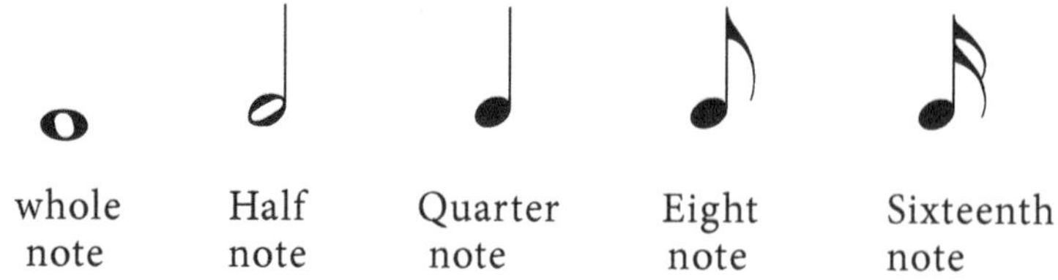

whole note	Half note	Quarter note	Eight note	Sixteenth note

In theory, additional flags could be added to produce shorter note values. But as a practical matter, the use of notes beyond the thirty-second note is rare. The above notes do not represent exact duration.

The precise length of a half note is impossible to determine without the time signature (to be discussed later). The notes do, however, represent relative duration. For example, we can say a "whole note is equal to 2 half notes" or a "quarter note is equal to 4 sixteenth notes."

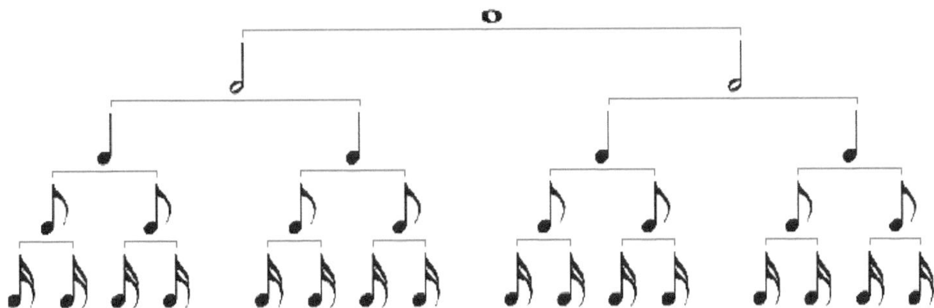

Note duration: the above chart displays the relationship of all five note types discussed in this lesson.

Activity 7:

Whole notes: Write ten more

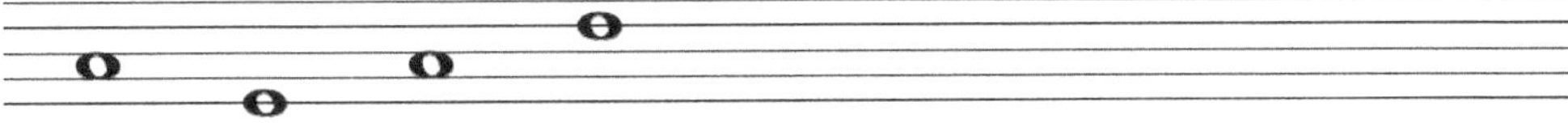

Half notes: Write ten more

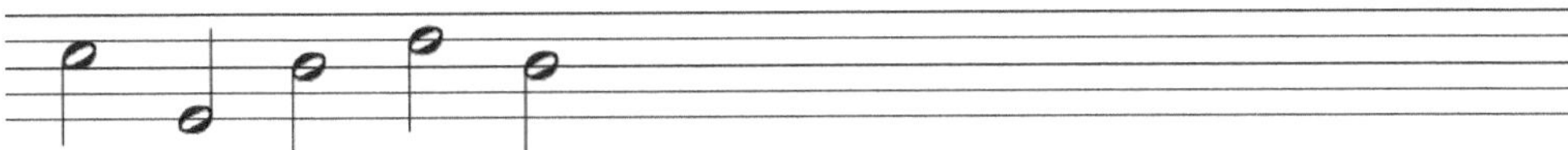

Quarter notes: Write ten more

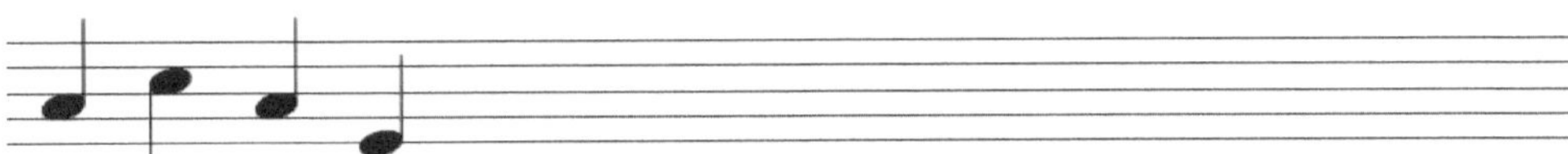

Eight notes: Write ten more

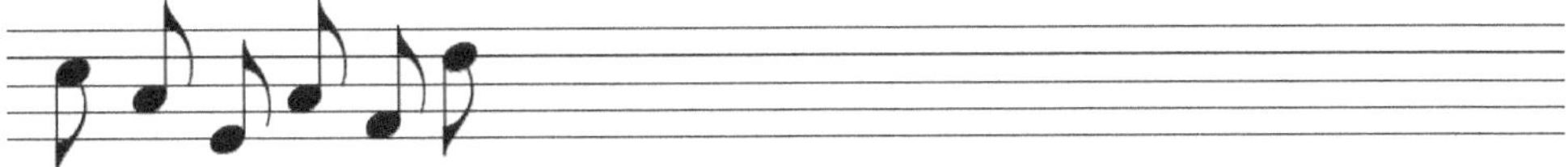

Name:____________________

Date:__________________

Lesson 6: Practice Exercises

Notes values are defined in relationship with each other. A quarter note is twice the duration of an eight note but half the duration of a half note. The commonly used rhythm values, in order from longest to shortest are:

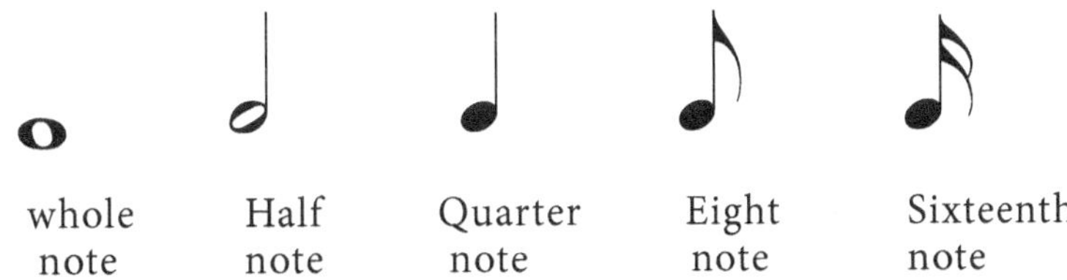

A. Write one note in each blank to complete the equations.

𝅘𝅥 + 𝅘𝅥 = ____

𝅗𝅥 + 𝅗𝅥 = ____

𝅘𝅥𝅮 + 𝅘𝅥𝅮 = ____

𝅘𝅥𝅯 + 𝅘𝅥𝅯 + 𝅘𝅥𝅯 + 𝅘𝅥𝅯 = ____

𝅘𝅥 + 𝅘𝅥 + 𝅘𝅥 + ___ = 𝅝

𝅘𝅥𝅮 + 𝅘𝅥𝅮 + 𝅘𝅥 + 𝅗𝅥 = _____

𝅘𝅥𝅯 + 𝅘𝅥𝅯 + 𝅘𝅥𝅮 + 𝅘𝅥 = _____

𝅘𝅥𝅮 + 𝅘𝅥 + ___ = 𝅗𝅥

𝅘𝅥𝅮 + 𝅘𝅥𝅯 + 𝅘𝅥𝅯 + 𝅘𝅥𝅮 = _____

B. Give the equivalent number on indicated values for the note shown.

𝅝 ______ half notes

𝅝 ______ quarter notes

𝅝 ______ eighth notes

𝅝 ______ sixteenth notes

𝅗𝅥 ______ quarter notes

𝅗𝅥 ______ eighth notes

𝅗𝅥 ______ sixteenth notes

𝅗𝅥 ______ thirty-second notes

♩ ______ sixteenth notes

♩ ______ eighth notes

♩ ______ thirty-second notes

♪ ______ sixteenth notes

♪ ______ thirty-second notes

𝅘𝅥𝅯 ______ thirty-second notes

Lesson 7: Dots and Ties

Dot

Not all durations are represented by the notes themselves. Additional signs must be used to indicate other values. The **dot**, which follows to the right side of the note head, adds half the value of the note.

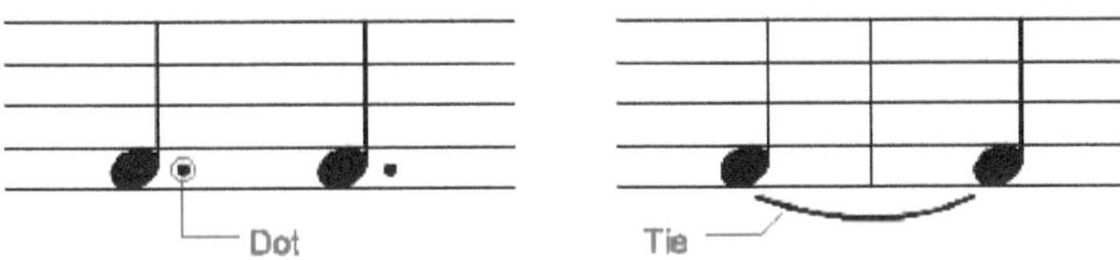

A dot increases duration by one half ♩. = ♩ + $\frac{1}{2}$

Since an eighth note is half the duration of a quarter note, we will substitute it for the 1/2 symbol above. ♩. = ♩ + ♪

As you can see, a dotted quarter note is equal to a quarter note plus an eighth note.

♩. = ♩ + ♪

A dotted quarter can also equal three eighth notes. ♩. = ♪ + ♪ + ♪

A second dot can add half the value of the first dot. Dots may also be added to rests to achieve a wider variety of rest durations. The value of dotted rests is determined in the same way that the value of dotted notes is determined.

Dots may be added to any note value:

𝅝. = 𝅝 + 𝅗𝅥

𝅗𝅥. = 𝅗𝅥 + ♩

♩. = ♩ + ♪

Tied

A **tie** merge multiple notes of the same pitch. They are used to let the duration of a note travel across barriers (such as the measure line in the example below).

Ties can also be used to combine durations that can't also be expressed using dots. Any two notes may be tied together, within or between measures.

Activity #8:

Give the equivalent number of indicated values for the note shown.

𝅝.	_____ half notes	♩.	_____ sixteenth notes
𝅝.	_____ quarter notes	♩.	_____ eighth notes
𝅗𝅥.	_____ eighth notes	♪.	_____ sixteenth notes
𝅗𝅥.	_____ quarter notes	♪.	_____ thirty-second notes
𝅗𝅥.	_____ sixteenth notes	𝅘𝅥𝅯.	_____ thirty-second notes

Name:____________________

Date:__________________

Lesson 7: Practice Exercises

Slurs and Ties

A **slur** is a curved line connection *two or more* notes of *different* pitches. **Slurred** passages should be played as smoothly as possible.

A **tie** is a curved line which connects *two* notes of the *same* pitch.

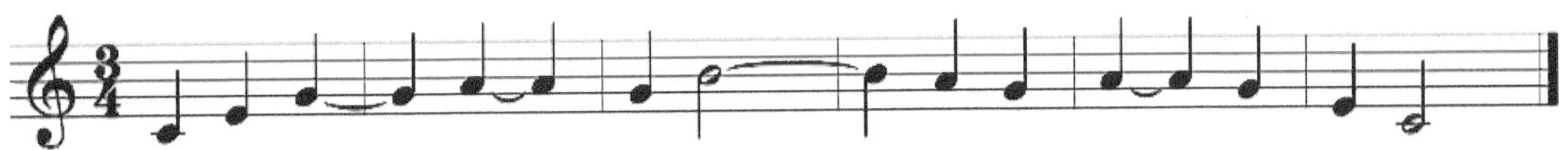

Tied notes are played as one note. The rhythmic value is the sum of the two notes.

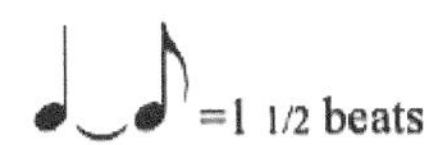

---

1. Circle the ties in this example.

2. Circle the slurs in this example.

3. Write the number of beats each pair of tied notes should receive.

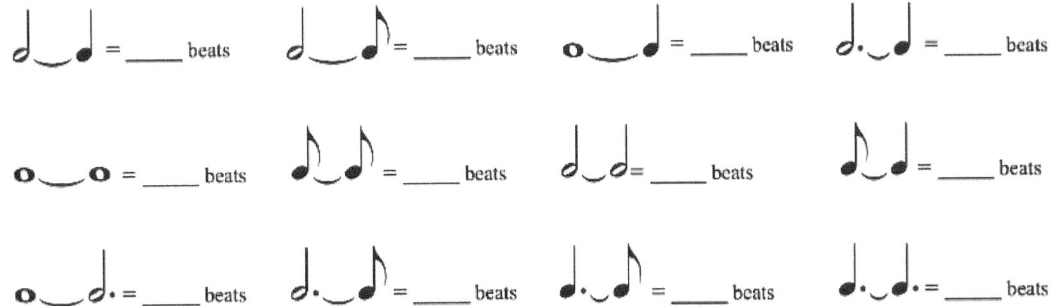

Lesson 8: Rests

Rests

In music **rests** are just as important as note events. It is a symbol used to denote silence or a pause in music. The symbols used to represent relative duration of rests are shown below. Again, you are probably familiar with some of these. You should also be able to draw each of these symbols.

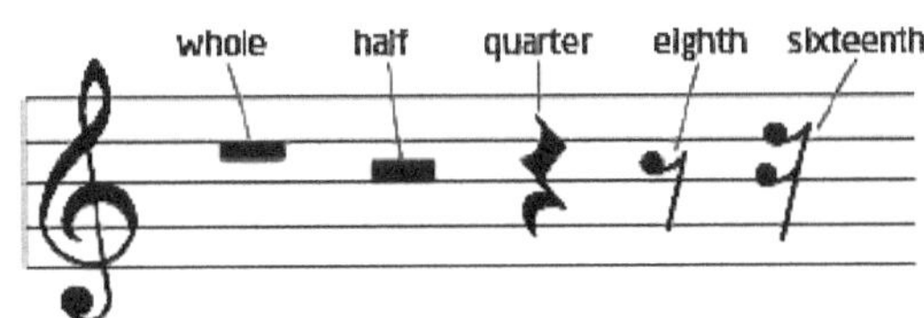

Rest symbols and names

Study the whole rest and the half rest, as they are easily confused. The whole rest "hangs heavily" from the fourth line while the half rest "sits lightly" on the third line.

Rest are used in music to indicate silence.

A **quarter rest** (𝄽) = 1 beat
A **half rest** (▬) = 2 beats
A **whole rest** (▬) = 4 beats

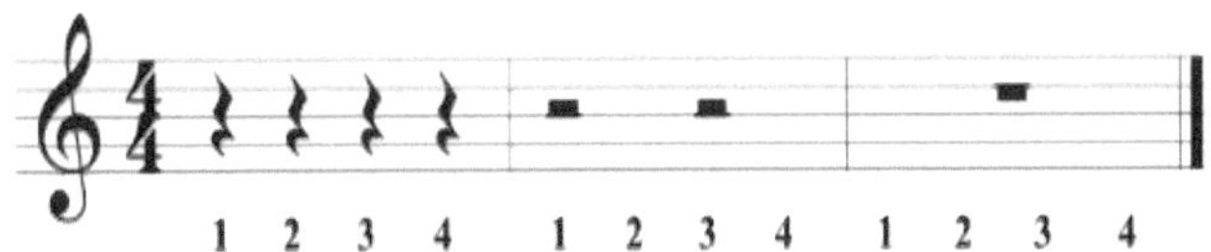

We will now discover some of the relationships that exist between the above notes and rests values.

Note Duration

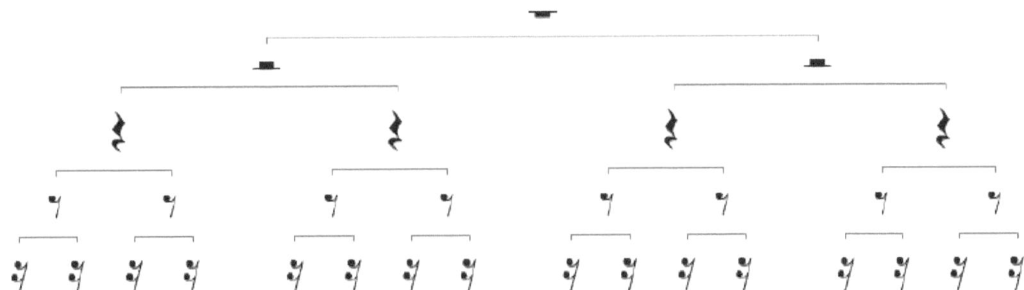

Activity #9:

1. Practice drawing quarter rests by tracing over the outlines.
Draw four quarter rests in each blank measure.

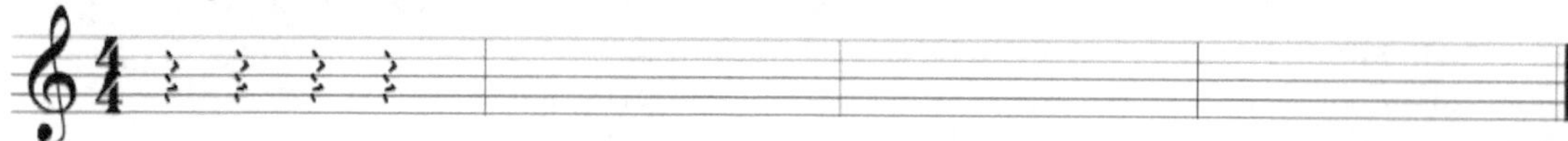

2. Draw two half rests in each blank measure.

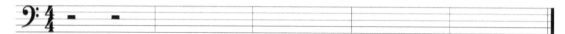

3. Draw one whole rest in each blank measure.

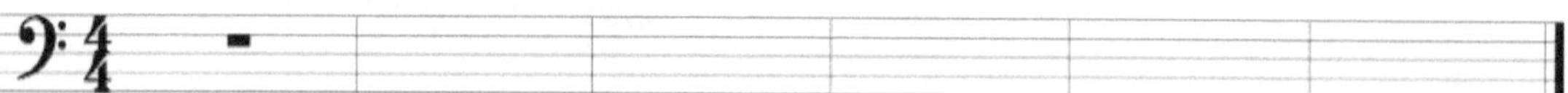

4. Write the count below the rests.

5. Write the count below the notes and rests, then clap and count the rhythm out loud.

6. Write the count below the notes and rests, then add the missing bar lines.

Lesson 9: Simple Meter

Time Signature or Meter Signature

The **time signature** or **meter signature** as it is also called, is made up of two numbers, one above the other. It is notated always at the beginning of a piece. The time signature provides information of how many beats are in each group of notes (meter) and which note value receives the beat. The top number indicates the type of meter of the piece; the bottom number indicates the rhythmic note value that represents that beat. A meter can be either simple of compound. Depending of the type of meter these two numbers can be read in different ways. A continuation, we will learn how to read a time signature in simple and compound meters.

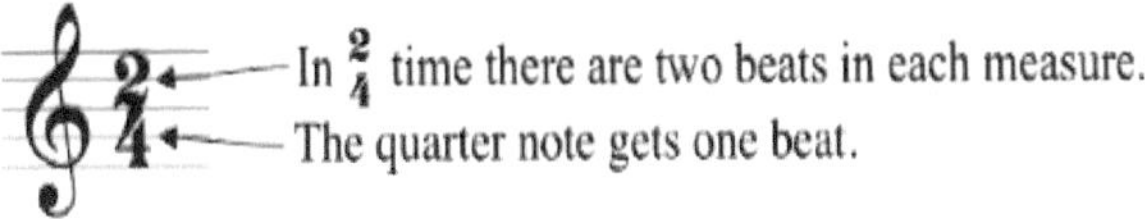

In 2/4 time there are two beats in each measure.
The quarter note gets one beat.

Rhythmic values
- An eighth note (♪) = 1/2 beat
- A quarter note (♩) = 1 beat
- A half note (𝅗𝅥) = 2 beats

Simple Meter
Duple
Triple
Quadruple

Each time signature can be classified into a certain meter. The terms duple, triple, and quadruple refer to the number of beats in a measure. In simple meter, each beat is normally subdivided into two parts; the note receiving the beat is always a standard single note value (i.e. a quarter, half, eight, etc.)

In **Simple Meter**:

"The top number indicates the numbers of beat per measure"
"The bottom number indicates the note value that receives that beat"

For example, in the example shown below, a meter with 2 beats per measure with the quarter note receiving the beat is called "2/4" time, and is notated with a "2" as the top number and a "4" for the bottom number at the beginning of the score.

This 2/4 time is classified as **simple duple**

"**Duple**" refers to the two beats per measure

"**Simple**" states that each of these beats can be divided into two notes as shown to the right

2/2 and 2/8 are also simple duple

Let's try another example. In the figure below, a meter with 3 beats per measure with the quarter note receiving the beat is called "3/4" time, and is notated with a "3" as the top number and a "4" for the bottom number.

This 3/4 time is classified as **simple triple.**

"**Triple**" refers to the three beats per measure

Again, "simple" states that each of these beats can be divided into two notes

3/2 and 3/8 are also simple triple

Common
Cut time

Let's try our last example. In figure below, a meter with 4 beats per measure with the quarter note receiving the beat is called "4/4" time, and is notated with a "4" as the top number and a "4" for the bottom number. The time signature of "4/4" is so commonly used that publishers and composers often abbreviate it with a "C" for "**common time**". Note: a "C" with a slash through it indicates "**cut time**" which is equal to "2/2".

$$\mathbf{C} = \begin{matrix}4\\4\end{matrix} \qquad \mathbf{¢} = \begin{matrix}2\\2\end{matrix}$$

The 4/4 time is classified as simple quadruple due to its four beats which can be divided into two notes.

4/2 and 4/8 are also simple quadruple

Simple meters are "***simple***" because each beat is divisible into "***two equal parts***." If the top number is a 2, then it is simple duple meter; if the top number is a 3, then it is simple triple meter, and so on. The following chart may help you understand several different simple meters.

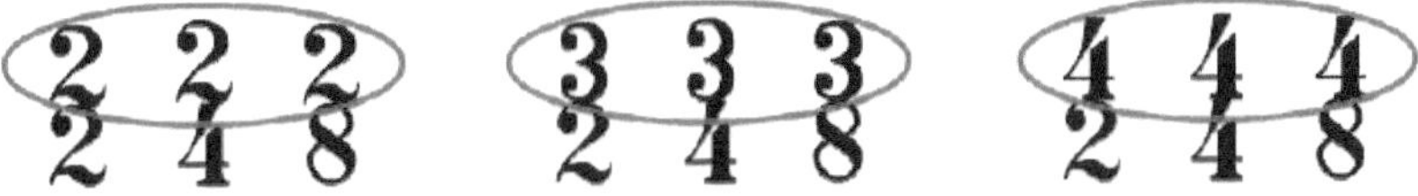

Counting Time In Simple Meters

Sometimes it must seem that musicians spend the greatest part of their lives counting. Counting is the best way we have of establishing the durational relationships of the notes and performing them evenly and correctly. There are many different ways we can count rhythms, all of which supply a verbal equivalent for each metric unit. We count the beats by number:

For notes of several beats' duration, we vocalize the count only where notes occur, but we must keep the beat going to ensure precision and uniformity in the note values. We can do this by clapping or tapping the pulse while vocalizing.

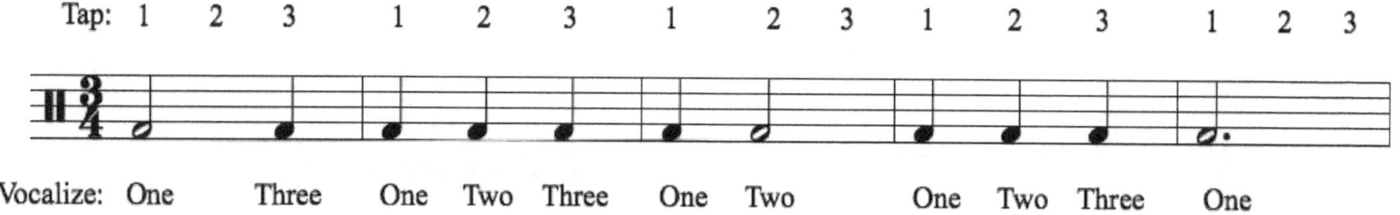

For simple divisions using eight and sixteenth notes, it might help to use a counting system that associates distinctive syllables with particular durations. For notes with ***half-beat*** duratoins, add "**&**" [**and**] halfway between the beats:

For subdivisions, (notes with ***quarter-beat*** durations) subdivide the space between beats into four equal parts by adding "**e-&-a.**"

Here's how the syllables would be used in a full rhythm exercise:

1 2 1 - & 2 1 - & 2 - e - & - a 1 2 - e - & - a 1 - e - & - a 2 1 2

In order to fit the syllables the words one and two will be replaced by numbers

1 2 3 (4) 1 - & 2 3 4 - & 1-e-&-a 2 3 - & 4 1 (2 3 4)

* Numbers in ( ) are not meant to be vocalized. It is just a beat indication *

The Use of Beams

You may noticed that beans are a tremendous aid to the eye in seeing the metric organization of a measure, quickly locating the beat, and easily parsing the divisions of the beat. For this reason, most music makes use of beamed groups rather than using single flags. One general exception to this is vocal music, where the individual flags are used to indicate where the syllables of the lyrics fall, but even there it is becoming much more common to use the beams. Beams should be used to group any and all small values failing ***within*** a beat:

This is what it would look like using beams:

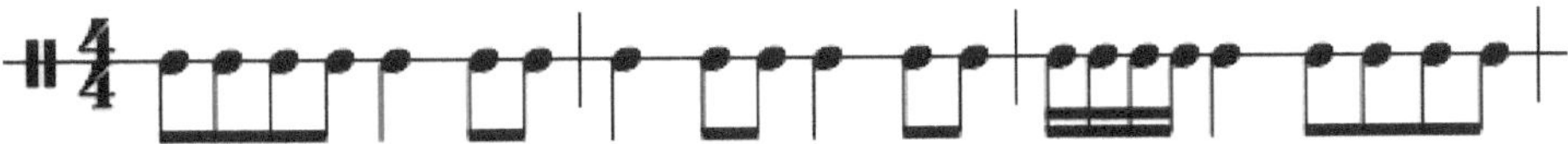

Activity #10: Rhythm Reading

I. Write the count below the notes and rests. Clap the rhythms whole counting out loud.

1.
2.
3.
4.
5.
6.
7.
8.
9.

10.
11.
12.
13.
14.
15.
16.
17.
18.

19. 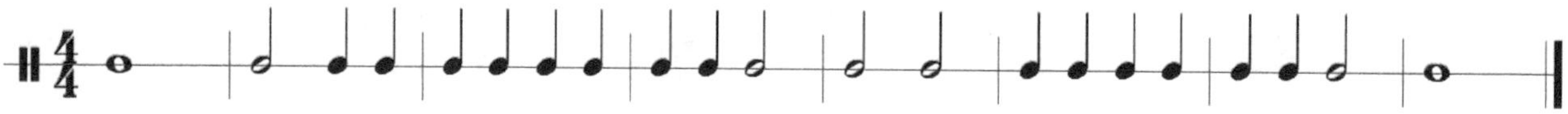 4/4

20. 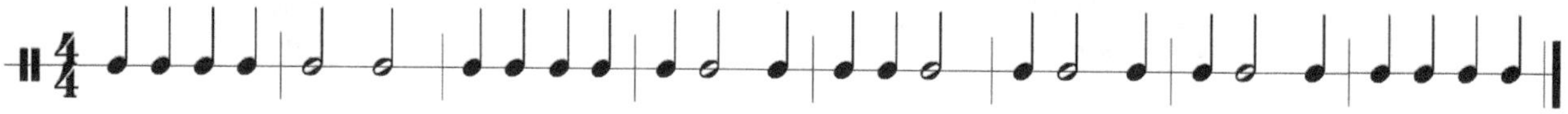 4/4

21.  4/4

22.  2/4

23.  2/4

24. 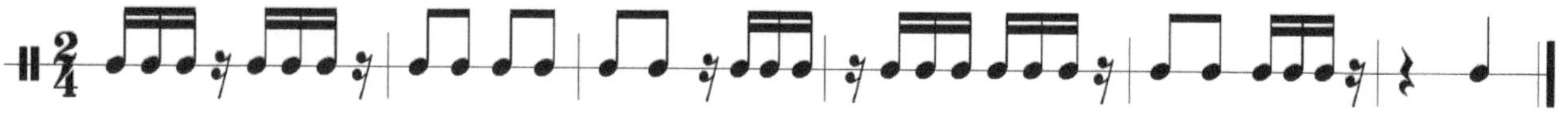 2/4

25.  3/4

26.  3/4

27.  3/4

II. Now lets keep practicing rhythms using the "***tie***". Write the count below the notes and rests. Clap the rhythms while counting out loud.

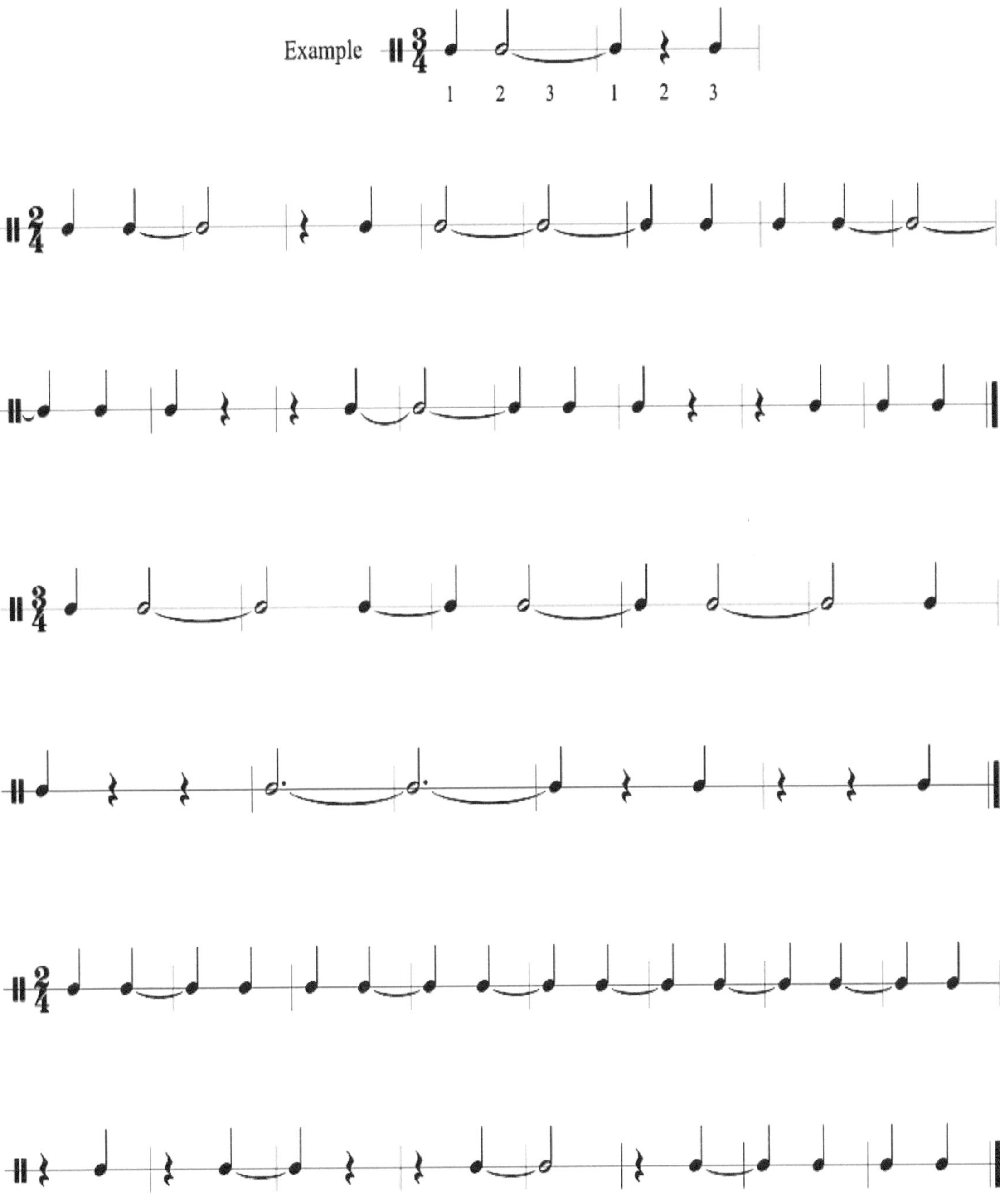

III. Write the count below the notes and rests. Clap the rhythms while counting out loud.

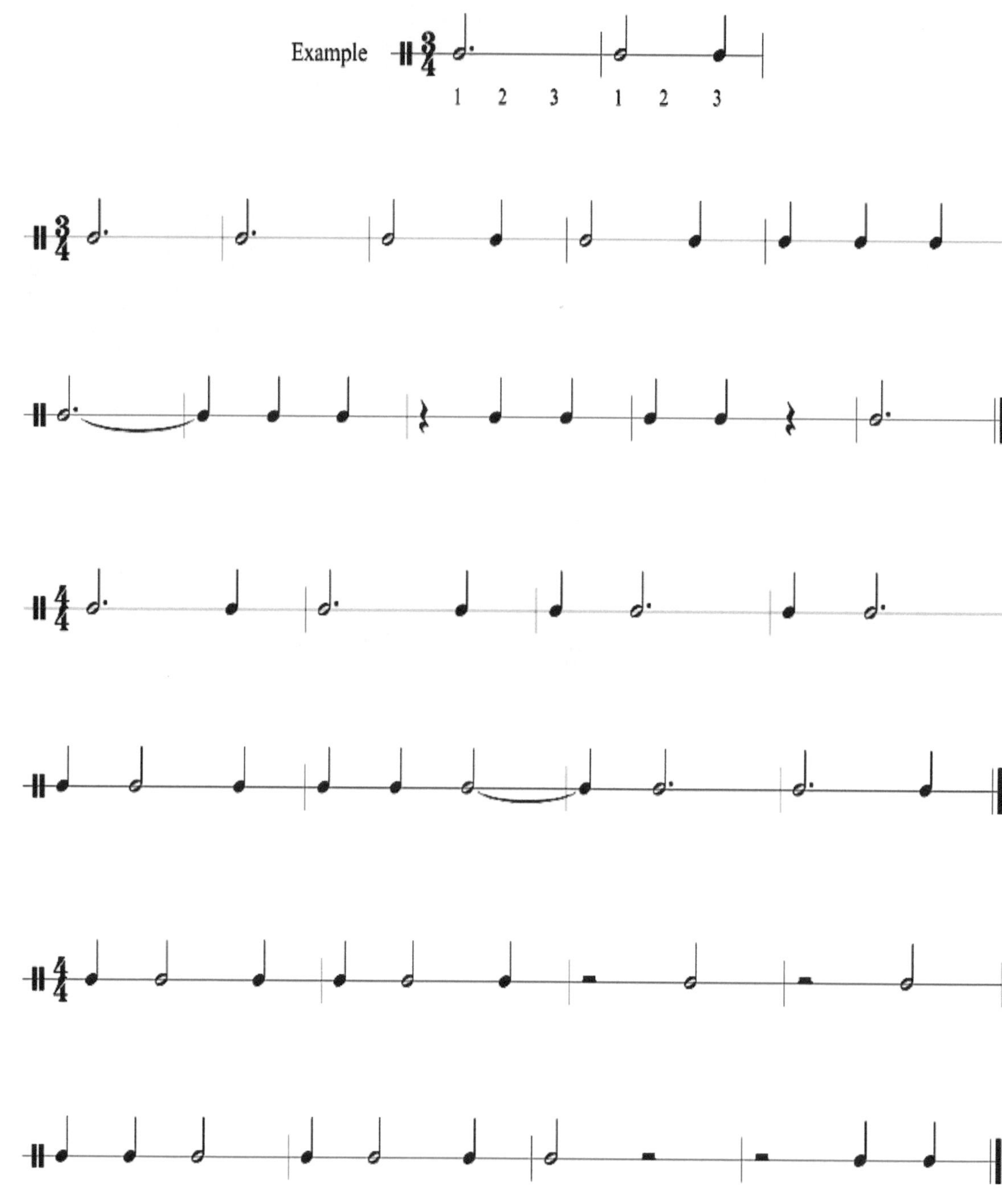

IV. Write the count below the notes and rests. Clap the rhythms while counting out loud.

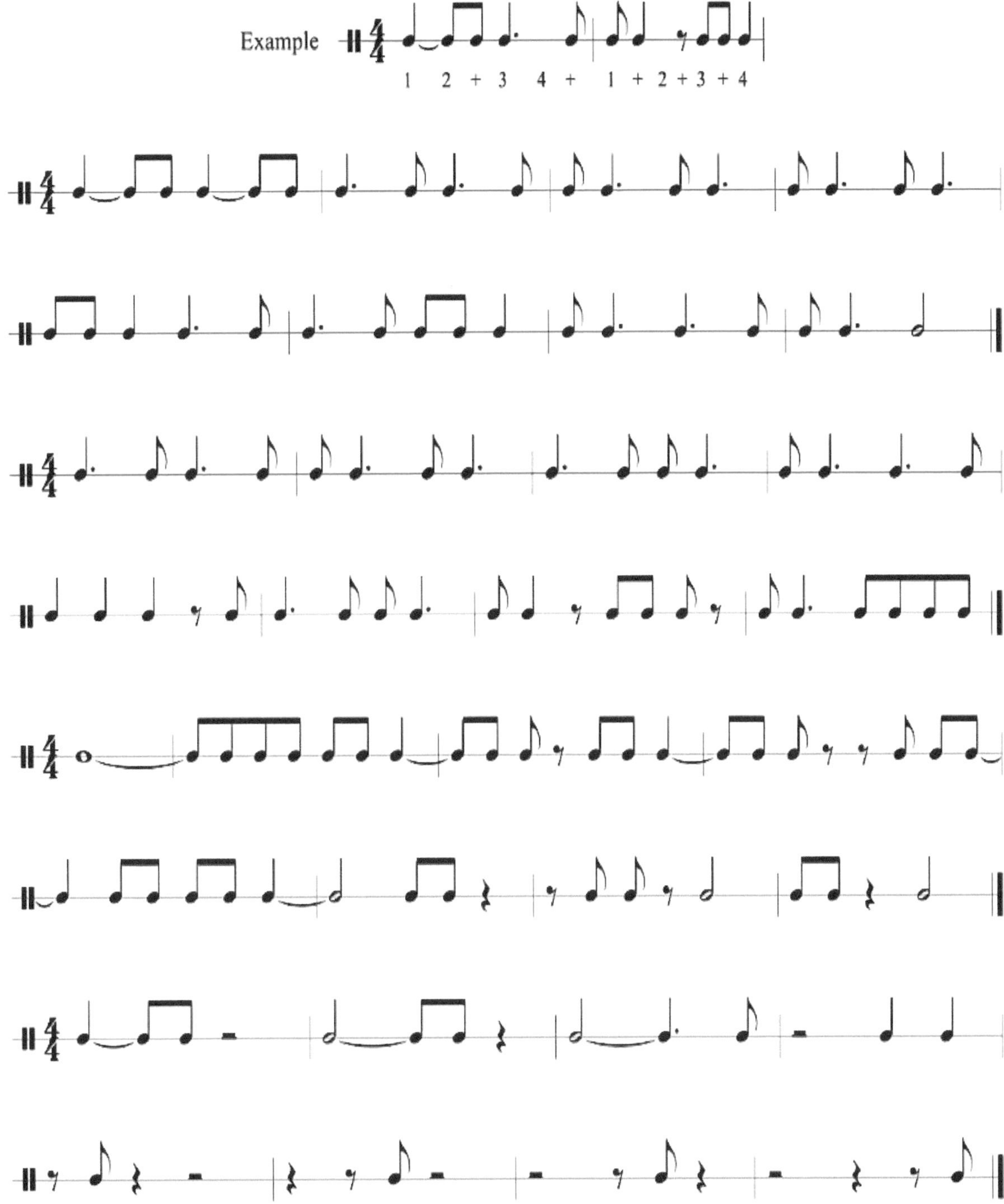

V. Write the count below the notes and rests. Clap the rhythms while counting out loud.

Simple Meter Listening Exercises

Write out and count the rhythms of each of the following melodies. Identify the meter of each. Observe that the meter signature is placed in only the first measure and is not repeated on subsequent staves. How many beats in a measure? What is the unit of the beat? (You will find any unfamiliar tempo terms defined in the Glossary.)

First, count the rhythms aloud, using a neutral pitch. Then, count along as the tune is played or sung.

EXAMPLE 1

EXAMPLE 2

EXAMPLE 3

EXAMPLE 4

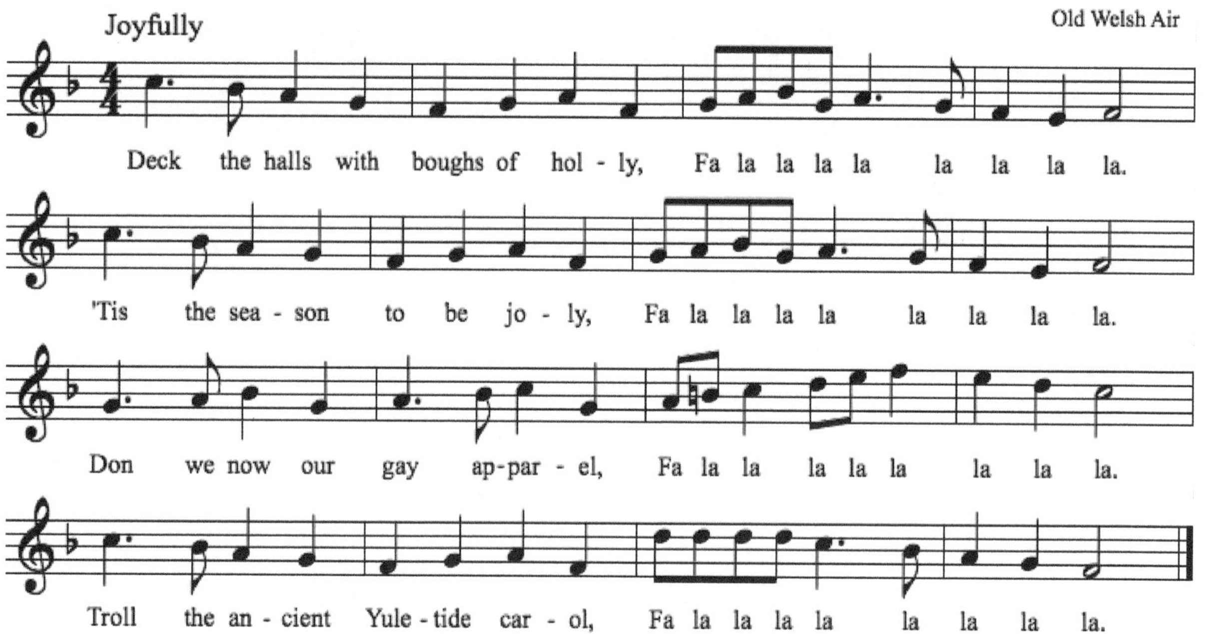

EXAMPLE 6

Counting with Rests: We have observed that the beat is felt to continue steadily under the music, regardless of the actual note values being used, even when the beat is only very subtly implied. In fact, so strong is the sense of the beat, we feel it even during brief stretches where there is no sound at all.

Count the rhythms in the following melodies. As before, first just count, using a neutral pitch. Then, count as the melodies are played or sung. Tap the beat to assure rhythmic accuracy with the rests.

EXAMPLE 7

EXAMPLE 8

THE ANACRUSIS (PICKUP MEASURE)

Now, there is something interesting about this next example.

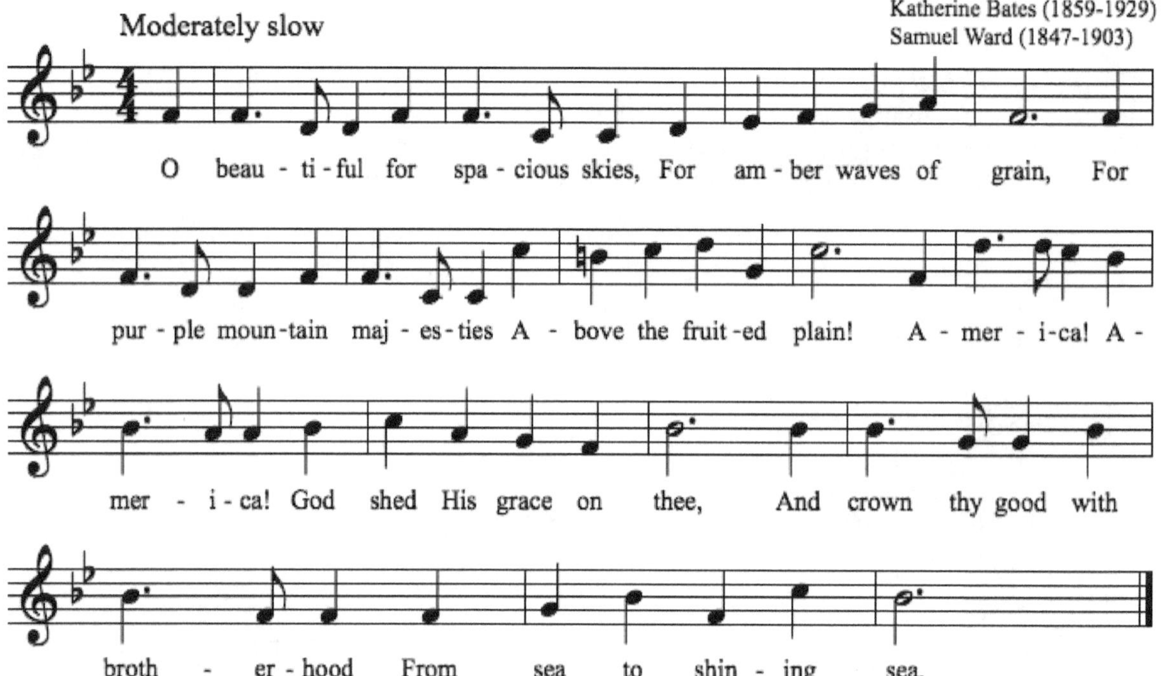
America the Beautiful
Moderately slow
Katherine Bates (1859-1929)
Samuel Ward (1847-1903)
O beau - ti - ful for spa - cious skies, For am - ber waves of grain, For
pur - ple moun-tain maj - es - ties A - bove the fruit -ed plain! A - mer - i-ca! A -
mer - i - ca! God shed His grace on thee, And crown thy good with
broth - er - hood From sea to shin - ing sea.

Pickup
Upbeat
Anacrusis

We immediately notice one big different with the stress pattern of this song. We sing "O **beaut**-i-ful for spa-cious skies," not "**O** beaut-iful for spa-cious skies...." That first note ("**O**") that precedes the first stressed note is called **upbeat** or **pickup** or **anacrusis**.

The pickup note ("**O**") is notated as an incomplete first measure. By custom, the last measure of the entire song should also be incomplete, the pickup plus the final measure should combine to form one complete measure. In this case, because the pickup measure is one beat, the last measure contains three beats.

For more information about musical symbols and terminology see APPENDIX A "*A brief guide to common musical symbols and signs.*"

Study Questions for Chapter 2

1. Define the following terms:

Common time
Rhythm
Cut time
Bar line
Beat
Measure
Meter
Time signature
Anacrusis
Tie
Dot
Slur
Rests

2. What numbers you expect to find as the lower values in a time signature? What numbers you will never find as the lower values of a time signature? Why?

3. Describe the difference in the appearance of these notes:

Quarter note and half note
half note and eight note
eight note and whole note
whole note and half note

Name:______________________________

Date: ______________________________

Chapter 2: Self-Test

Simple Meter

I. Complete the following measures. You may use a single note or several notes, as appropriate.

1.

2.

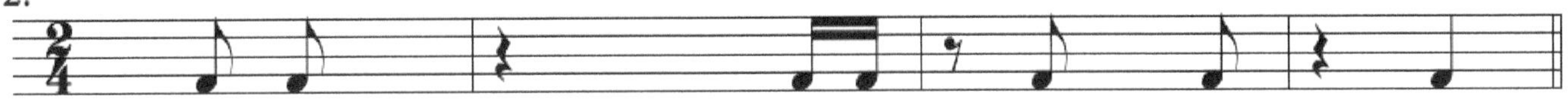

3.

4.

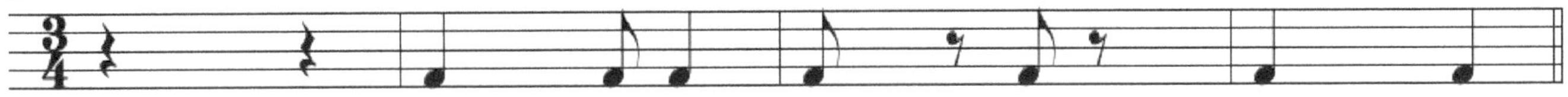

5.

6.

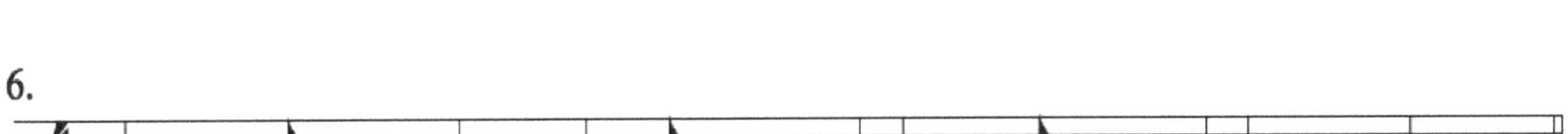

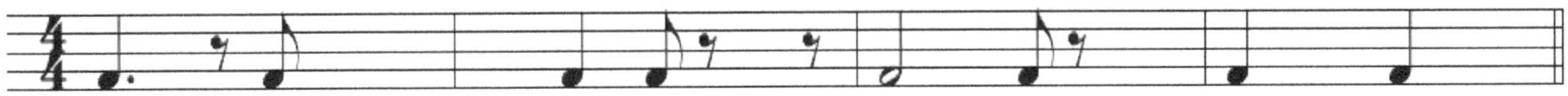

II. Draw the bar lines in the proper places as indicated by the time signature.

1.

2.

3.

4.

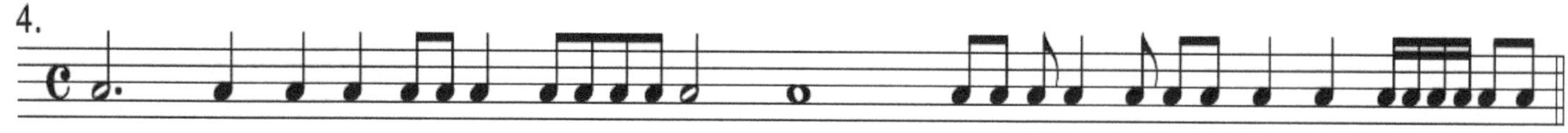

5.

6.

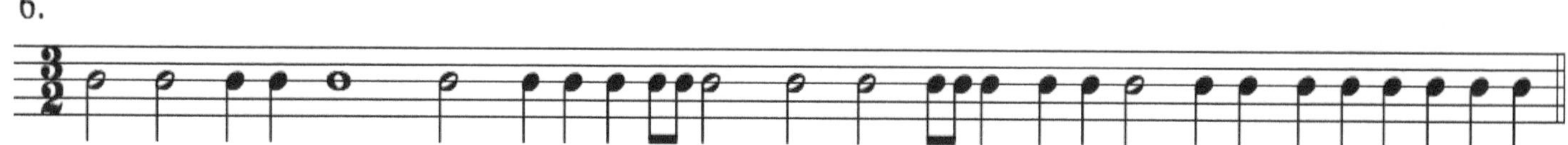

Name: ________________ Date: ______________________

III. Identify the following time signatures by indicating the number of beats, note value receiving one beat, the division of the beat, and the type of meter.

Time Signature	Beats	Unit of Beat	Division of the Beat	Meter type
2 4	Two	♩	♪♪	Simple duple
3 4				
2 8				
4 4				
C				
3 8				
4 8				
3 16				
₵				

IV. Complete the Chart Below

Time Signature	Beats	Unit of Beat	Division of the Beat	Meter type
4	2			
				Simple duple
3 8				
			𝅘𝅥𝅯𝅘𝅥𝅯	Simple ________
2 8				
	3	𝅗𝅥		Triple ________

CHAPTER 3

COMPOUND METER

Lesson 10: Compound Meter

In **compound meter** each beat is normally subdivided into ***three equal parts***, and the note receiving the beat is always a dotted note value (i.e. a dotted quarter, a dotted half, a dotted eight, etc.) This is because a dotted note value may always be easily divided into three equal notes (i.e. a dotted quarter = 3 eighth notes). Because time signatures consist of whole numbers only, the top numbers in a compound meter time signature indicate the number of subdivided values. In compound meter:

Compound Meter

6/8

"The top number indicates the number of subdivided beats per measure."
"The bottom number indicates the rhythmic note value that receives the subdivided beat."

The most common compound meter is "6/8." This compound meter may be confusing at first because the time signature seems to indicate that there are six beats in a measure and that the eight note gets the beat. This is true, but 6/8 meter is normally counted and performed with the six eight notes grouped into two sets of three. As a result, 6/8 "feels" like duple meter, with the unit of beat represented by a dotted quarter note and each of the units of beat are divisible into three parts.

a) Notice that the six eighth notes can either be divided into two beats (compound duple).

b) Notice that each beat in 6/8 is a dotted quarter note. In fact, all compound meters will have some dotted note as its beat.

c) Any time signature with a 6 on top is compound duple. Of the above time signatures, 6/8 and 6/4 are the most commonly used.

d) 9/8 time is classified as compound triple. There are three beats (three dotted quarter notes), thus making the meter triple. Since each beat is comprised of three notes, the meter is compound.

g) Any time signature with a 9 on top is compound triple. Although 9/8 is the most common; 9/2, 9/4, and 9/16 can also be used.

h) Finally, 12/8 time is classified as compound quadruple. There are four beats, thus making the meter quadruple. Since each beat is comprised of three notes, the meter is compound.

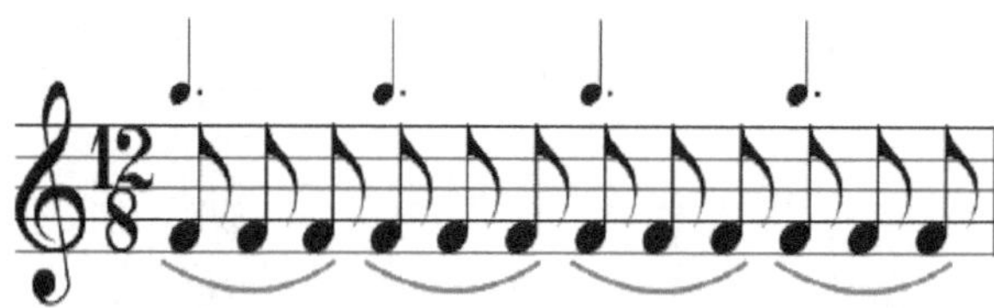

i) Any time signature with a 12 on top is compound quadruple. Of the above time signatures, 12/8 and 12/16 are the most commonly used.

COUNTING TIME IN COMPOUND METERS

A compound meter represents several problems. We know from our earlier discussion that our basic note-value symbols are always divided into *two* of the next smallest value, and we can't divide a note into three parts using any of the standard note value.

There are two possible solutions to this problem. First, we can use what we call a **triplet** figure. This is a type of proportional notation that means to play three notes in the time of two. Stated as a ratio, it would be 3:2, but simply use the 3, along with a slur or bracket for unbeamed notes.

3

♪♪♪ = ♫ or ♩

However, in an entire piece uses these divisions, the triplet becomes very cumbersome. The second possibility is to work up from the value of the division itself, what we call the **background unit**. If we need three background units for every beat, it follows that we can then sum these values into a single ***dotted note***, and this value can then be used to ***represent the beat*** in compound meters:

Background Unit

(background Unit) ♪♪♪ = ♩. (beat Unit)

But how do we express this organization in a meter signature. In a simple meter, we can designate the beat unit by a digit 4 for ♩, 2 for 𝅗𝅥, and so on. But a dotted note would become a fractional number: ♩. = 4 1/2 (?).

Instead, we must represent the background unit in the meter signature. As we mentioned earlier the upper number is then derived by counting the total number of background units:

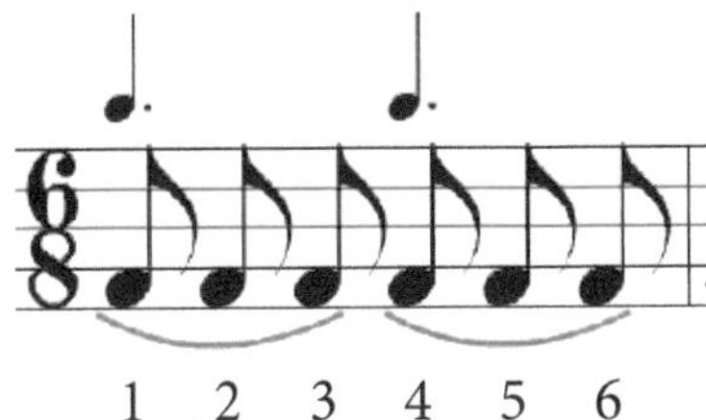

The trick in counting rhythms is to keep simple and compound meters distinct. Certain patterns are difficult to distinguished clearly and must be counted with care, always mentally keeping the smallest value clear and steady. For example:

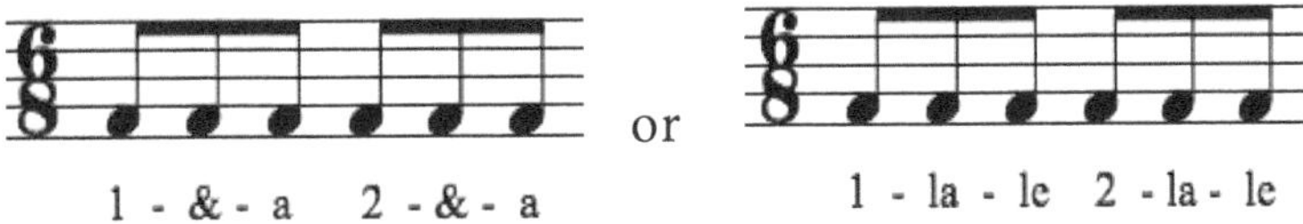

If you find the use of the same vocables for both simple and compound meters confusing, try using this traditional system for counting compound meter:

Activity #11:

As a class or individually, clap and count the following rhythmic examples in simple and compound meters. Begin by saying two measures of the beat aloud before clapping. When you are comfortable with the counting system, also try playing the rhythms on an instrument or keyboard while counting mentally. Remember to always keep the basic beat steady.

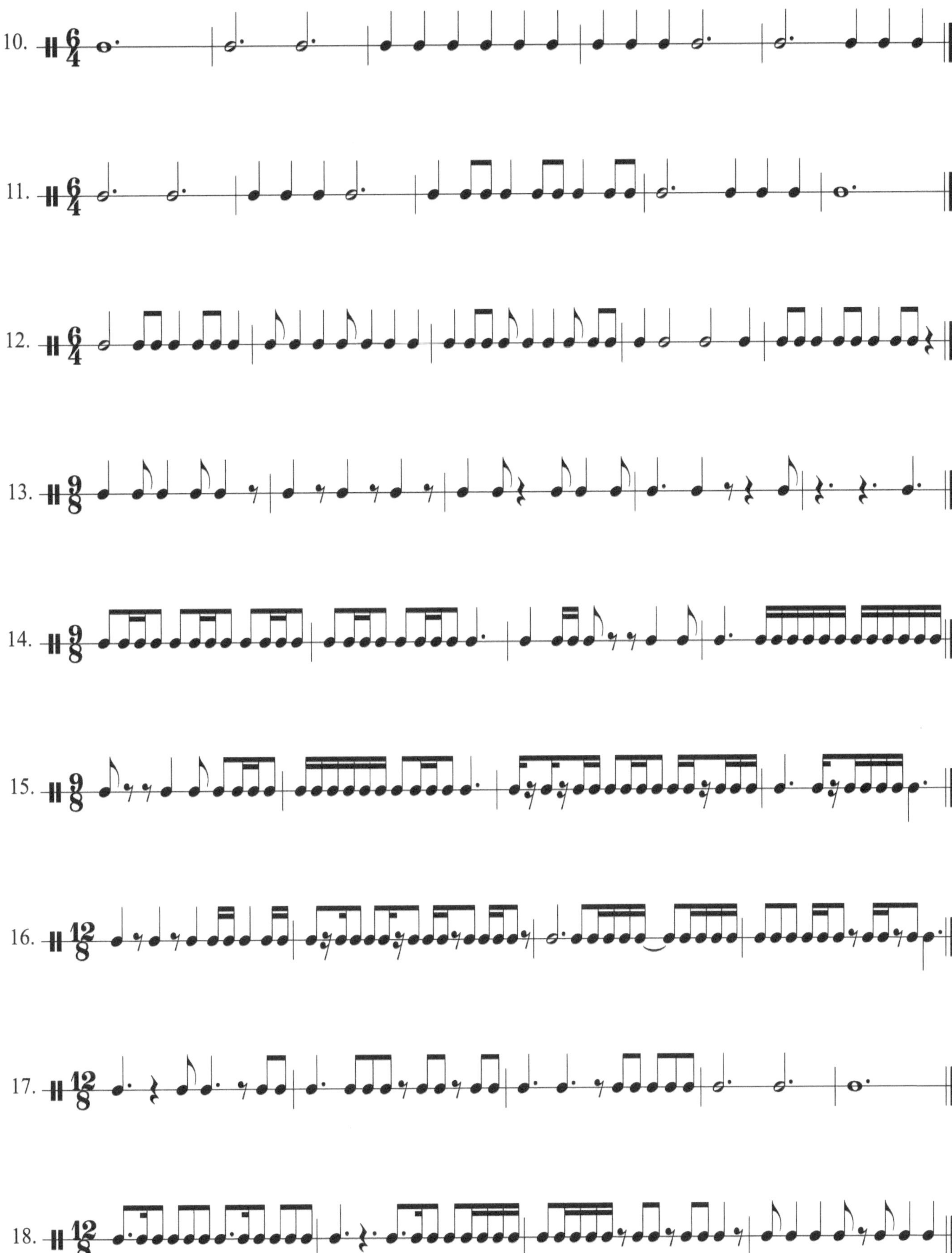
10. 6/4
11. 6/4
12. 6/4
13. 9/8
14. 9/8
15. 9/8
16. 12/8
17. 12/8
18. 12/8

Activity #12: Rhythm Reading

I. Write the count below the notes and rests. Clap the rhythms while counting out loud.

II. Write the count below the notes and rests. Clap the rhythms while counting out loud.

III. Write the count below the notes and rests. Clap the rhythms while counting out loud.

IV. Write the count below the notes and rests. Clap the rhythms while counting out loud.

Compound Meter Listening Exercises

As Before, write out and count the rhythms of the following melodies. Identify the meter of each. How many beats is a measure? What is the unit of the beat? What is the background unit? Does it seem more comfortable to count the beat unit, or the background unit?

Here are a few of the most common patterns you will encounter. Count each of them in two ways: first, counting the beat unit, and second, counting the background unit.

EXAMPLE 1

EXAMPLE 2

EXAMPLE 3

STUDY QUESTIONS FOR CHAPTER 3

1. Using the symbols (>) for strong or accented beats and (-) for unaccented beats, give the stress patterns of the meters indicated.

a. Triple ___ ___ ___

b. Duple ___ ___

c. Quadruple ____ ____ ____ ____

2. The lower number in the time signature refers to a note value.
True ______ False______

3. A lower number four (4) in the time signature refers to a __________note (note value).

4. In all time signatures, the upper number indicates the numbers of beats per measure.
True ______ False _______.

5. The "common time" signature is indicated by the symbol ________.

6. In compound meter, the beat unit is always a __________ note.

7. Time signatures having an upper number ____, _____, _____, or _____ are considered to be compound time signatures.

8. Time signatures having an upper number ____, _____, _____, or _____ are considered to be simple time signatures.

9. The "Cut time" signature is indicated by the symbol ______.

10. A lower number eight (8) in the time signature refers to a __________note (note value).

Name:_____________________________
Date: ______________________________

Chapter 3: Self-Test

Compound Meter

I. Complete the following measures. You may use a single note or several notes, as appropriate.

1.

2.

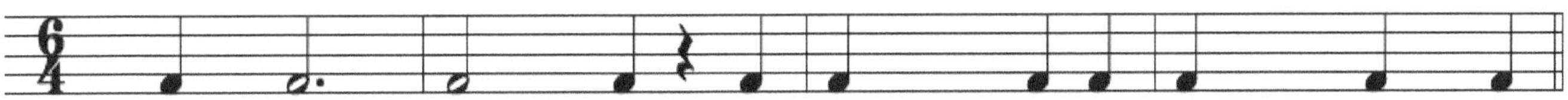

3.

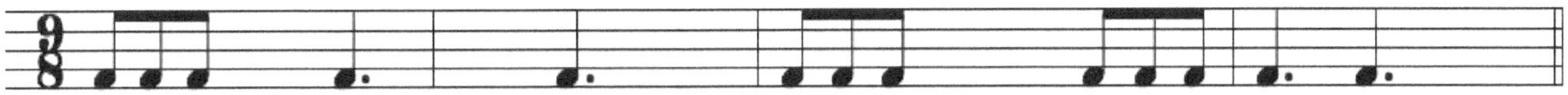

4.

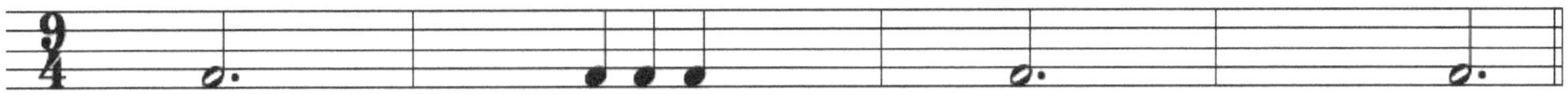

5.

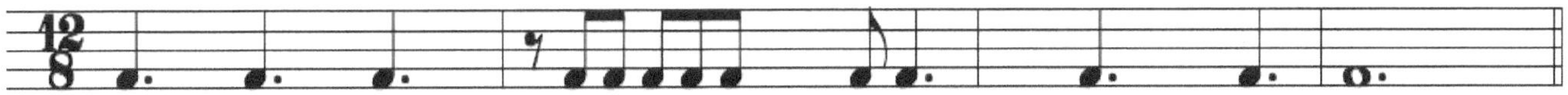

6.

II. Draw the bar lines in the proper places as indicated by the time signature.

Name: _______________ Date: _____________________

III. Identify the following time signatures by indicating the number of beats, note value receiving one beat, the division of the beat, and the type of meter.

Time Signature	Beats	Unit of Beat	Division of the Beat	Meter type
6 4	Two	♩.	♪♪♪	Compound duple
9 8				
6 8				
12 4				
12 8				
9 4				

Complete the chart Bellow:

Time Signature	Beats	Unit of Beat	Division of the Beat	Meter type
6 4	2			
				Compound duple
6 8				
			𝅘𝅥𝅯𝅘𝅥𝅯𝅘𝅥𝅯	Compound ________
12 8				
	4	♩.		Compound ________

IV. Write rhythms in each of the following time signatures. Be sure to Include the correct number of beats per measure.

Name: ___________________ Date:_______________________

Identifying Simple and Compound meter

V. Write the correct time signature for each of the following rhythms.

answer:

Ex. 2/4

1. answer:

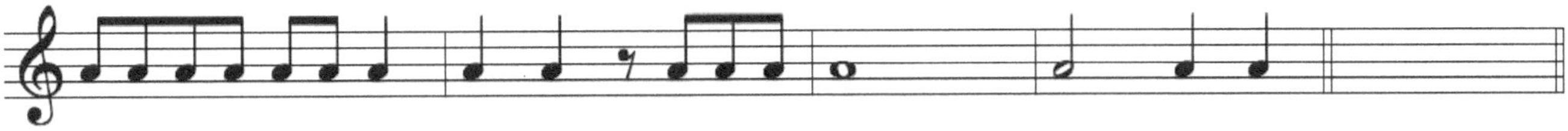

2. answer:

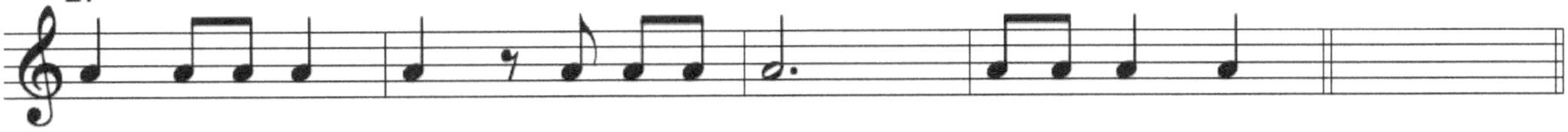

3. answer:

4. answer:

5. answer:

6. answer:

7. answer:

8. answer:

CHAPTER 4

MAJOR SCALES AND KEYS

Lesson 11: Scales and Scale Types: Chromatic, Whole-Tone, and Major

The term **scale** (from Italian *scala*, ladder) refers to a stepwise arrangement of pitches in ascending or descending order spanning an octave. The scale is a fundamental building block of music, much as the skeleton is the foundation of the human body. The fact that music of one culture sounds different in comparison to another culture is largely due to an unfamiliarity with the scales upon the music is created. Western music is based almost entirely on two scales, major and minor scales. Both of them are constructed out of whole and half steps. The music written using these two types of scales is called **tonal music.**

Scale

Although the great majority of western music written from the seventeenth through the nineteenth centuries is based on the major and minor scales, a number of other scales are found occasionally. The following descriptions are some of these scales.

Pentatonic Scale

As its name suggests, the ***pentatonic scale*** is a five-tone scale. It is an example of a gapped scale, one that contains intervals of more than a step between adjacent pitches. It is convenient to think of the common pentatonic scale as an incomplete major scale.

Pentatonic

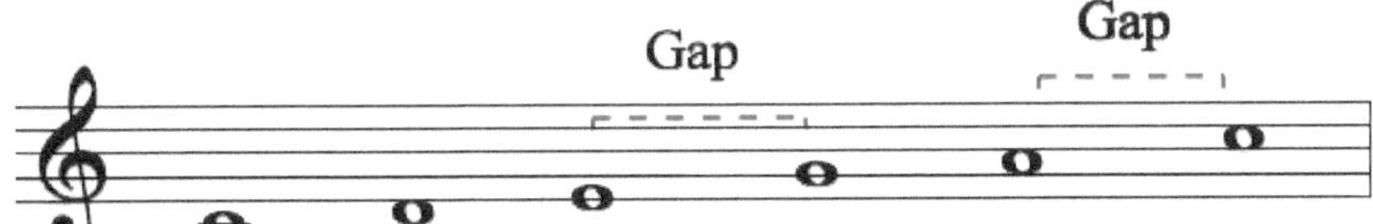

Note: The sequence of black keys on the keyboard coincides with the interval relationship of the pentatonic scale.

Chromatic Scale

Chromatic

A ***chromatic scale*** is a nondiatonic scale consisting entirely of half-step intervals. Since each tone of the scale is equidistant from the next, it has no tonic.

Whole-Tone Scale

Whole-tone

A ***whole tone scale*** is a six-tone scale made up entirely of whole steps between adjacent scale degrees.

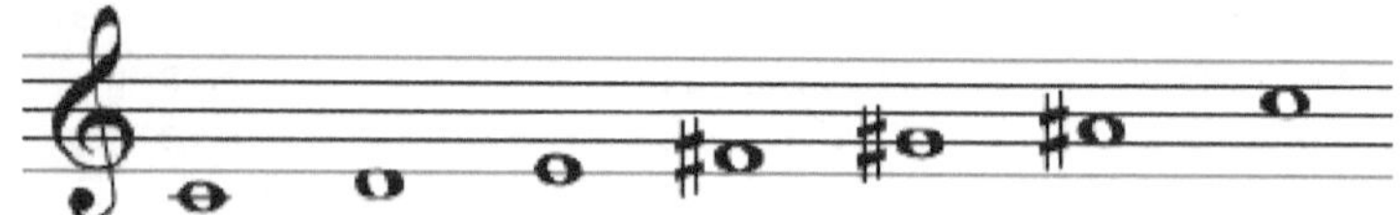

Blues Scale

Blues scale

The ***blues scale*** is a chromatic variant of the major scale with a flat third and a flat seventh. These notes, alternating with the normal third and seventh scale degrees, create the blues inflection. These "blue notes" represent the influence of African scales on this music.

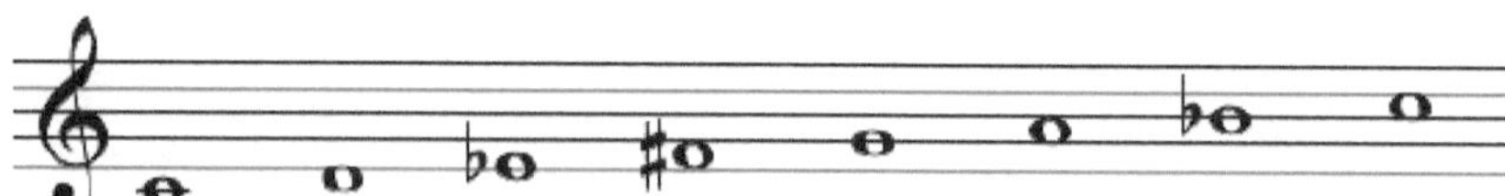

Octatonic (Diminished) Scale

Octatonic or Diminished

The ***octatonic scale*** is an eight-note scale composed of alternating whole steps and half steps. Jazz musicians refer to this scale as **diminished** because the chords resulting from this scale's pitches are diminished.

DIATONIC SCALE

Diatonic
Tonic

Diatonic (literately "***across the tones***") defines a scale of mixed half and whole steps (and occasional step and a half) in which each individual tone plays a role. The first tone of a scale is called **tonic**, is a point of rest and is considered to be the most stable. Other tones lead toward or away from it, creating varying degrees of tension or relaxation. Since the tonic is the focal point of the scale, the most stable note, and the point of greatest relaxation, diatonic melodies frequently end on the tonic note. At times the word diatonic is used to indicate a tone that is part of a particular scale pattern – as distinguished from a non-diatonic tone that does not belong to the pattern. This is the the type of scale that forms the Major scale.

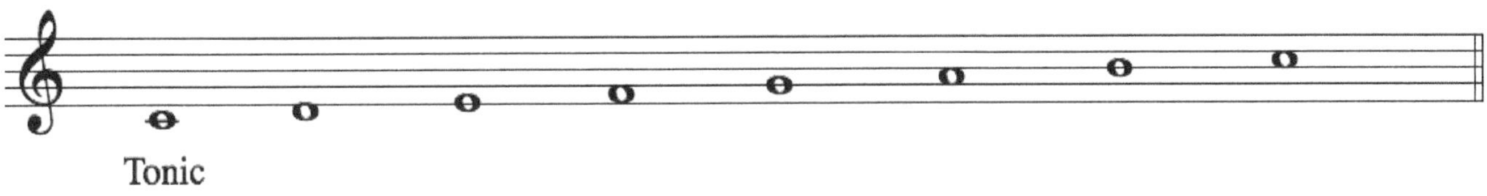

LESSON 12: SCALES DEGREES

Scale Degree
Scale Step

Each of the diatonic scale is a **scale degree**, or **scale step**. Each degree of the seven-tone diatonic scale has a name that relates to its function. The following table describes each degree and function.

SCALE DEGREE	NAME	MEANING
1st	TONIC	Tonal Center – the final resolution tone.
2nd	SUPERTONIC	One step above the tonic
3rd	MEDIANT	Midway between tonic and dominant
4th	SUBDOMINANT	The lower dominant – the fifth tone down from the tonic (also the fourth tone up from the tonic).
5th	DOMINAT	So called because its function is next in importance to the tonic.
6th	SUBMEDIANT	The lower mediant – halfway between tonic and lower dominant (subdominant). The third tone down from the tonic.
7th	LEADING TONE	Strong affinity for and leads melodically to the tonic. Used when the seventh tone appears a half step below the tonic.

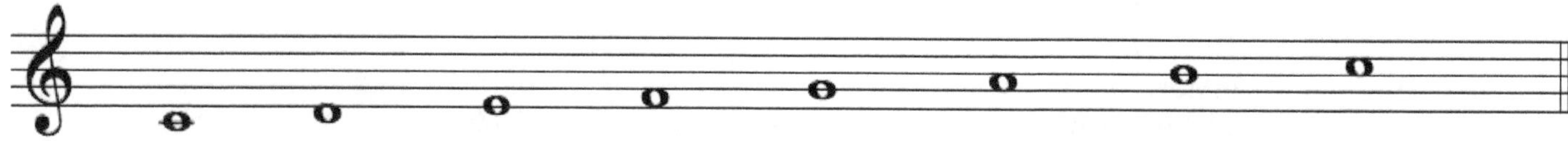

Notice that each scale contains a different arrangement of intervals between each note of the scale. The intervalic relation of notes in a scale provides a unique character to that scale. Our current concern is that of diatonic scales.

When you look at the figure at the above diatonic scale, you should notice several things:

1) The notes are stepwise (alphabetically) ascending. They may also be descending.

2) All the basic notes are represented including the octave duplication. No notes are missing.

3) Eight notes are required for a complete, one-octave diatonic scale.

LESSON 13: MAJOR SCALES

Major Scale

The major scale consists of seven different pitches. There are half steps between the third and fourth and seventh and eighth scale degrees; whole steps exist between all other steps.

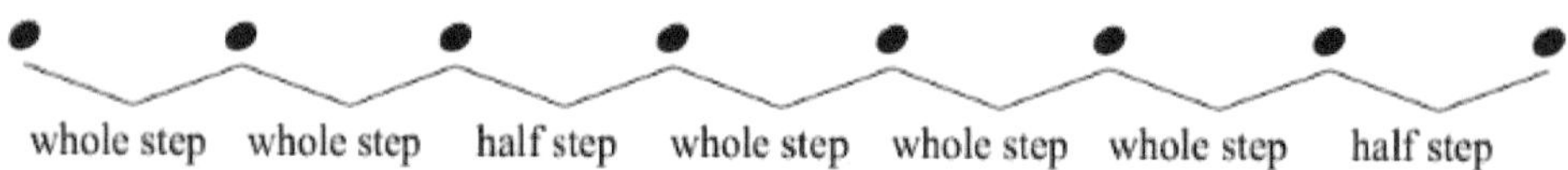

Below is the C major scale. The pattern of whole and half steps is the same for all major scales. By changing the first note, then using the pattern as a guide, you can construct any major scale. Likewise, if you know the pattern for any other scale, you can create them, too.

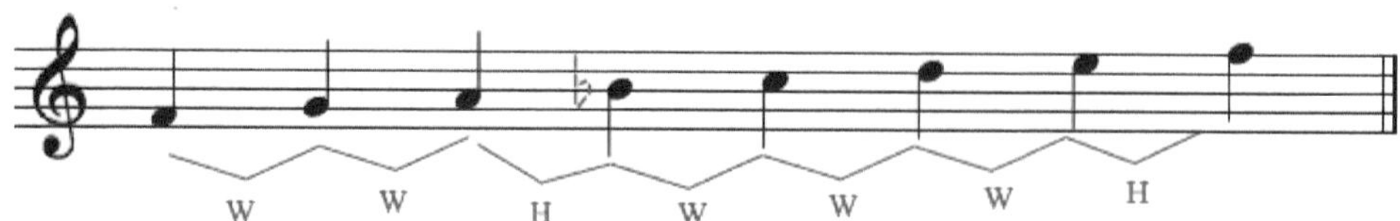

You may find it helpful to SAY THE PATTERN OUT LOUD:

WHOLE - WHOLE - HALF - WHOLE - WHOLE - WHOLE - HALF

Tetrachord

Some people prefer to learn major scales in terms of ***tetrachords***. A major scale consists of two tetrachords, two groups of four-note chords or scales.. The D major scale, for example, is shown below with its two tetrachords.

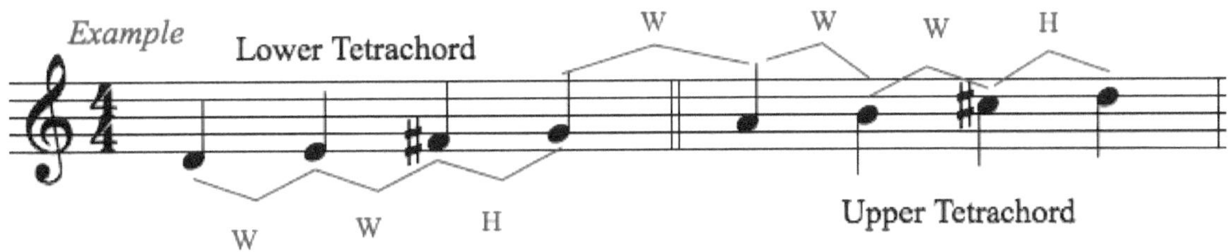

Several observations should be made about the example above.

1. There are two tetrachords in a major scale.
2. The two tetrachords are separated by a whole step.
3. Each tetrachord contains the same pattern of whole steps and half steps.

Activity #14:

Steps to write a major scale:

(a) Write the first note of the desired scale...in this case we picked the scale of F Major:

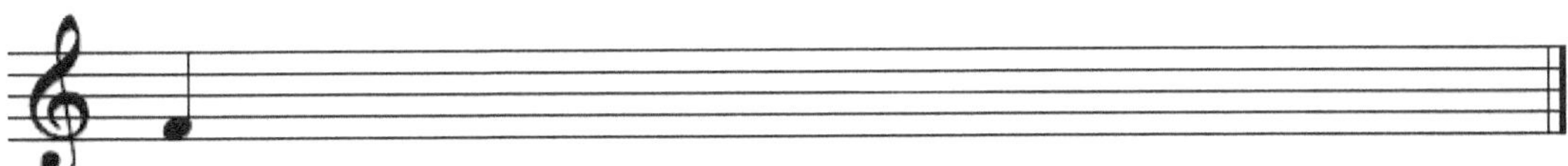

(b) Add the remaining notes.

(c) Write the whole/half step patter for a major scale

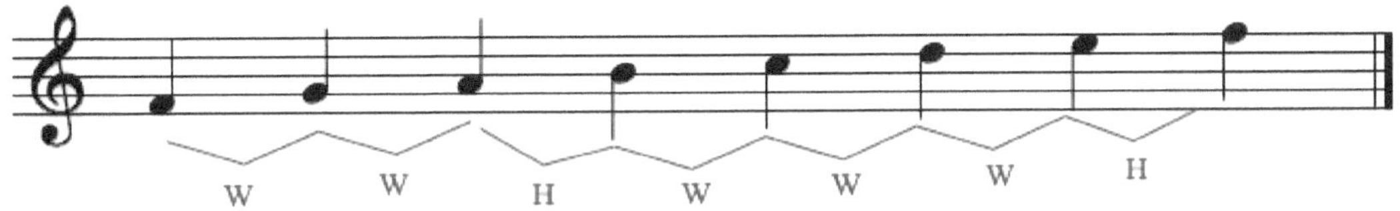

(d) Add accidentals, if needed.

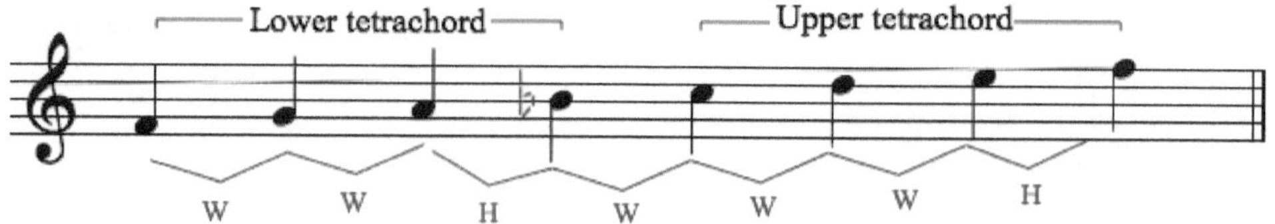

KEY CONCEPT: Any major scale you write should include eight pitches - All seven letters plus the tonic at the end - and the accidentals should all be either ***sharps or flats***, **NOT** a mixture.

Another example: Let's write the Bb (B flat) major scale.

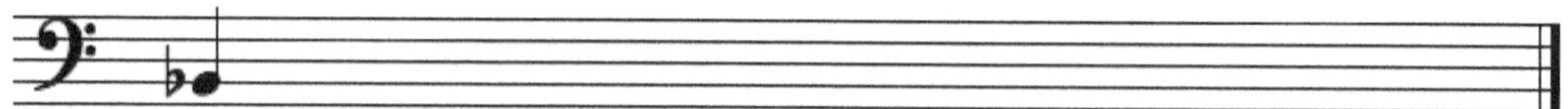

(b) Add the remaining notes.

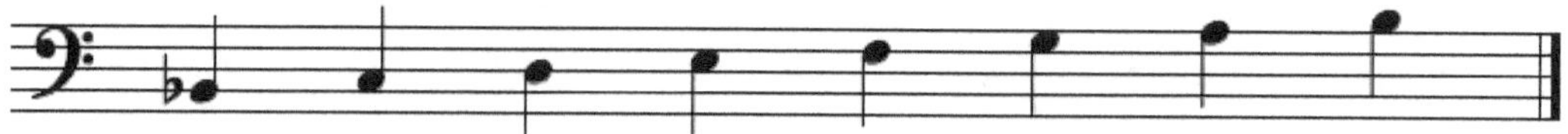

(c) Wite the whole/half step patter for a major scale

(d) Add accidentals. In the scale of Bb major we need one more accidental in addition to the Bb. We need Eb in order to complete the W-W-H-W-W-W-H pattern.

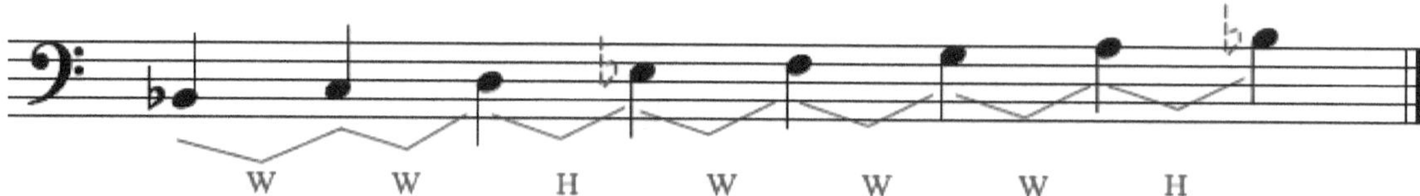

Written Exercises:

Spell each of these major scales by writing letter names in the blanks above the scale degrees. Use uppercase letters. For sharps and flats, draw the correct symbol after the letter name. The first example has been completed for you.

1. C major:	C	D	E	F	G	A	B	C
	1	2	3	4	5	6	7	8
2. A major:	___	___	___	___	___	___	___	___
	1	2	3	4	5	6	7	8
3. G major	___	___	___	___	___	___	___	___
	1	2	3	4	5	6	7	8
4. D major:	___	___	___	___	___	___	___	___
	1	2	3	4	5	6	7	8
5. F major:	___	___	___	___	___	___	___	___
	1	2	3	4	5	6	7	8
6. E major:	___	___	___	___	___	___	___	___
	1	2	3	4	5	6	7	8
7. Bb major:	___	___	___	___	___	___	___	___
	1	2	3	4	5	6	7	8
8. Ab major:	___	___	___	___	___	___	___	___
	1	2	3	4	5	6	7	8
9. Db major:	___	___	___	___	___	___	___	___
	1	2	3	4	5	6	7	8
10. Eb major:	___	___	___	___	___	___	___	___
	1	2	3	4	5	6	7	8

MAJOR SCALES WITH SHARPS

G major:

D major:

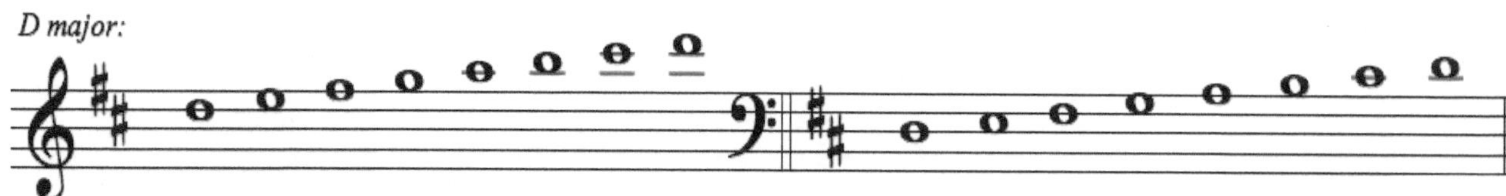

A major:

E major:

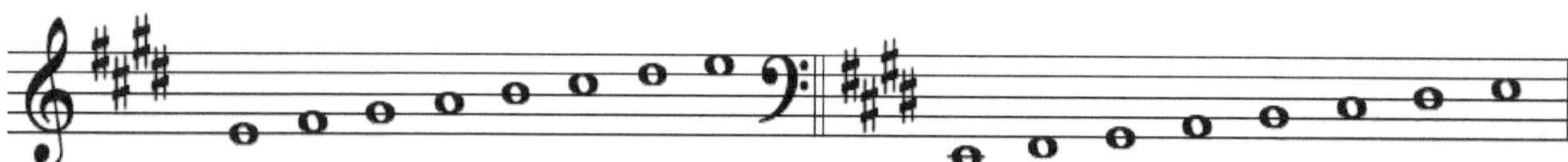

B major:

F# major:

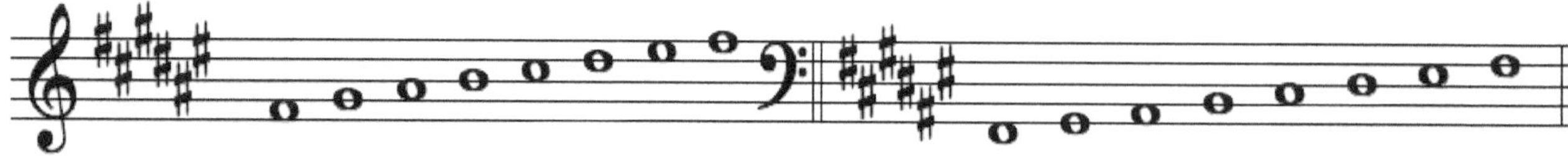

C# major:

Major Scales with Flats

F major:

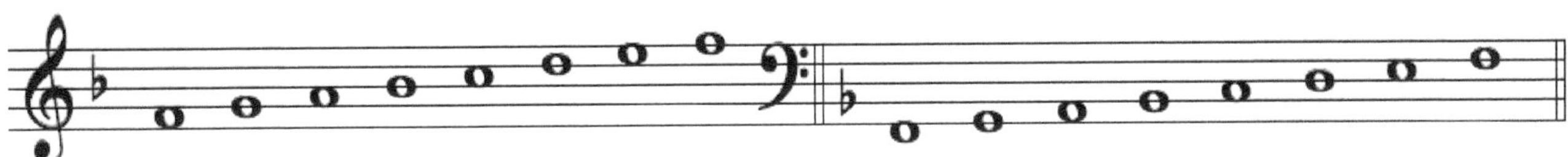

Bb major:

Eb major:

Ab major:

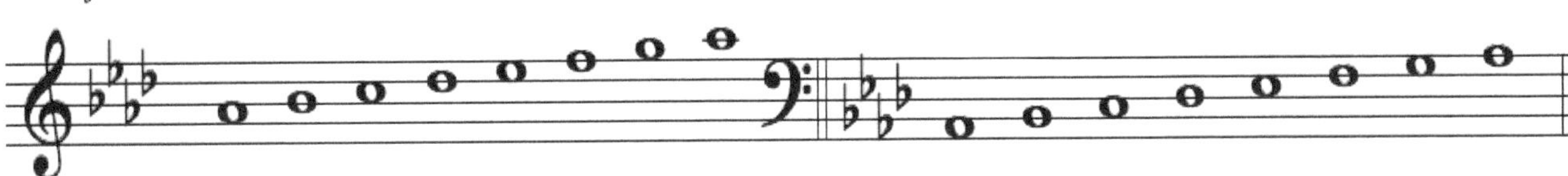

Db major:

Gb major:

Cb major:

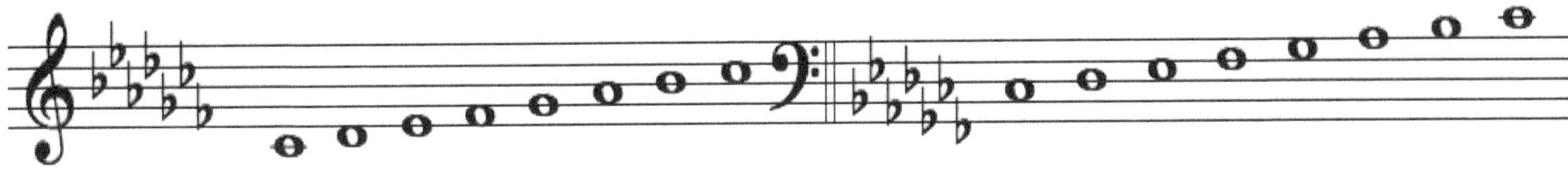

Below are shown two major scales, C and E, and how these scales appear on the piano keyboard.

C MAJOR:

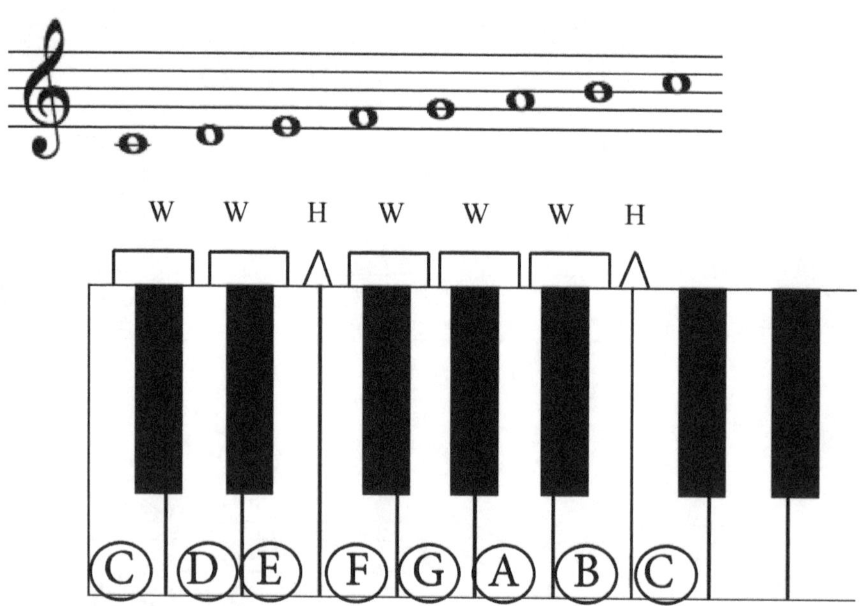

E MAJOR:

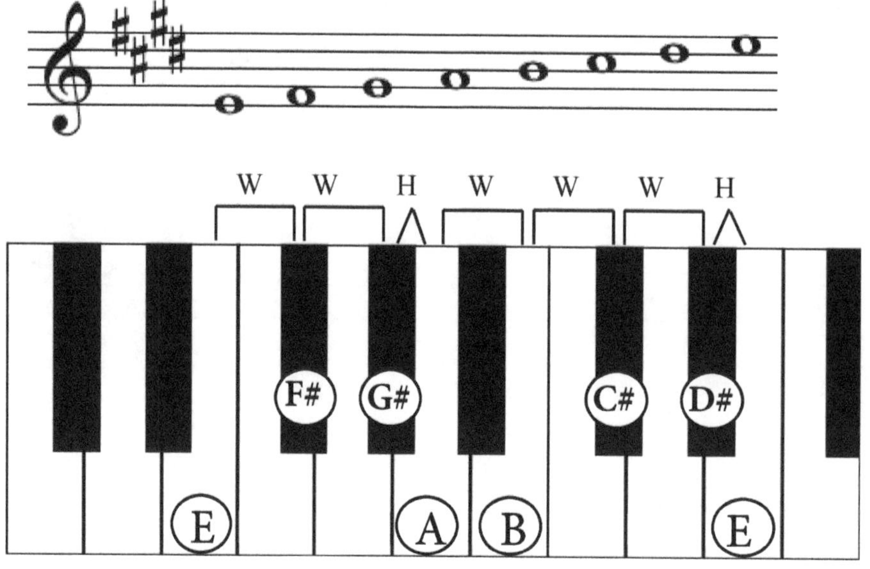

Name: ______________________

Date: ______________________

Lesson 15: Practice Exercises

Add sharps or flats to the exercises below to create major scales. Use the pattern of whole and half steps to determine which accidentals you will need to add.

Add sharps or flats to the exercises below to create major scales. Use the pattern of whole and half steps to determine which accidentals you will need to add.

Lesson 14: Major Key Signatures

Key Signature

In the previous lesson, we constructed major scales from the diatonic scale pattern. Patterns of whole steps and half steps were the key to creating those scale types. As we produced the correct patterns of whole steps and half steps for each scale, accidentals were added to the mode or basic scale. Those accidentals (sharps or flats) may be grouped together at the beginning of the music immediately after the clef sign. When sharps or flats are grouped together in this manner, they are referred to as the ***key signature***. When a key signature is used, there is no need to apply accidentals to the notes within the body of the music, resulting in music that is less cluttered from excessive use of accidentals. A particular sharp or flat in the key signature applies to every occurrence of that note, regardless of the octave (unless it is altered by an accidental in the music).

Key

Key

The terms **key** refers to the tonal system based on the major and minor scales. This system is by far the most common tonal system, but tonality can be present in music not based of the major and minor scales. By first learning to construct major and minor scales, you have already discovered what sharps or flats are in a given scale or key. The tonic, or keynote, of a scale is the same as the name of the key in which it is the main scale.

An important point to remember is that an accidental appearing in the key signature applies to that note in all octaves. For instance, an F# in the key signature indicates that all Fs encountered in the piece are to be played or sung as F#s. A similar rule holds for chromatic alterations within a measure. That is, once an accidental is introduced in a measure, it remains in force for the entire measure unless canceled by a natural sign. But unlike an accidental in the key signature, an accidental within a measure affects only the same note in the same register and in the same voice. This is an important distinction between the sharps or flats of a key signature and those introduced as accidentals.

Major Key Signatures

Sharp Keys

Each key signature can indicate either a major key or a minor key. We will begin with major keys. Since there are a total of seven (7) basic notes, there are a total of seven (7) sharps and a total of seven (7) flats. Logically it follows that there are 14 major keys with sharps or flats in them. The number and placement of sharps and flats in a key signature is not arbitrary; there is a definite order that makes key signatures easy to read and remember.

The following figure shows the order for the sharp keys. Notice the invariable pattern for sharps key signatures. If there is only one sharp that sharp is always F#; if two sharps, they are always ***F#*** and ***C#***, and so on. The complete order of sharps is ***F#-C#-G#-D#-A#-E#-B#.*** You should learn both the order and the location of the sharps in both the treble and bass clefs. Fortunately, once you have learned them, you know them; they never change.

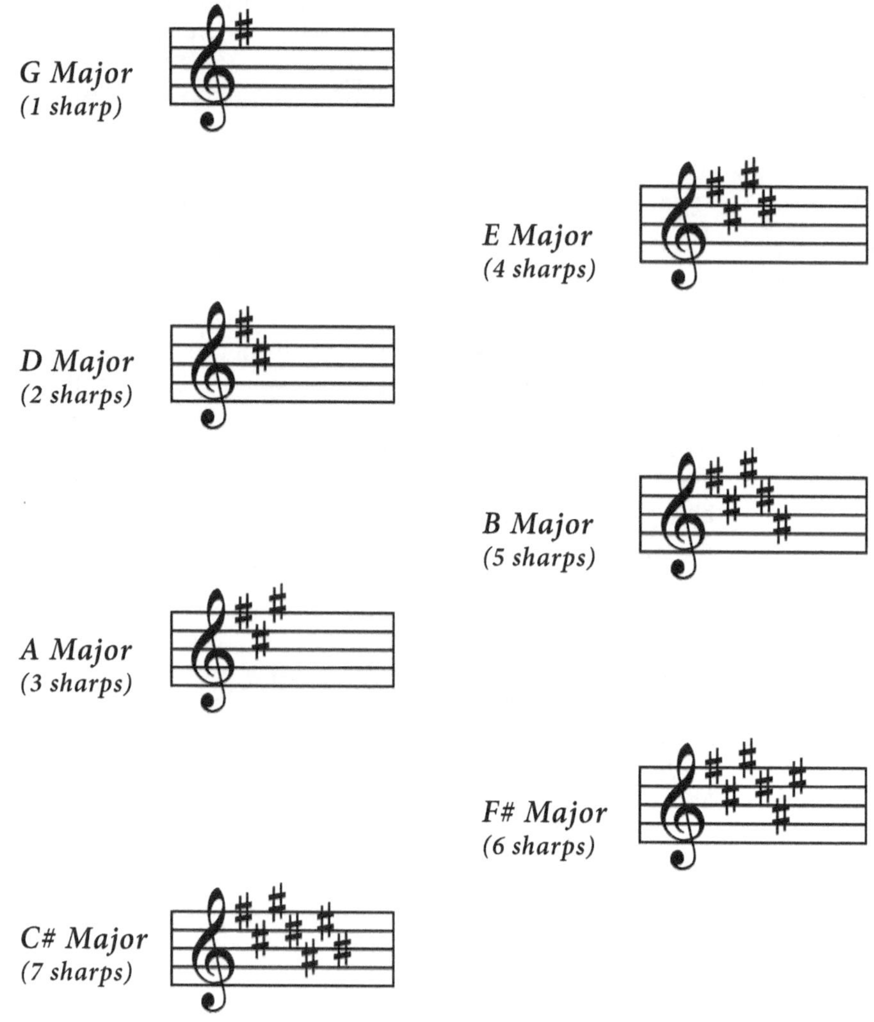

In identifying major key signatures that use sharps, the key is always the pitch a half step above the last sharp indicated in the signature. This is because the last added sharp is always the leading tone of that key. This method of identifying sharps keys is useful, but you should also memorize the number of sharps associated with each major key as shown in the above example.

Flat Keys

Flat key signatures, like sharp key signatures, have a consistent order and location on the staff. Notice that the last added flat is always the subdominat of that key. The complete order of flats is ***Bb-Eb-Ab- Db-Gb-Cb-Fb.*** The order of flats in major keys is shown below:

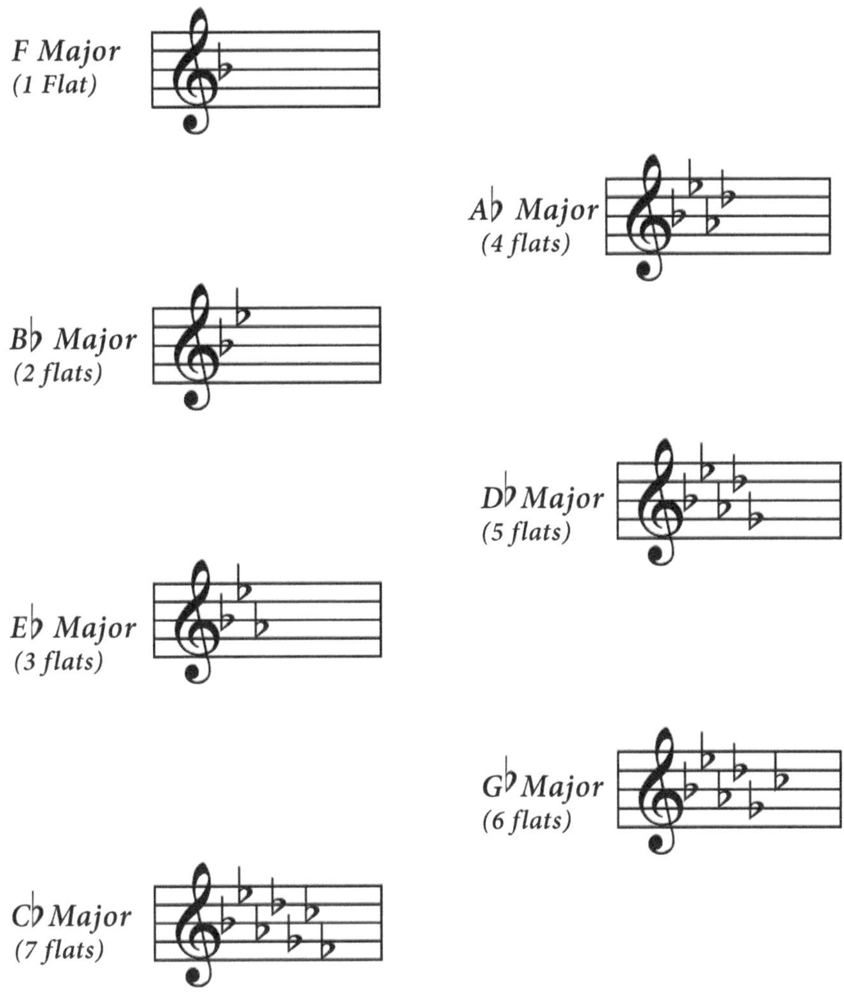

When identifying major key signatures that use flats, we cannot use the system that we learned for major keys that use sharps. Instead, with the last flat key signatures the name of the key is the same as the name of the next-to-last flat.

Name: ______________________

Date: ______________________

Lesson 14: Practice Exercises

1. Name the major key for each of the following key signatures. (see example)

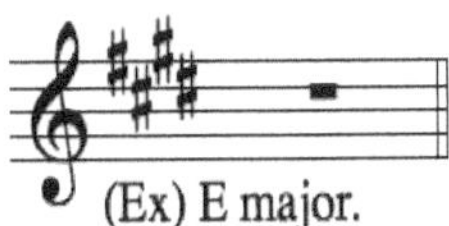

2. Write the proper key signature for each of the following examples.

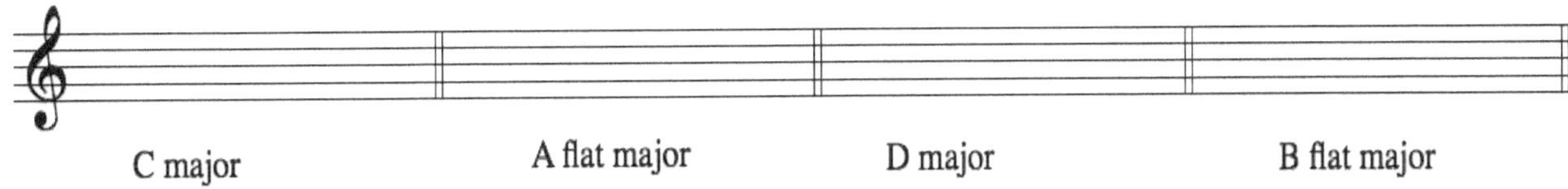

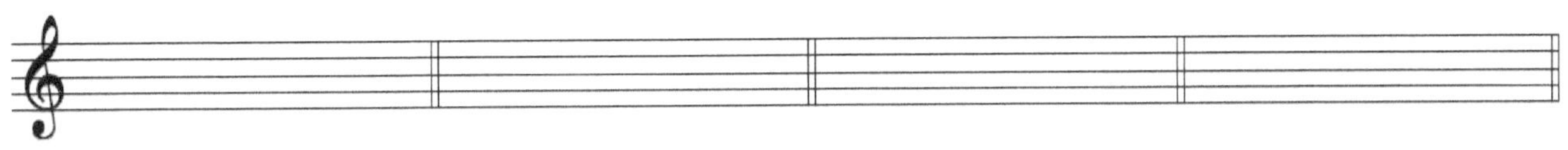

3. Write the order of sharps for both clefs.

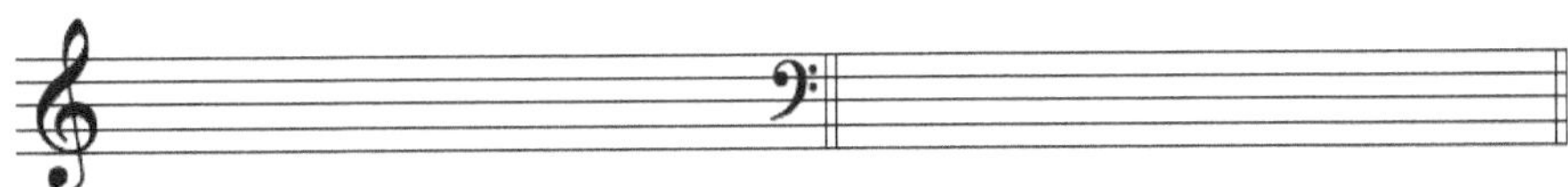

4. Write the order of flats for both clefs.

Lesson 15: Circle of Fifths

Circle of Fifths

You may have noticed that each time a new sharp is added, the new key is five scale steps higher that the last; and each time a new flat is added, the new key is five scale steps lowers than the last. That is, C major has no sharps or flats, G major (five steps higher) has one sharp, D major (five step higher than G) has two sharps, and so on. This relationship between keys is sometimes represented around a circle, like the one shown below, called the ***circle of fifths***.

The circle of fifths is a chart that can help you remember the number of sharps or flats in a given key. When you learn the circle of fifths and remember the order of sharps (and flats), you will be able to figure out any major key signature. A certain amount of logic is inherent in the design of the circle of fifths.

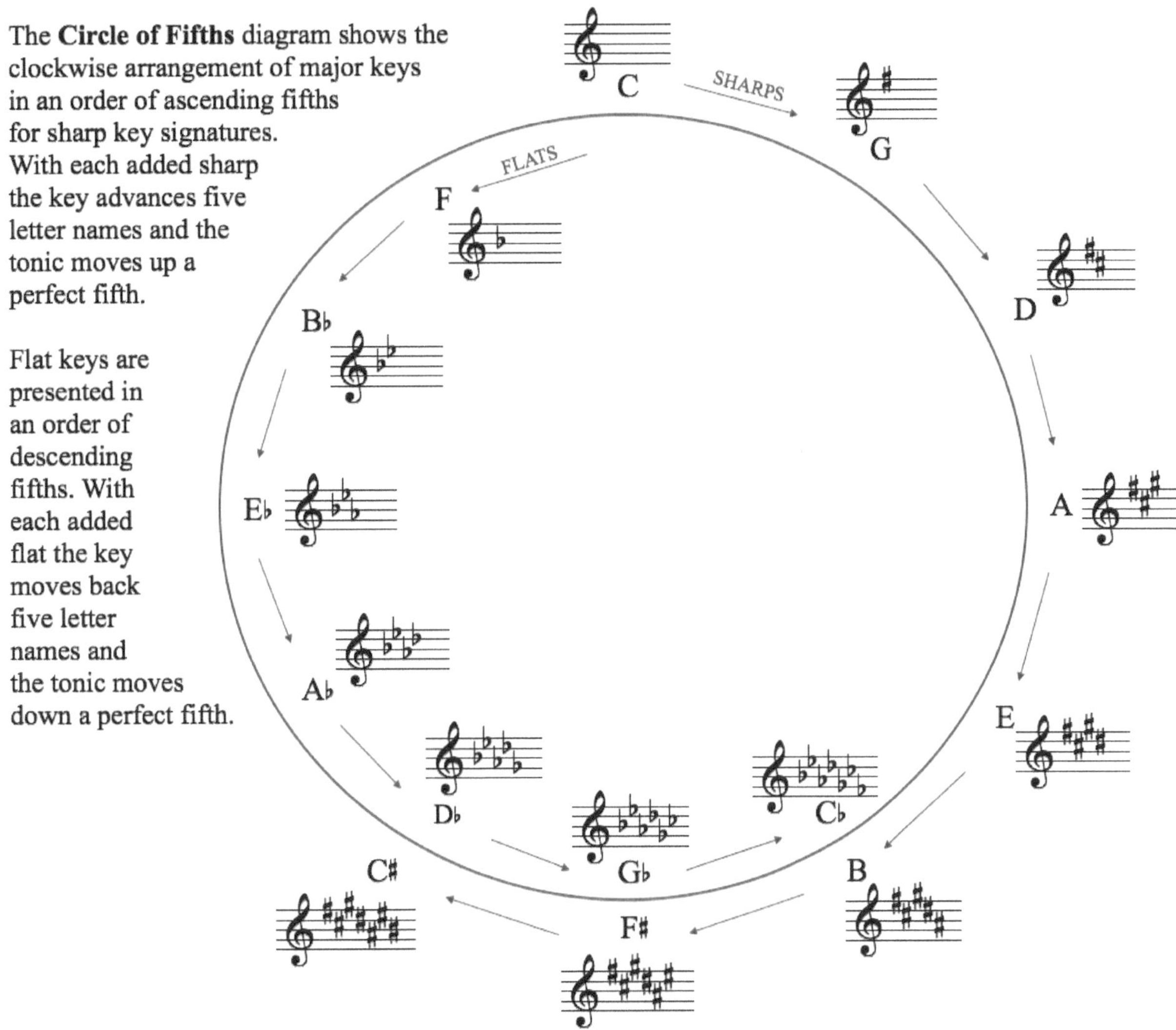
The Circle of Fifths diagram shows the clockwise arrangement of major keys in an order of ascending fifths for sharp key signatures. With each added sharp the key advances five letter names and the tonic moves up a perfect fifth.
Flat keys are presented in an order of descending fifths. With each added flat the key moves back five letter names and the tonic moves down a perfect fifth.
C
SHARPS
G
D
A
E
B
F♯
C♯
FLATS
F
B♭
E♭
A♭
D♭
G♭
C♭

Activity #15:

1. Write the flats in the order in which they are added as you go around the circle of fifths.

Bb ___ ___ ___ ___ ___ ___

2. Write the sharps in the order in which they are added as you go around the circle of fifths.

F# ___ ___ ___ ___ ___ ___

3. Write the names of the keys with sharps in order as they appear on the circle of fifths.

G ___ ___ ___ ___ ___ ___

4. Write the names of the keys with flats in order as they appear on the circle of fifths.

F ___ ___ ___ ___ ___ ___

5. Complete the circle of fifths by writing the name of the missing key signatures.

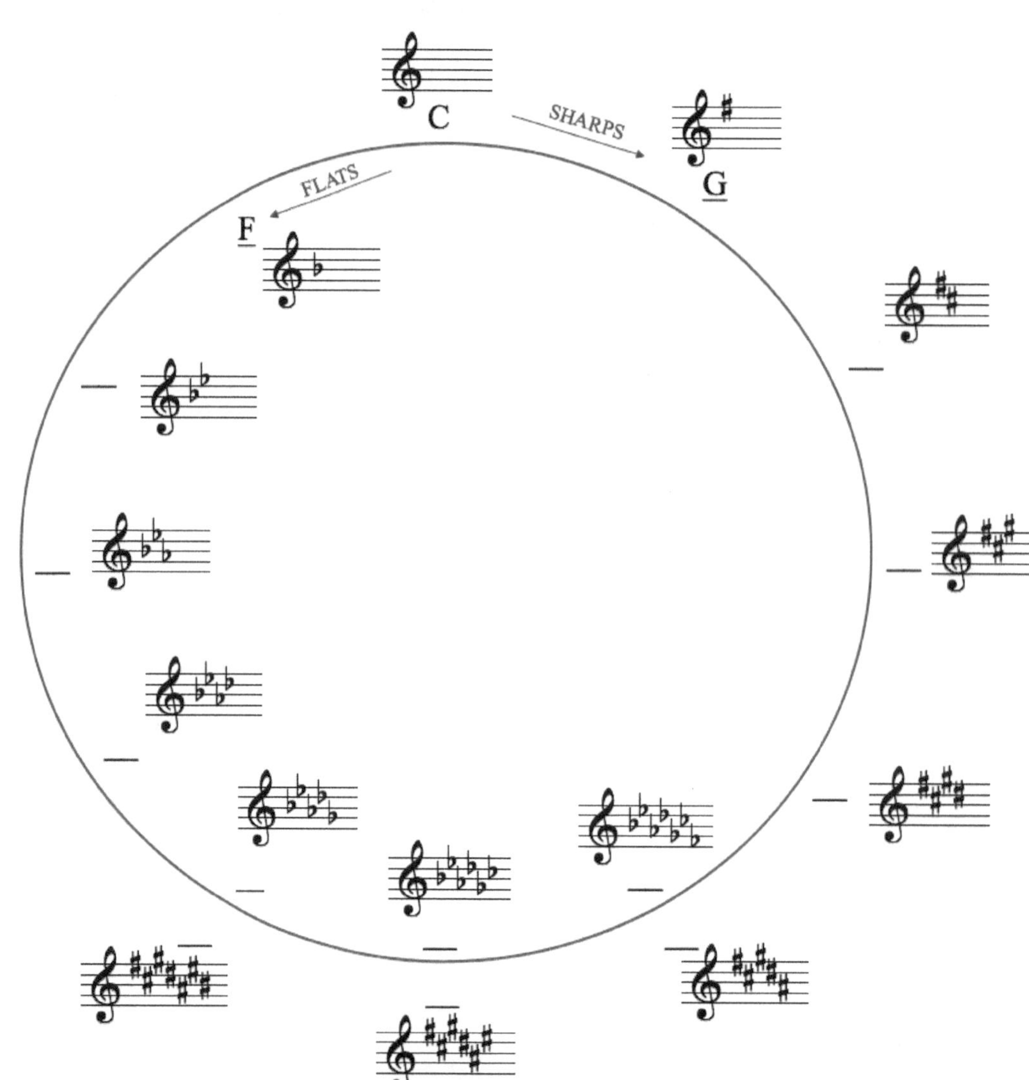

STUDY QUESTIONS FOR CHAPTER 4

1. Define the following terms:

   Scale
   Diatonic
   Scale degrees
   Tetrachord
   Key signature
   Circle of fifths

2. In the major scale, between what scale degrees do half steps occur?

3. What is the pattern of whole and half steps of all major scales?

4. What is the order of sharps when writing a key signature?

5. What is the order of flats when writing a key signature?

6. What is the purpose of the circle of fifths?

Name: ________________ Date:_______________

Chapter 4: Self-Test

Name the major key and write the tonic on the staff for the following key signatures.

Write the key signatures for the following major keys.

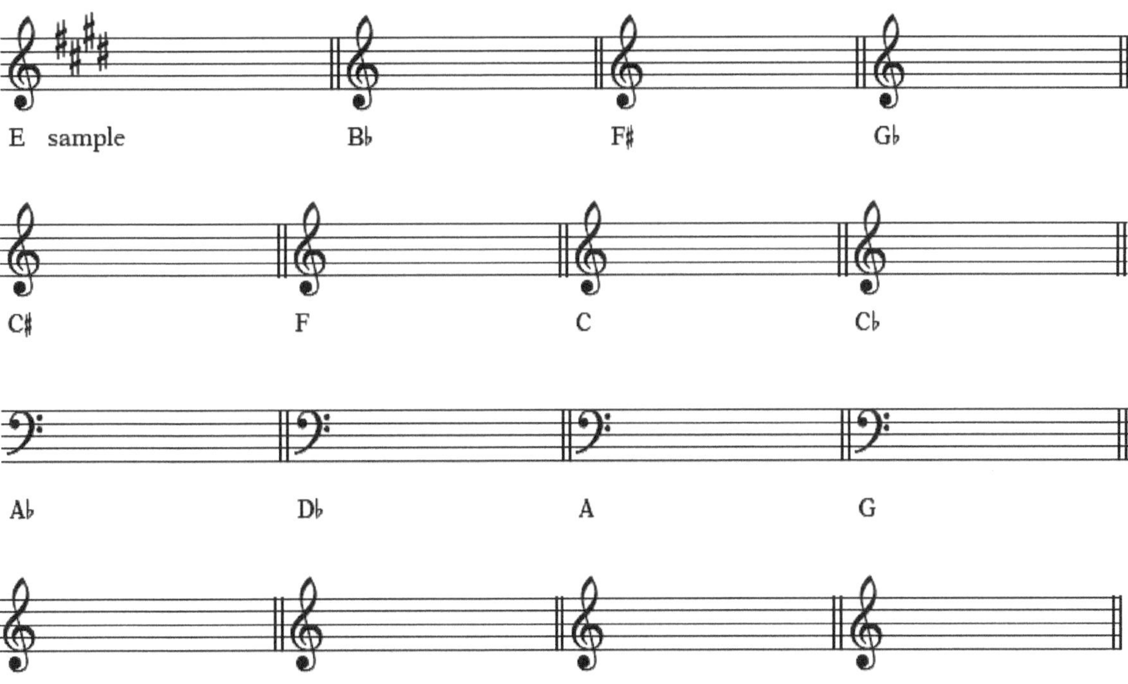

Major Scales:

Add sharps or flats to the exercises below to create major scales. Use the pattern of whole and half steps to determine which accidentals you will need to add.

Name:_____________________________
Date:___________________

Write ascending major scales starting from the given tonic pitches. When you have written the scales, check that the half steps occur between the third and fourth degrees and between the seventh and first degrees. Indicate the half steps for each scale. A keyboard is given to help you visualize the intervals.

Write the following scales. Please only use eight notes. (see Example)

1. Db major

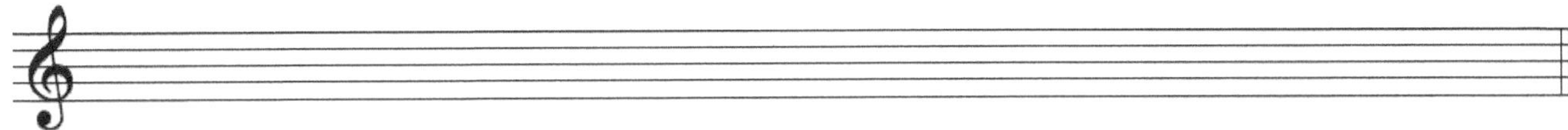

2. C# major

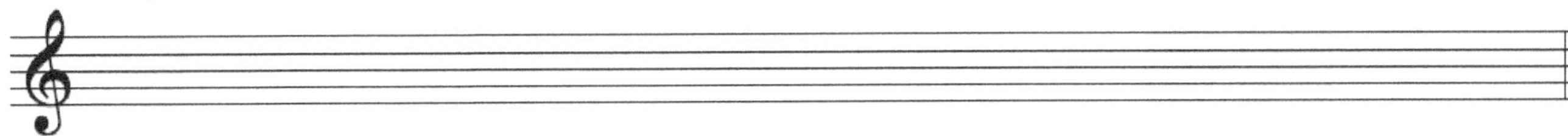

3. Eb major

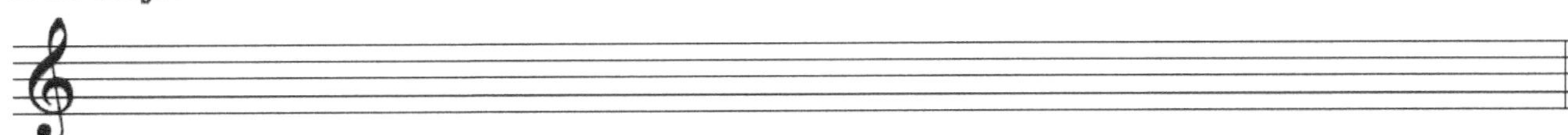

4. Bb major

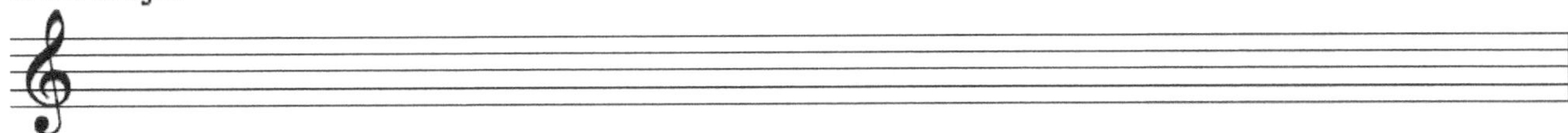

5. D major

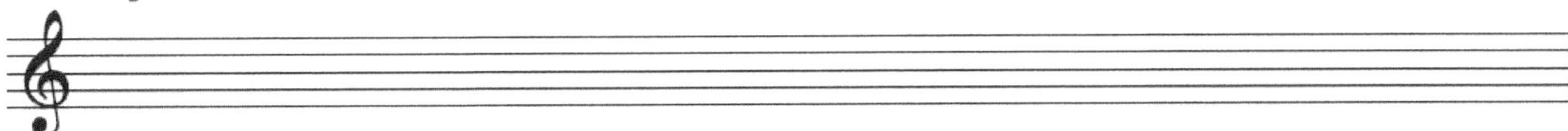

Complete the circle of fifths by adding the missing key signatures.

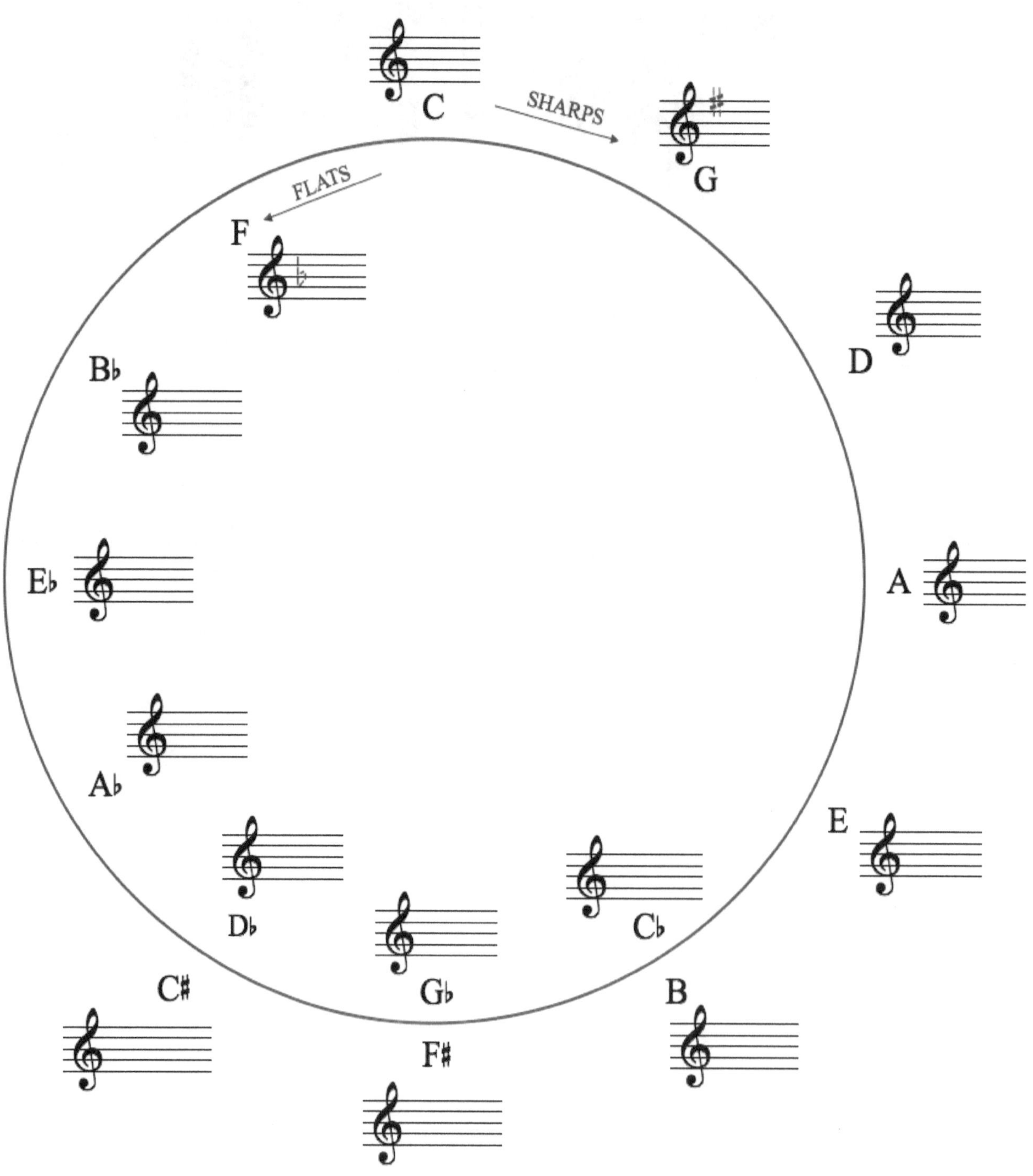

CHAPTER 5

MINOR SCALES AND KEYS

Lesson 16: Parallel and Relatives Keys

Parallel Keys

Major and minor scales that share the same tonic are called ***parallel keys***. Parallel keys share not only the same tonic but also the same supertonic, subdominant, and dominant as well. C Major and C minor, Bb major and Bb minor, D major and D minor are all parallel keys. They differ only in scale degrees 3, 6, and 7. But those differences can have a powerful expressive effect. Many compositions create a change of mood by shifting from minor to major, or vice versa, while retaining the same tonic.

Parallel Keys

Relatives Keys

Two scales that share the same key signature are called ***relative scales.*** We say that F major is the relative major of d minor, and that d minor is the relative minor of F major. Key signatures can specify major or minor keys. To determine the name of a minor key, find the name of the key in major and then count backwards three half steps. For example, the relative minor of "F" major is "D" minor because from "F" we count backwards three half steps and we end up in "D". Remember that sharps and flats affect names.

Relatives Keys

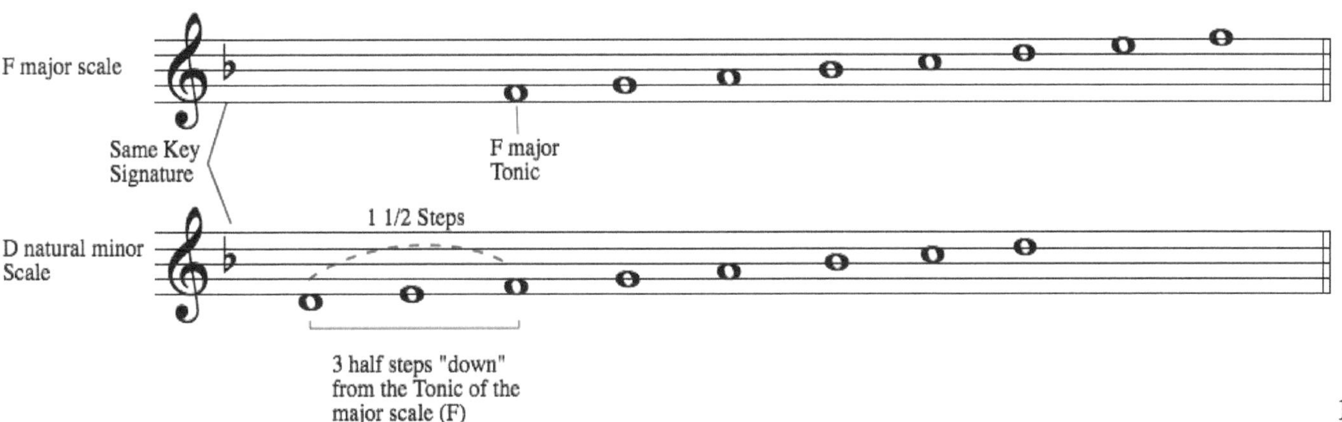

Both scales have one and the same accidental, Bb. In fact, if you begin on the sixth degree of any major scale and follow its note pattern for one octave, the result will always be a new, natural minor scale. This relationship, which is constant for all major keys, means that there are pairs f keys – one major, one minor – related by the same pitch content, hence by the same key signature. Such keys are called relative keys.

Relative Minor

The term ***relative minor*** refers to the minor key or scale that is relative to a particular major scale be having the same key signature. The term relative major refers to the major key or scale with the same key signature as a particular minor scale. The relative minor-major relationship may be remembered in two ways: (1)The relative minor scale always begins on the sixth degree of the major scale. (2)The relative minor scale always begins three half steps (a minor third) below its relative major scale.

LESSON 17: MINOR SCALES

Unlike the major scale, the minor scale has three different and distinct forms. Each form of the minor scale has a unique pattern of whole steps and half steps. Each form of the minor scale has a unique name also: natural minor, harmonic minor and melodic minor. Each form will be presented in turn.

NATURAL MINOR SCALE

It contains seven different pitches with whole steps separating adjacent tones, except for half steps between the second and third degrees and between the fifth and sixth degrees. Its pitches are those of the white keys of the piano from A to A:

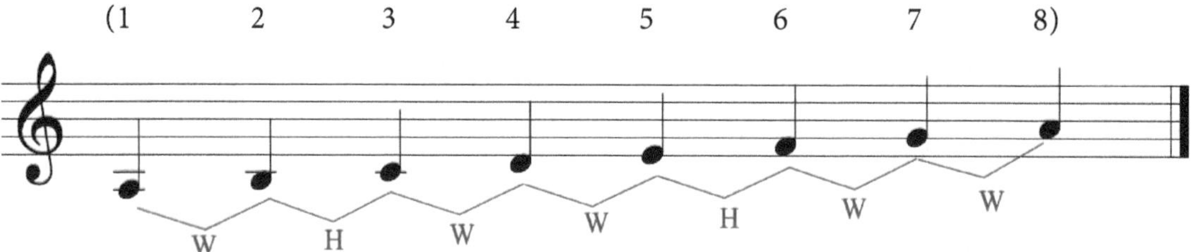

All natural minor scales are made up of the following pattern of whole and half steps:

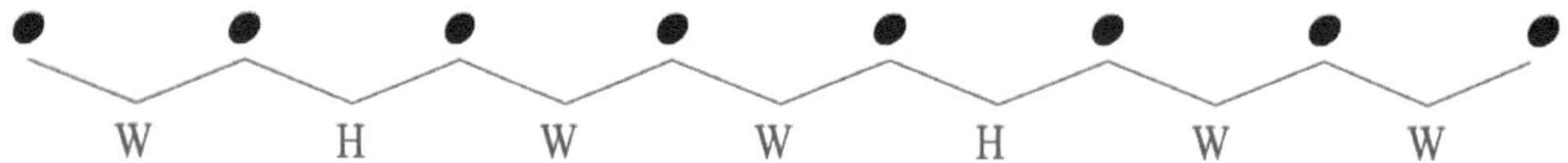

Another way to spell a natural minor scale is by taking the parallel major scale and lowering the 3, 6, and 7 scale degree by half step. For example, we are going to construct a C natural minor scale out of its parallel major, see below:

From this C major scale lets lower the 3. 6. and 7 scale degree.

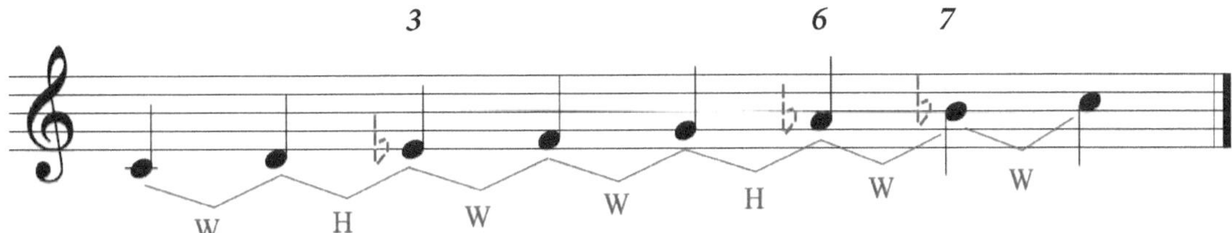

Our finished C natural minor scale will look like this:

Activity #16:

Write the specified major scale on the left-hand side in whole notes. Then rewrite the scale on the right-hand side, lowering the 3, 6, and 7 scale degree to make it a natural minor scale.

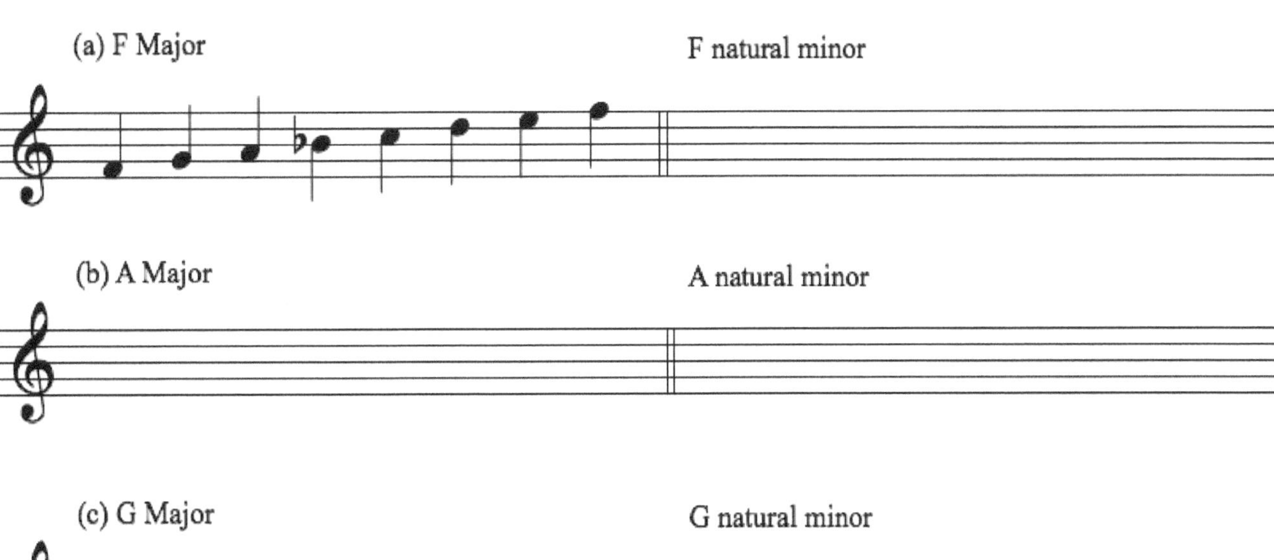

HARMONIC MINOR SCALE

Harmonic Minor

Harmonic Minor scale has a raised seventh degree. The added impetus of a raised seventh degree gives more melodic thrust toward the tonic. Raising the seventh degree creates a step and a half between the sixth and seventh degrees, and a half step between the seventh and Tonic. The difference between the natural minor and the harmonic minor is that the harmonic minor borrows the leading tone of the parallel major scale to replace its own leading tone. Composers do this tin order to create a stronger harmony, that is, a greater feeling of harmonic motion between chords.

Harmonic Minor scales apply the following rule to its pattern of half and whole steps: the 7 scale degree is raised by ***½ step***.

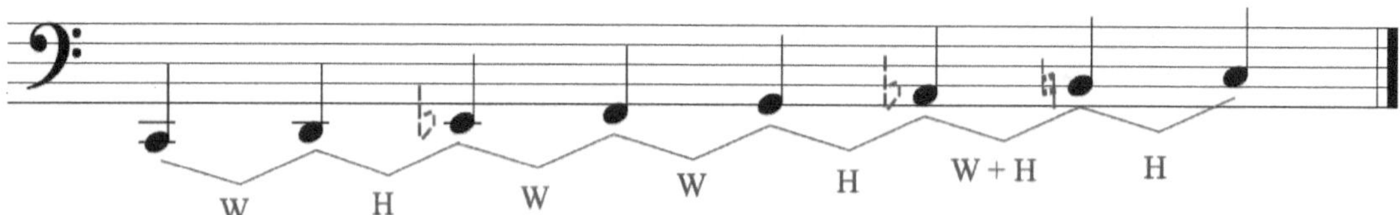

All harmonic minor scales are made up of the following pattern of whole and half steps:

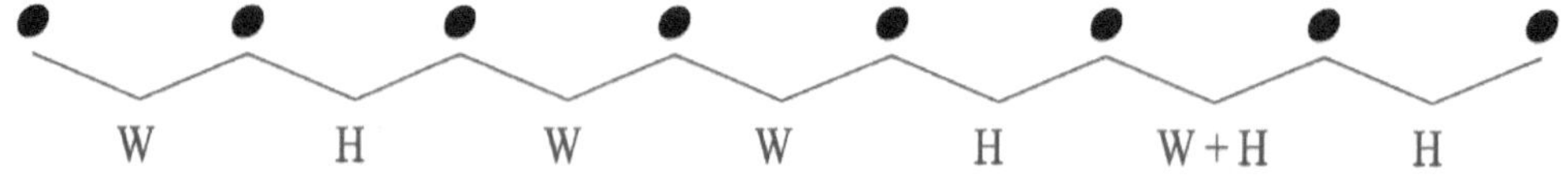

Another way to spell the harmonic minor scale is by writing the the natural minor and raise the 7 scale degree a chromatic half step.

We start with the natural minor scale. In this case we are using C natural minor.

In order to create the harmonic minor scale we need to raise the 7 scale degree from the natural minor scale:

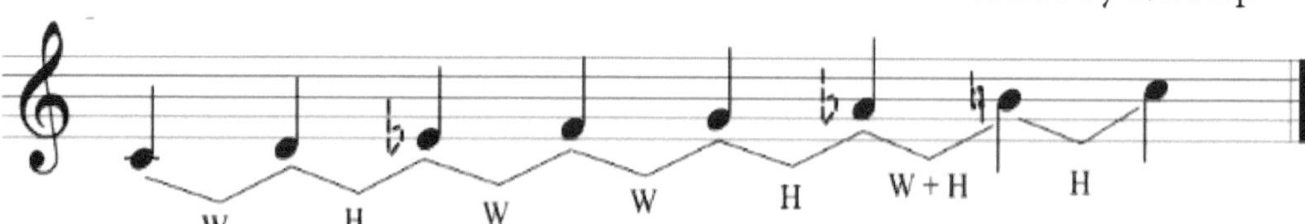

Our finished harmonic minor scale will look like this:

Activity #17:

Write the following natural minor scales, then change them to harmonic minor by raising the 7 scale degree. Circle the 7 scale degree.

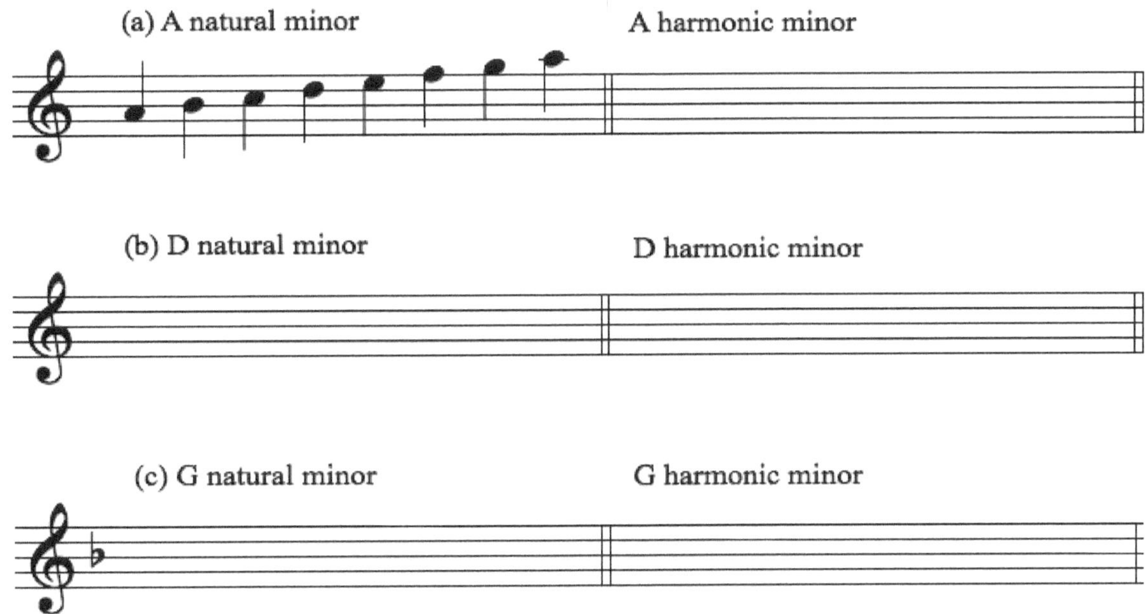

Melodic Minor

Melodic Minor

Melodic Minor scale appears in both ascending and descending form. When ascending, the 6 and 7 scale degree are raised by ½ step each. When descending, they do so in the natural minor form. The melodic minor scale developed because composers liked the urgency of the raised seventh, but found the step-and-a-half interval between the sixth and seventh degrees of the harmonic minor scale to harsh, especially for smooth vocal writing. In descending melodic passages, no need exists for the raised seventh, so composers most often used the natural minor with the lowered seventh and sixth degrees.

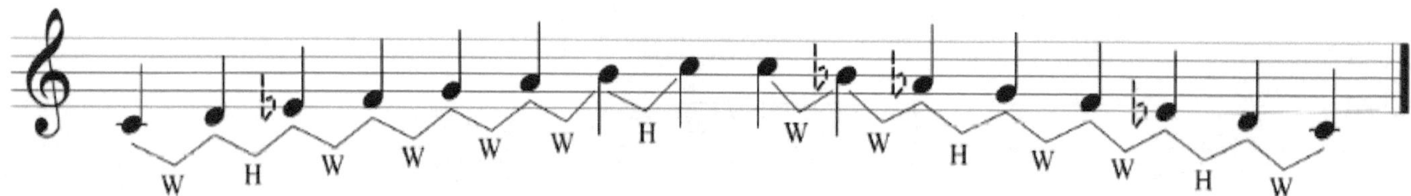

The pattern of whole and half steps used in the Melodic Minor scale varies depending if the scale is ascending or descending.

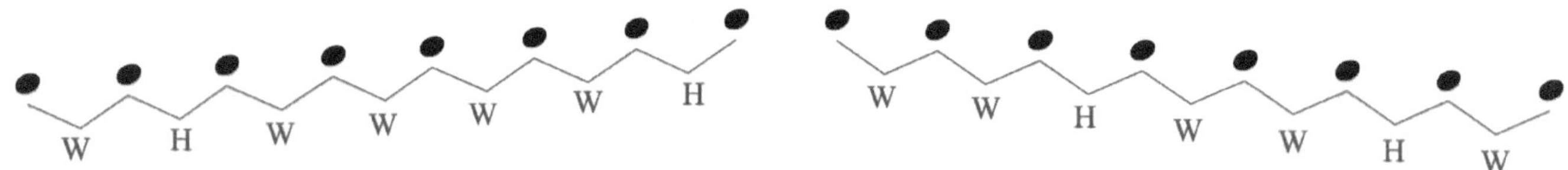

Compare the ascending pattern with the descending pattern. The descending pattern is the same pattern for the Natural Minor scale. *(For more information about how to play major and minor scales on the keyboard see* Appendix B*)*

Summary Of The Minor Scales

The unaltered ***natural*** form of minor is a rearrangement of the notes of its relative major; both have the same key signature. To convert the natural form to the ***harmonic*** form, raise the 7 scale degree by one chromatic half step. To convert the natural form to the ***melodic*** form, raise both the 6 and 7 scale degree by one chromatic half step:

Name: ______________________

Date: ______________________

Lesson 17: Practice Exercises

Add sharps or flats to the exercises below to create natural minor scales.

Add sharps or flats to the exercises below to create harmonic minor scales.

Add sharps or flats to the exercises below to create melodic minor scales.

Lesson 18: Minor Key Signatures

The minor key signatures, for sharp keys and flat keys, are given below. Notice that the lowercase letters are used to indicate minor keys, which is an acceptable practice. Notice also that last sharp added to each sharp key is the supertonic, and the last flat added to each flat key is the submediant. As you study these minor key signatures, make a mental association with the relative major for each hey.

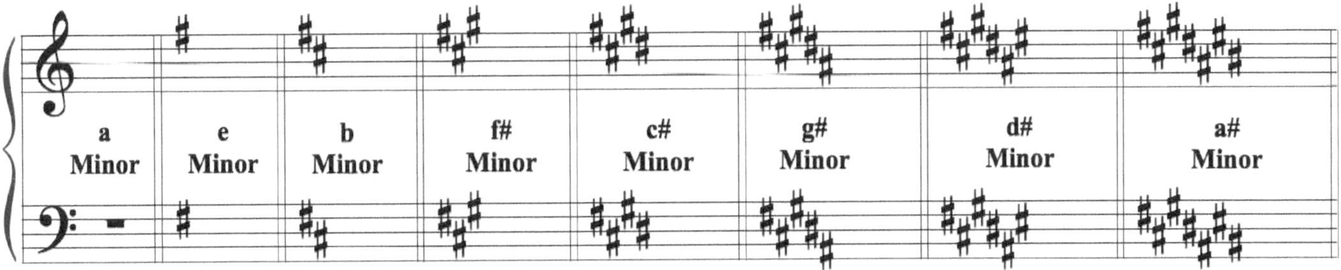

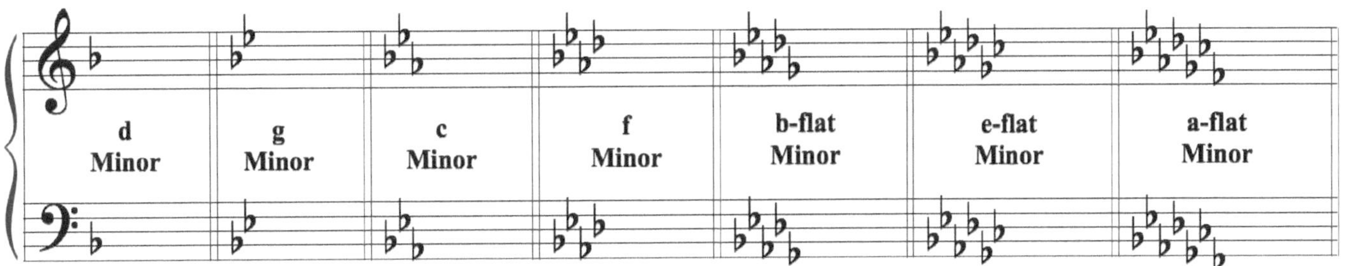

Another way to write a natural minor scale is to think of the relative major and its key signature:

(1) Write the pitches from the first scale degree to the octave of the minor scale without accidentals.
(2) Find its relative major (count up three half steps and three letter names).
(3) Write the relative major key signature next to the clef.

For harmonic or melodic minor, add the appropriate accidental (e.g., a sharp or natural for the 7 scale degree (leading tone).

For speed and facility in sight-reading and analysis, memorize the minor key signatures just as you have the major ones. The circle of fifth can also show the key signature shared by relative major and minor keys. It may help you memorize the minor key signature. It may also help to remember that key signatures for parallel keys differ by three accidentals. For example, A major has 3 sharps, A minor has 0; B major has 5 sharps, B minor has 2; D major has 2 sharps, D minor has 1 flat.

The following figure shows the circle of fifth with major and minor key signatures.

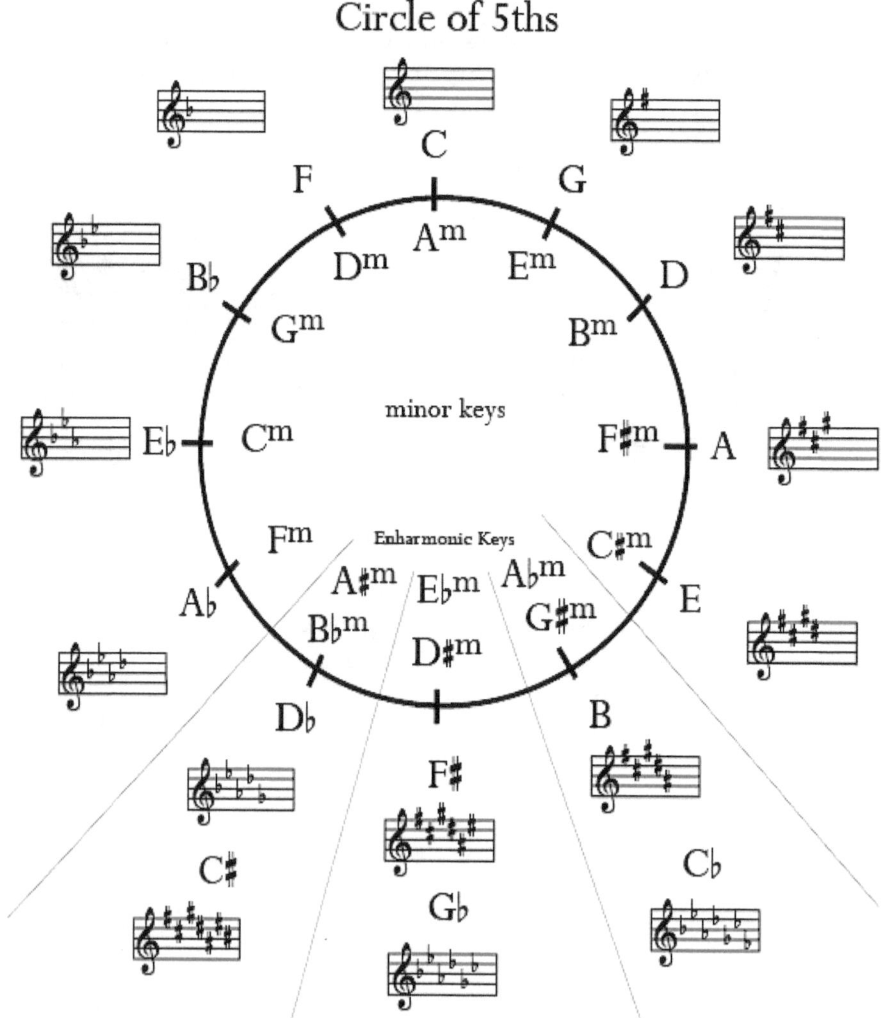

The major key names are on the outside, separated by fifths. The corresponding minor key names are on the inside. The number and position of the sharps or flats is in the middle.

(For more information about the circle of fifths see APPENDIX G)

Study Questions for Chapter 5

1. Define the following terms:

   Natural minor

   Relative keys

   Parallel Keys

   Harmonic Minor

   Melodic Minor

2. What is the difference between parallel keys and relative keys?

3. In terms of whole and half steps, what is the upper tetrachord structure of:

   a. Natural minor:

   b. Ascending melodic minor:

   c. Harmonic minor:

   d. Major:

4. Types of minor scales:

   ____

   ____

   ____

5. In a ______________________ the 7th scale degree is raised.

Name:______________________________

Date:_____________________

Chapter 5: Self-test

Name the minor key and write the tonic on the staff for the following key signatures. If possible without the ledger lines, write the tonic in two different octaves.

c♯ sample

Write the key signatures for the following minor keys.

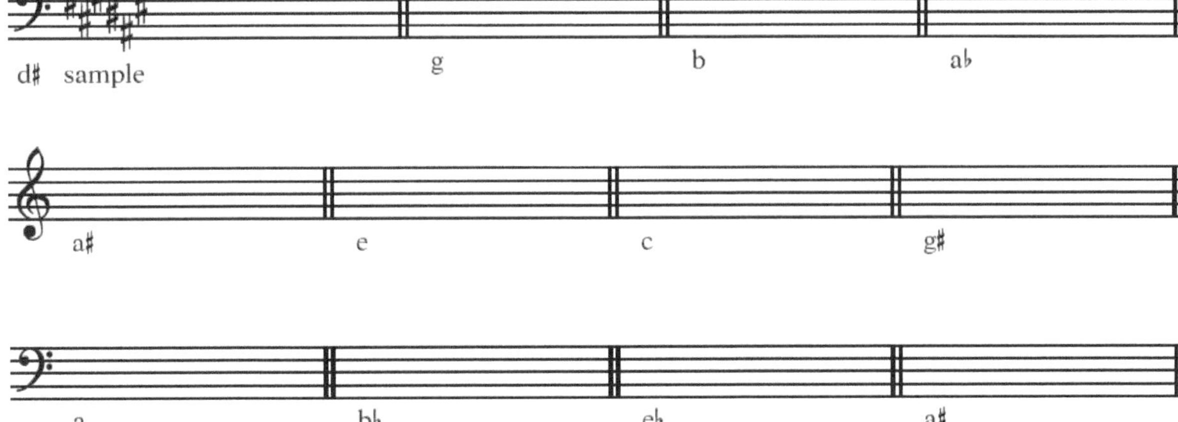

Write the ascending relative minor scales for the following ascending major scales in all forms indicated.

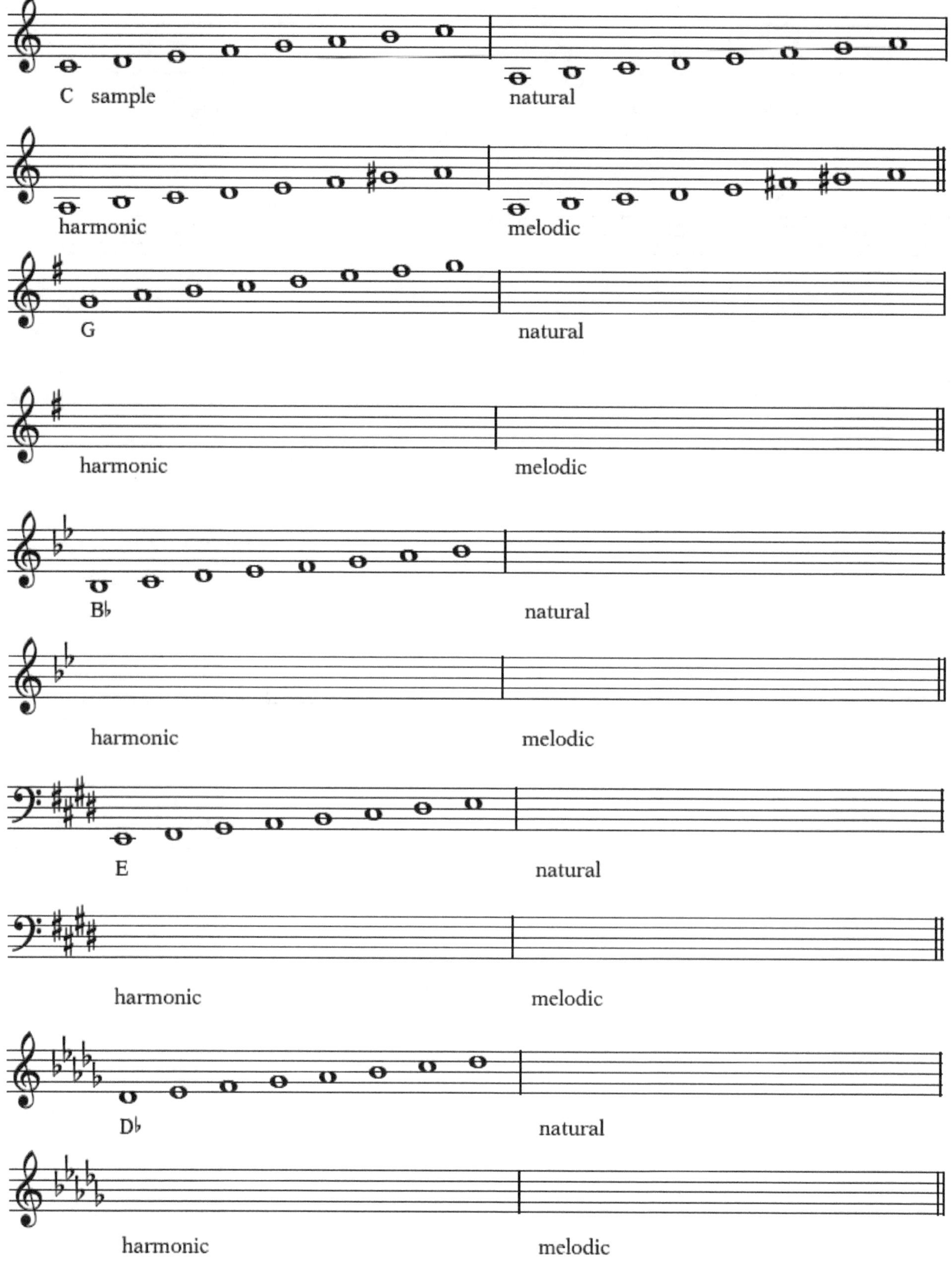

Name:____________________________
Date:___________________

Using the proper key signatures, write the ascending parallel minor scales for the following major scales in all forms as indicated.

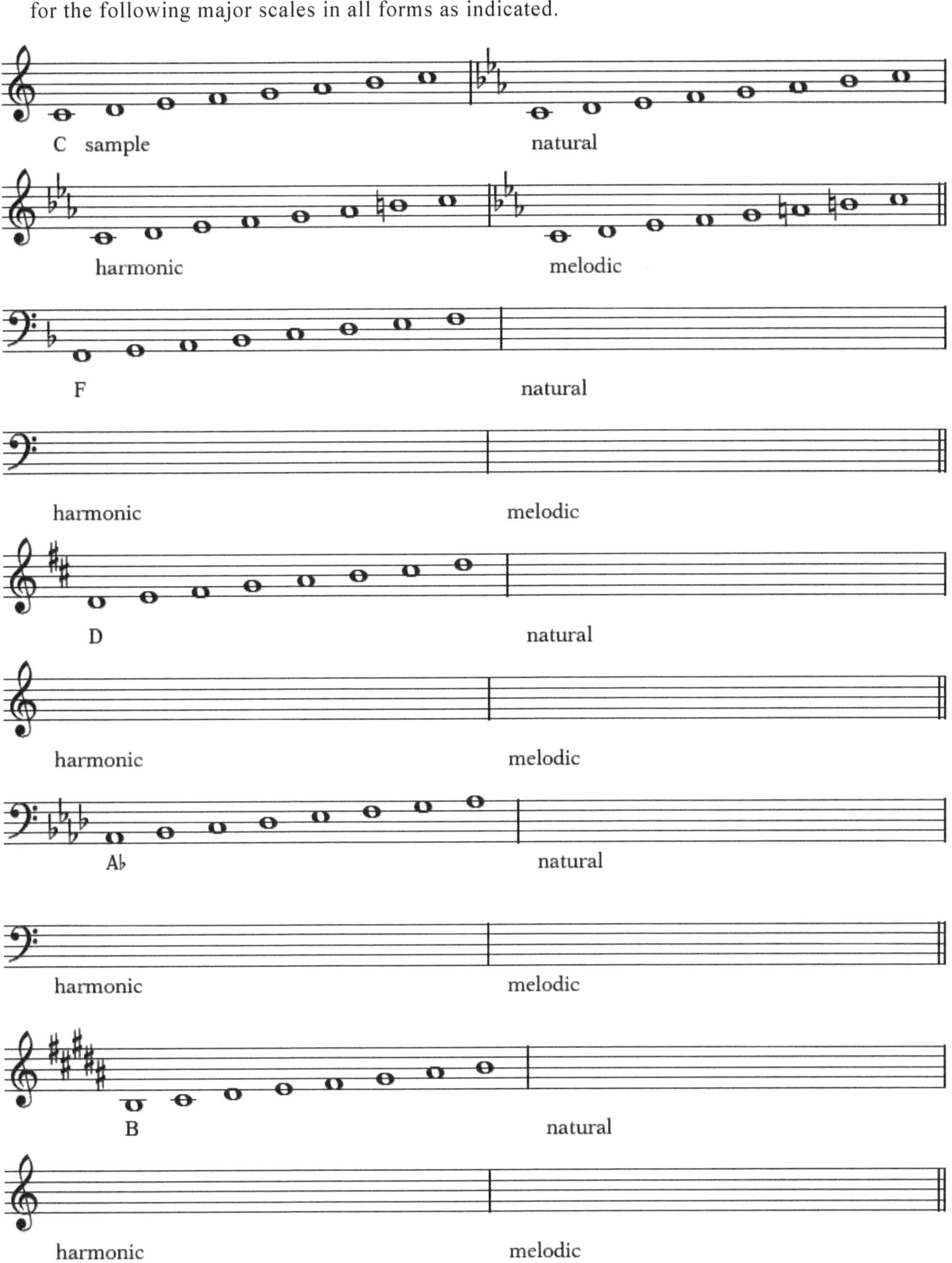

CHAPTER 6

INTERVALS

Lesson 19: Interval Size

Sound combinations are classified in music with names that identify the pitch relationships. Learning to recognize these combinations by both eye and ear is a skill fundamental to the foundations of music. Although there are many different tone combinations, the most basic pairing of pitches is the interval. Musical intervals require a lot of practice and memorization. Every time we listen to any type of music, we are listening to intervals. What we hear and define as music is actually combinations of interval patterns. Therefore, intervals are the basic units of tonal music. In this chapter, we will learn how to recognize and identify intervals in tonal music.

Interval

An ***interval*** is a measurement of the distance in pitch between two notes. Intervals can be harmonic or melodic. An interval is harmonic when two pitches sound at the same time. An interval is melodic when two pitches sound one after another.

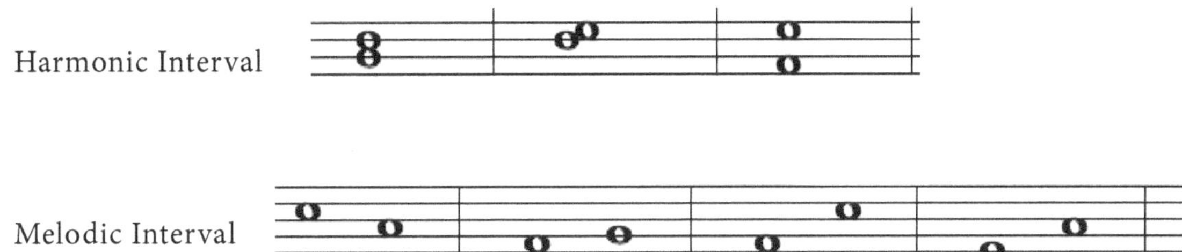

Numerical Size

In either position, there are two elements in identifying interval names: the ***numerical size*** and the ***quality***.

Let's first look at the numerical size of an interval. The numerical name is a measurement of how far apart the notes are on the staff. Identifying the numerical size of an interval can be done in two different ways:

1. By counting the letter names of the two pitches whose interval we are trying to determine plus the letter names of all the pitches in between

Or

2. By counting lines and spaces. (Remember to count both the bottom note and the top note when determining the numerical size)

The size of an interval is the number of steps it contains (or the number of different letter names it spans), ***disregarding any accidentals***. A ***unison*** contains a single step: its two notes have the same space of the staff.

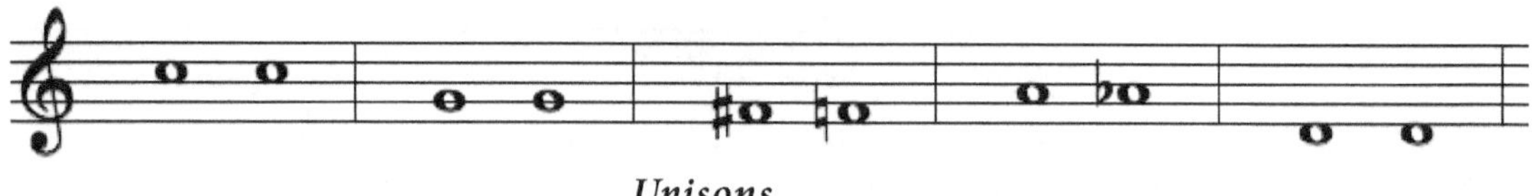

Unisons

A ***second*** contains two steps and consists of notes with adjacent letters names. The actual number of semitones between the notes may vary, but is one note is on a space and the other is on the adjacent line (or vice versa), the interval is a second. We have previously referred to this interval as a step.

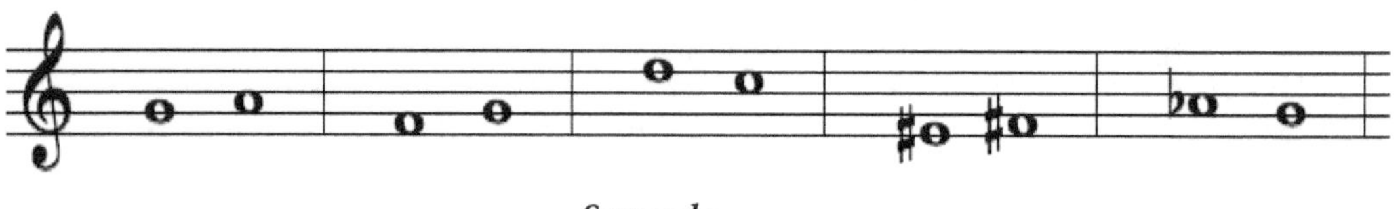

Seconds

A ***third*** contains three steps and spans three letter names. As with seconds, the actual number of semitones may vary, but if the two notes are on adjacent lines or adjacent spaces, the interval is a third.

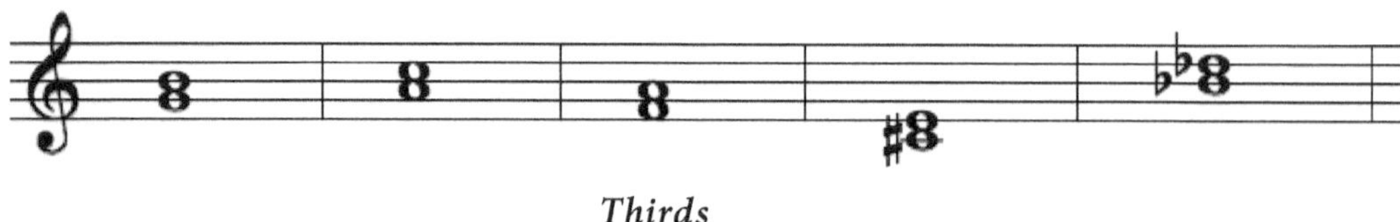

Thirds

The remaining intervals - ***fourths***, ***fifths***, ***sixths***, ***sevenths***, and ***octaves*** - are calculated in the exact same way.

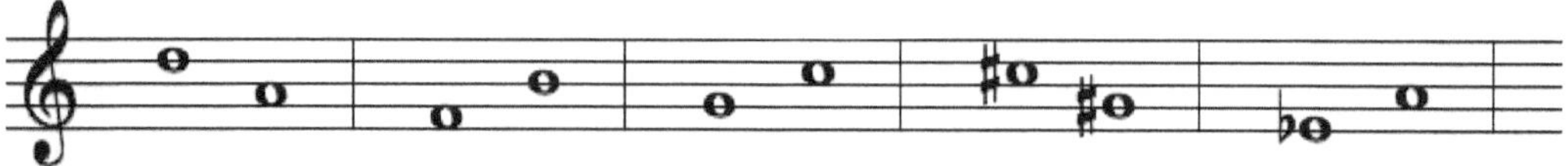

Fourths

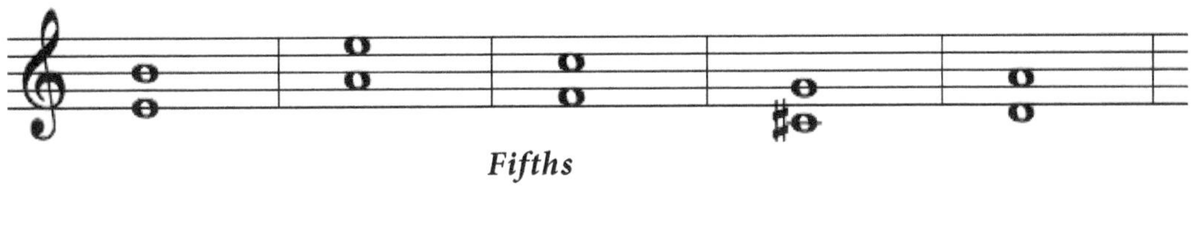

Fifths

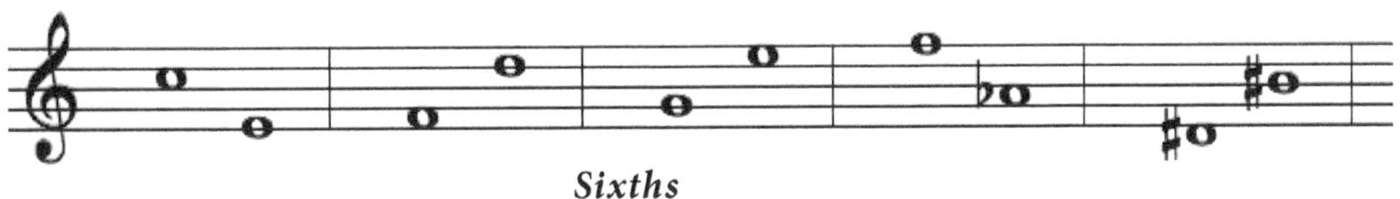

Sixths

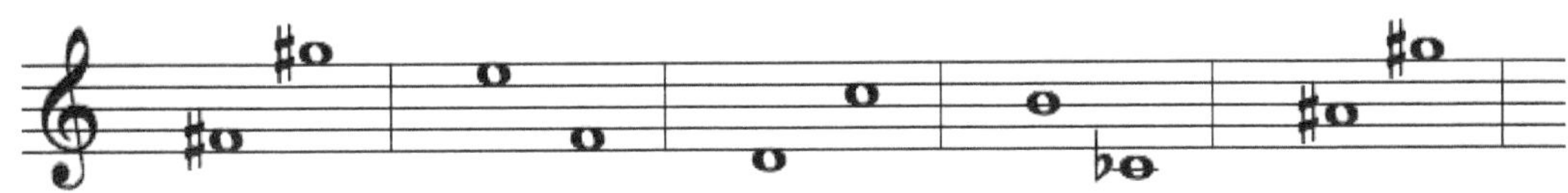

Sevenths

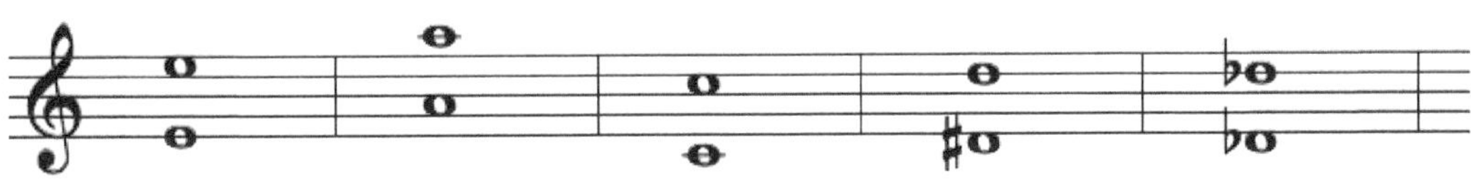

Octaves

Activity #18:

Identify the following intervals by their numerical size.

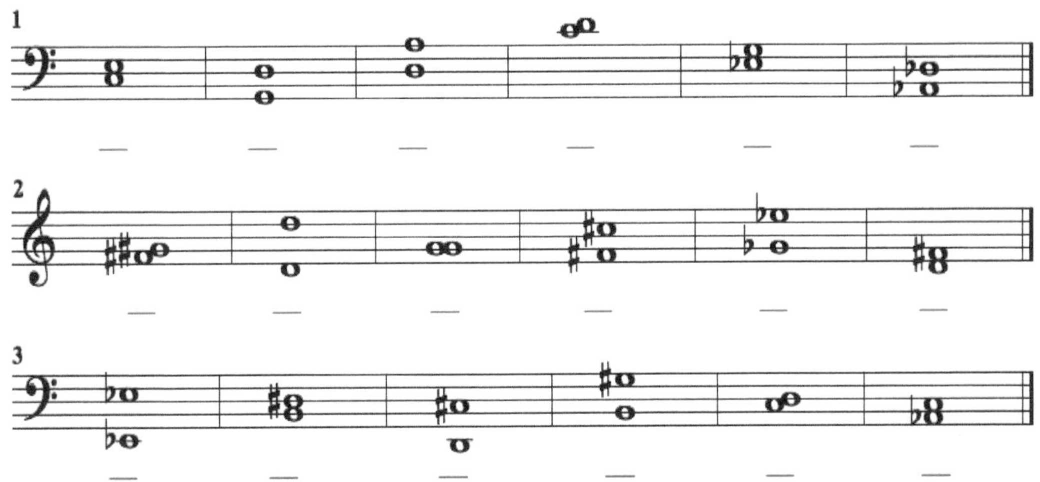

LESSON 20: SECONDS AND THIRDS

Quality

Intervals are given a second, mores specific, name depending on their sound quality. The ***quality*** of an interval is related to the number of half steps contained between the two pitches. In order to describe the quality of the intervals we will use the following terms:

Interval	*Abbreviation*
Perfect	P
Major	M
Minor	m
Augmented	A or +
Diminished	D or °

Determining the quality of an interval can be done by counting the numbers of ***half/whole steps*** contained within the two notes you are analyzing. This is the safest method to determine the quality of and interval. However, you need to understand that this method involves a lot of counting and memorizing. Be aware that counting whole/half steps is very accurate but you need to focus to avoid any errors.

Semitone

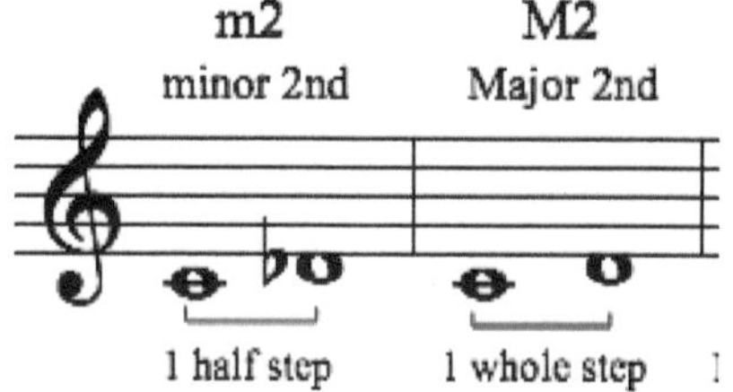

In this lesson we will focus only on seconds and thirds. If a second contains only **one semitone** (half step), it is a ***minor second***. If a second contains ***two semitones*** (two half steps or one whole step), it is a ***major second***.

Enharmonic

If a minor second, or any minor interval, is compressed by lowering the upper or raising the bottom note by a half step, it becomes ***diminished***. But diminished seconds - interval made up of adjacent letter names that are ***enharmonically*** (a term used to describe notes of the same pitch which have different names, e.g. C# and Db, F# and Gb.) the same pitch - are rare and we will not consider them further here. If a major second, or any major interval, is expanded by lowering the bottom note or raising the upper note by a half step, it becomes ***augmented***.

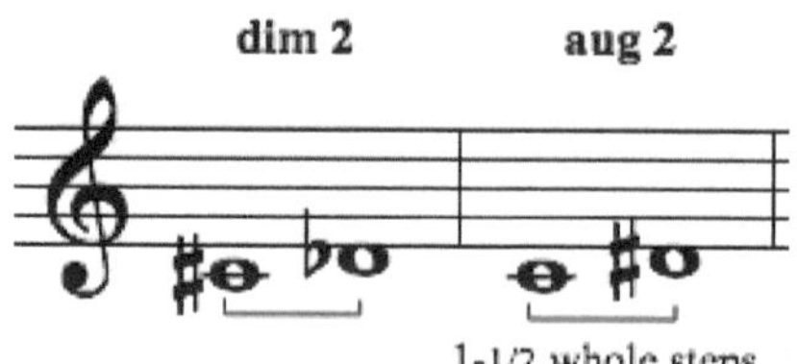

Like seconds, ***thirds*** can be ***major***, ***minor***, ***augmented,*** and ***diminished***. A major third contains four half steps (two whole steps) and a minor third contains three half steps (1+1/2 whole steps).

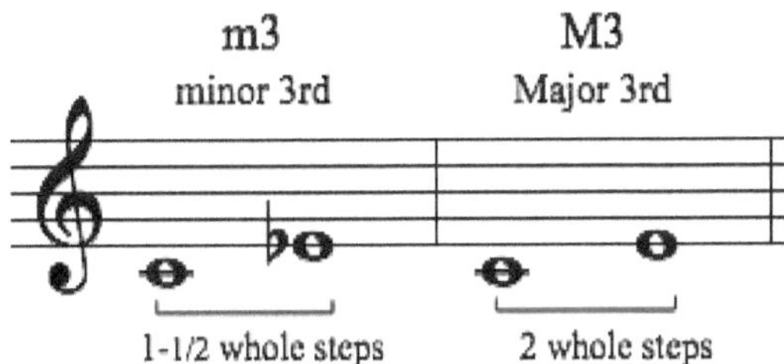

When a minor third is compressed by a half step, it becomes ***diminished***; when a major third is expanded by a half step, it becomes ***augmented***. These are relatively rare in music and will not concern us further here; instead, we will concentrate on major and minor thirds.

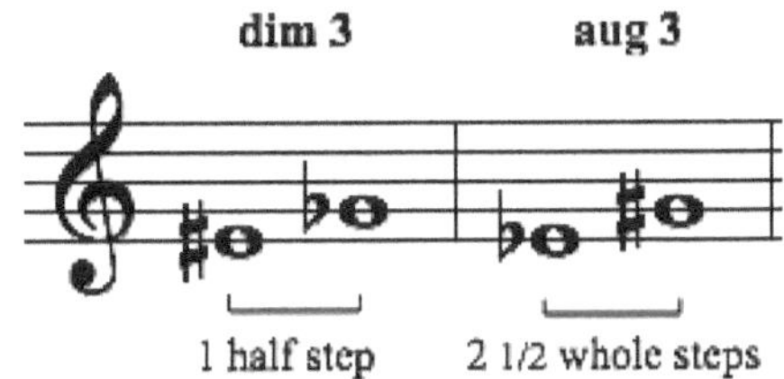

In sum, there are four kinds of seconds and thirds (major, minor, augmented, and diminished), but only minor, major, and augmented seconds and minor and major thirds are in common use. The number of half steps in each of the major intervals must be memorized. It then becomes simple to change the quality of any major interval to minor, augmented, or diminished. For example, when a major interval is raised by a half step, it becomes augmented. When a major interval is lowered by a half step, it becomes minor. When a major interval is lowered by two half steps, it becomes diminished. When a minor interval is raised by a half step, it becomes major. When a minor interval is raised by two half steps, it becomes augmented. When a minor interval is lowered by a half step, it becomes diminished.

KEY CONCEPT: While any interval can be augmented or diminished in quality, only the following intervals can have major and minor qualities: ***second, third, sixth,*** and ***seventh***.

Enharmonically equivalent

Intervals that span the same number of half steps but are spelled with different note names are ***enharmonically equivalent***. C-D# and C-Eb, for example, both span three half steps, but one is a second and the other is a third. They have correspondingly different musical role to play.

In music there are many notes that have more than one name. ***Enharmonic*** notes sound the same but are spelled differently.

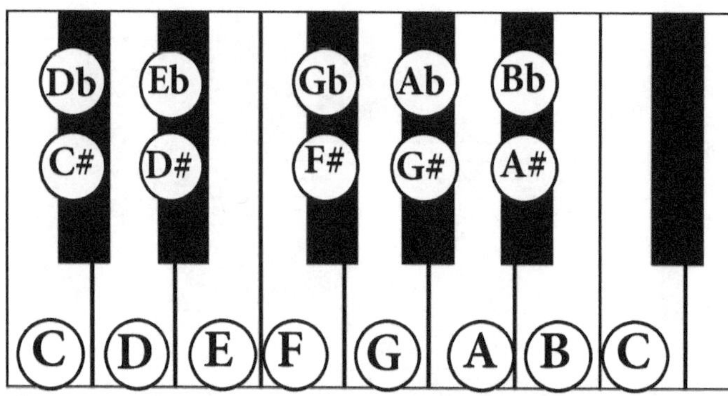

If you look at a piano keyboard you will see that D# and Eb are played with the same key.

In the example above we can say that each measure contains enharmonic notes because each measure will produce the same pitch (sound) but they are spelled differently. Try playing this exercise in the keyboard and you will notice that you will be playing the exact same note twice.

Name: ______________________

Date: ______________________

Lesson 20: Practice Exercises

Name each interval. Make sure to indicate if it is major (M) or minor (m).

Example

Add an accidental (sharp or flat) to the top note if needed to create seconds and thirds of the desired quality (m=minor, M=major, A=augmented.) Do not alter the bottom note.

Write the desired interval in the blank staff provided below.

Lesson 21: Sixths and sevenths

Sixths and sevenths behave like seconds and thirds. A ***minor sixth*** contains eight half steps, a ***major sixth*** contains nine half steps, a ***minor seventh*** contains ten half steps, and a ***major seventh*** contains eleven half steps.

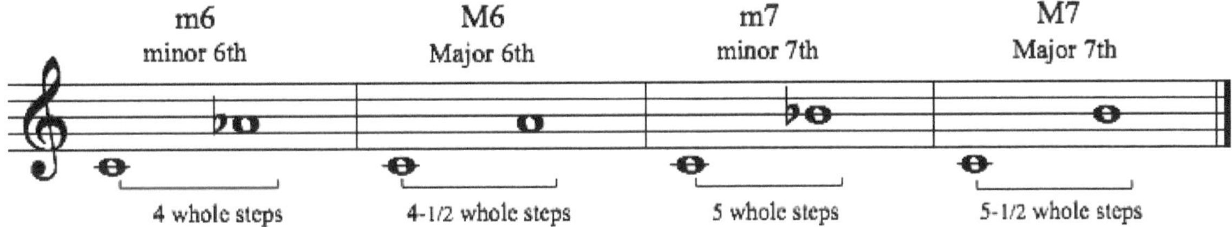

When a minor sixth or seventh is compressed by a half step, it becomes ***diminished***; when a major sixth or seventh is expanded by a half step, it becomes ***augmented***. These are relatively rare in music and will not concern us further: ***Augmented sixths*** are somewhat more common , but not enough to merit discussion and drill in an introductory textbook like this one. ***Diminished sevenths*** are also reasonably common.

Interval Inversion

Another way of identifying the quality of the sixths and sevenths is by using the ***inversion of the intervals***. When an octave is divided into two parts, each part is said to be the inversion of the other. Conversely, an interval can be combined with its inversion to make up an octave.

Intervals can be inverted, which basically means you turn them upside down. The lower note is raised up an octave so that the top note/bottom note relationship is reversed. The point to remember when inverting intervals is that one pitch remains stationary and the other moves an octave.

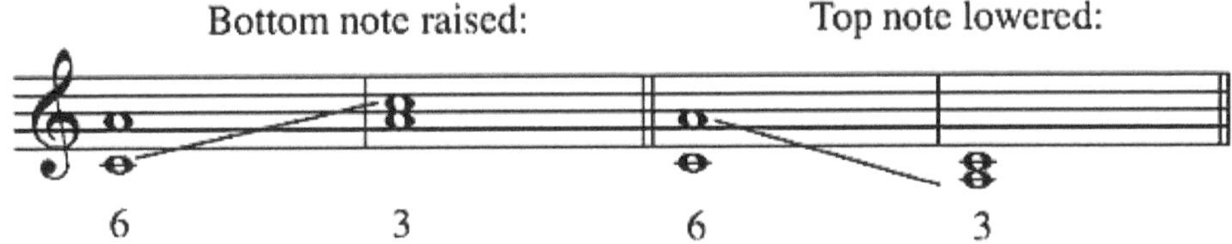

When a sixth is inverted, it becomes a third

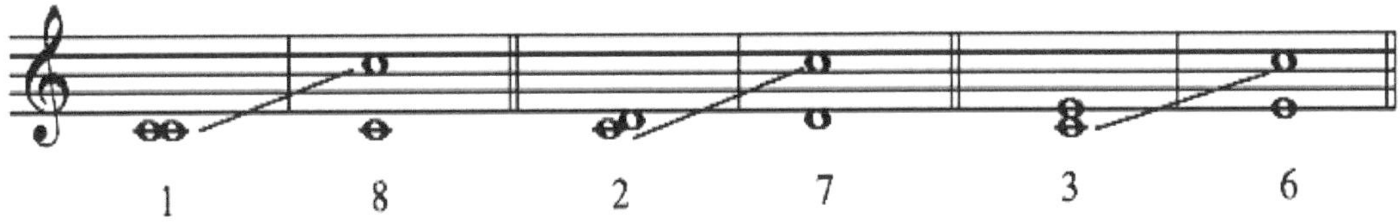

When a second is inverted, it becomes a seventh
Notice the effect of inversion on each of the intervals:

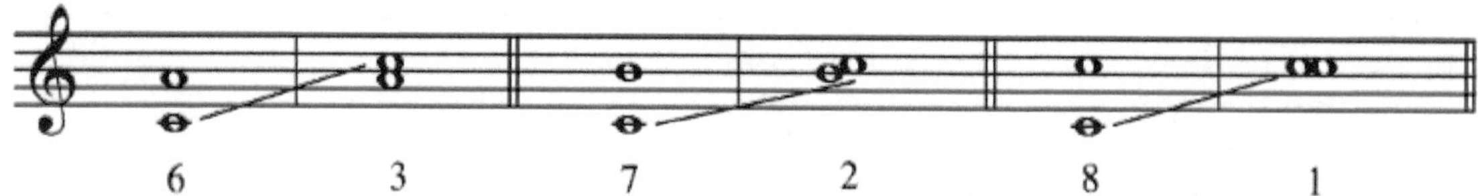

Now that we now how to invert a numerical interval we need to find out what happens to the quality of the interval once inverted.

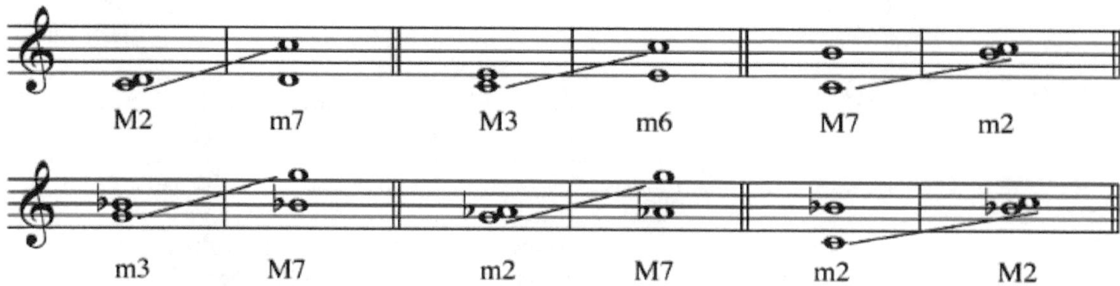

When inverted a major interval becomes minor, a diminished becomes augmented. When inverted a minor interval becomes, major, an augmented becomes diminished.

Another important point to remember is that inverted intervals can, in some ways, be considered to belong to the same interval family. That is, although the two pitches have changed location, and the interval between them has changed, the pitches themselves have not changed.

The chart below shows the inversions of intervals. The interval size changes when an interval is inverted. (*For more information about interval inversions see* APPENDIX C)

Size	Inversion	Size after Inversion
2nd	Becomes	7th
3rd	Becomes	6th
4th	Becomes	5th
5th	Becomes	4th
6th	Becomes	3rd
7th	Becomes	2nd

Quality	Inversion	Quality after Inversion
Major	Becomes	Minor
Minor	Becomes	Major
Perfect	**Remains**	**Perfect**
Augmented	Becomes	Diminished
Diminished	Becomes	Augmented

Name: ______________________

Date: ______________________

Lesson 21: Practice Exercises

Identify the quality if these sixths and sevenths (M=major, m=minor).

Example:

Identify the quality of these sixths and sevenths (M=major, m=minor). Then write the inversion and identify its quality.

Lesson 22: Fourths, fifths, unisons, and octaves

There are only four perfect intervals within an octave. These are the unison, the fourth, the fifth, and the octave. They are called perfect because in medieval and renaissance music they were considered the only intervals suitable for momentary or permanent stopping places within a piece. Although these intervals can be augmented or diminished, they cannot be either major or minor. The following figure shows the number of half steps in each perfect interval and the proper abbreviation symbols for identifying intervals, using letters for the quality and numbers for the numerical size.

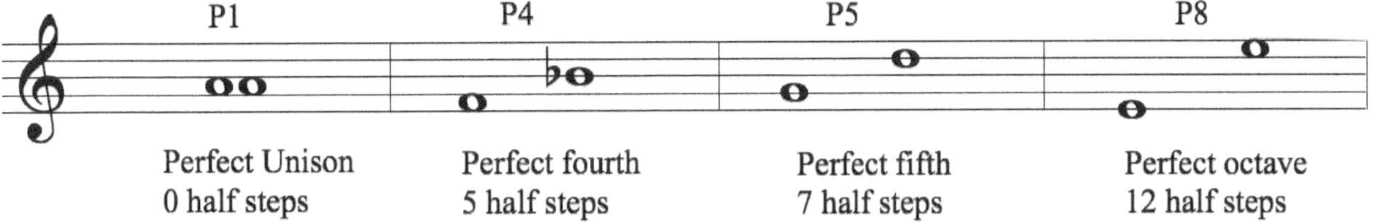

As mentioned before, perfect intervals can also be augmented or diminished in quality. For example, when a perfect interval is ***raised*** by a half step, it becomes augmented in quality.

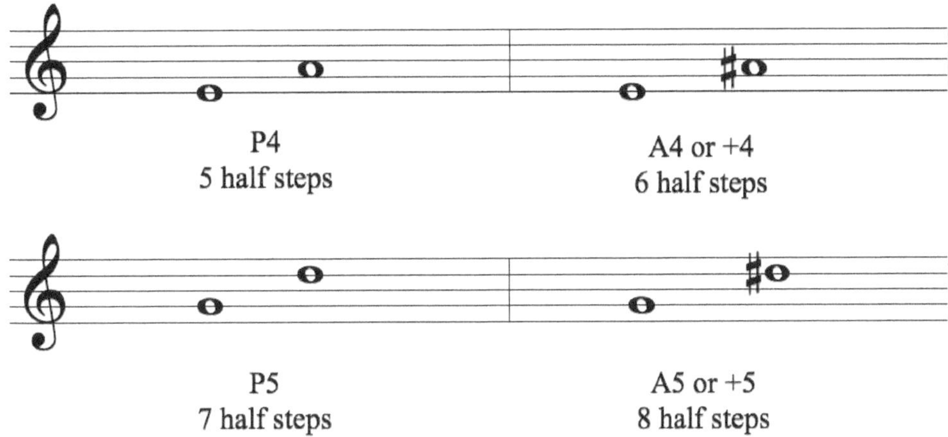

When a perfect interval is ***lowered*** by a half step, it becomes ***diminished*** in quality.

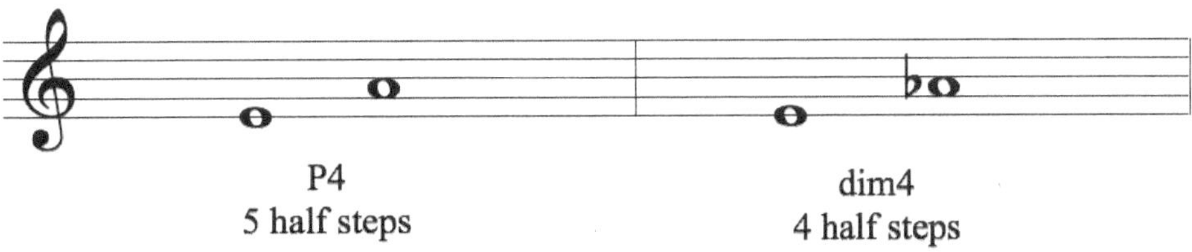

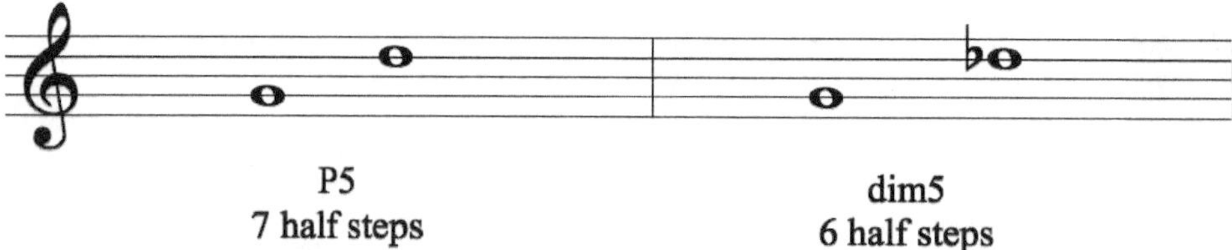

Notice that in both examples the augmented fourth and the diminished fifth both contain six half steps, one is identified as a fourth and the other as a fifth. This is because the numeric value of both intervals is not the same. Another important point to remember is that although perfect octave can be augmented or diminished, a unison can only be augmented by adding a half step, but it cannot be made diminished.

For any particular interval, both numerical value and quality must be correct in order for the interval itself to be correct. Remember that the numeric value is the total count of letter names included in the interval, while the quality is determined by counting whole or half steps.

KEY CONCEPT: Perfect intervals **cannot** be **major** or **minor**. They can only be diminished, augmented, or perfect. The augmented fourth is sometimes called the ***tritone*** because it spans three whole steps or 6 half steps, exactly half of the twelve half steps that forms the octave.

Fourths invert to fifths and unisons to octaves. Perfect intervals invert to perfect intervals and diminished intervals to augmented.

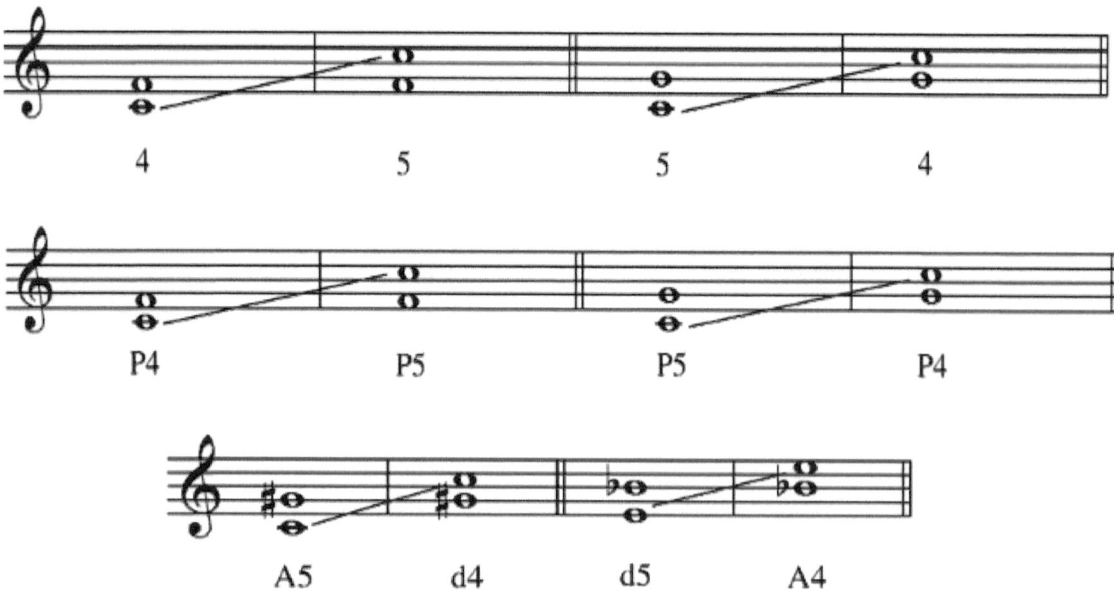

Name: ______________________

Date: ______________________

Lesson 22: Practice Exercises

Identify the quality if these fourth, fifths, unisons, and octave (P=perfect, A=augmented, Dim=diminished).

Example:

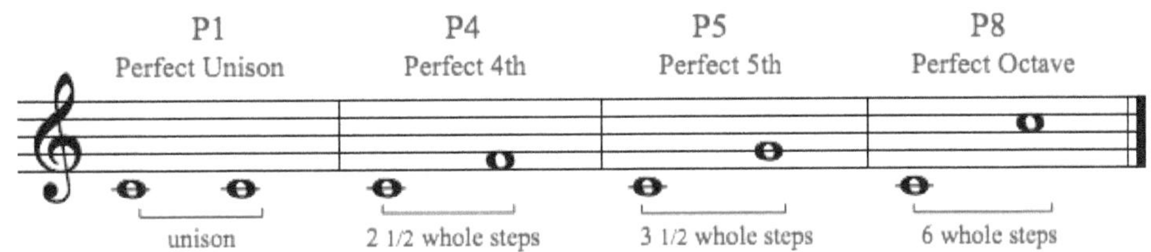

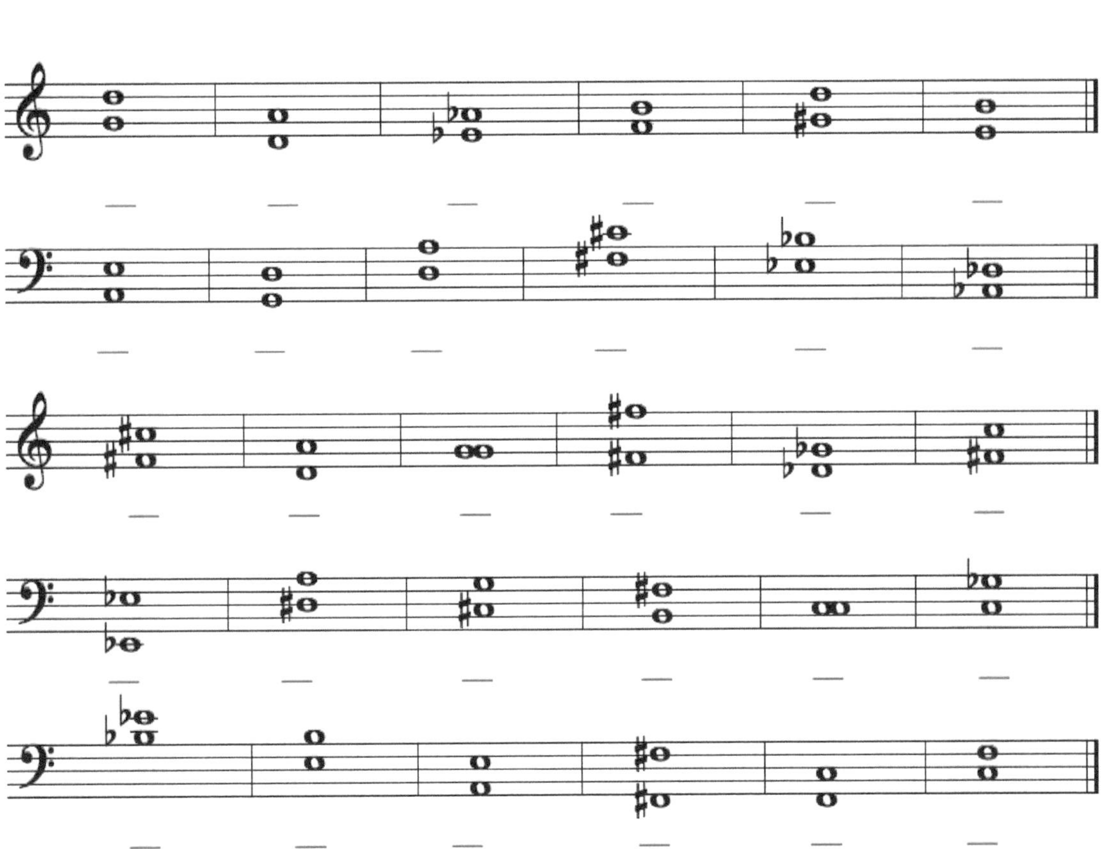

Write the desired interval in the blank staff provided below.

Lesson 23: Intervals Summary

1- When a major interval is raised by a half step, it becomes augmented.
2- When a major interval is lowered by a half step, it becomes minor.
3- When a major interval is lowered by two half steps, it becomes diminished.
4- When a minor interval is raised by a half step, it becomes major.
5- When a minor interval is raised by two half steps, it becomes augmented.
6- When a minor interval is lowered by a half step, it becomes diminished.
7- When a perfect interval is raised by a half step, it becomes augmented.
8- When a perfect interval is lowered by a half step, it becomes diminished.

Interval Name	Abbreviation	# of whole steps	# of half steps
Perfect Unison	P1	0	0
Minor Second	m2	½	1
Major Second	M2	1	2
Minor Third	m3	1 ½	3
Major Third	M3	2	4
Perfect Fourth	P4	2 ½	5
Augmented Fourth	A4	3	6
Diminished Fifth	d5	3	6
Perfect Fifth	P5	3 ½	7
Minor Sixth	m6	4	8
Major Sixth	M6	4 ½	9
Minor Seventh	m7	5	10
Major Seventh	M7	5 ½	11
Perfect Octave	P8	6	12

Interval Name	Example	# of half steps
Perfect Unison (P1)	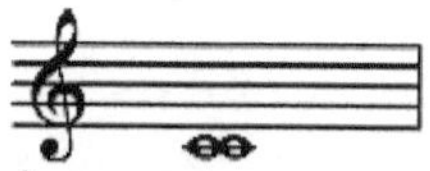	0
Minor Second (m2)	 2	1
Major Second (M2)	 3	2
Minor Third (m3)	 4	3
Major Third (M3)	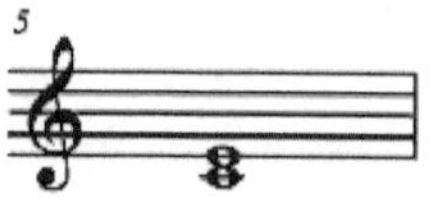 5	4
Perfect Fourth (P4)	 6	5
Augmented Fourth (A4)	 7	6
Diminished fifth (d5)	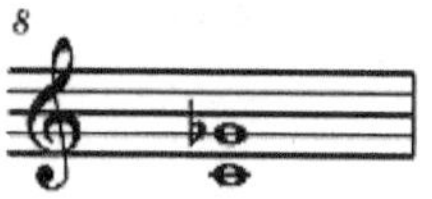 8	6
Perfect Fifth (P5)	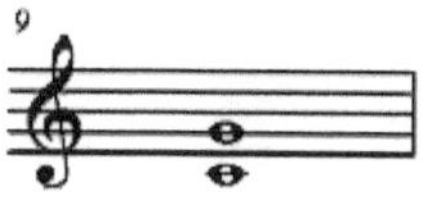 9	7
Minor Sixth (m6)	 10	8
Major Sixth (M6)	 11	9
Minor Seventh (m7)	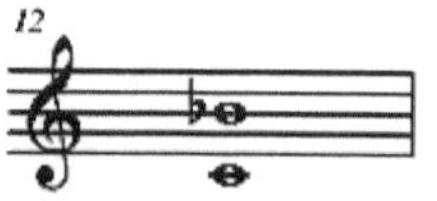 12	10
Major Seventh (M7)	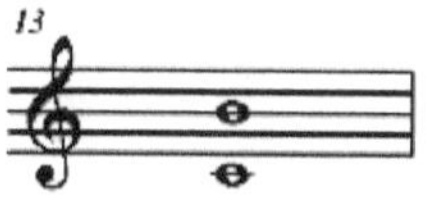 13	11
Perfect Octave (P8)	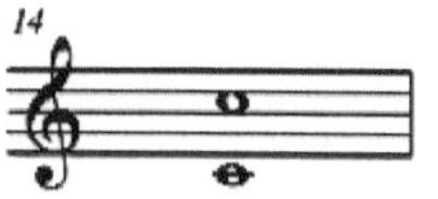 14	12

STUDY QUESTIONS FOR CHAPTER 6

1. Define the following terms:

   Interval

   Major Interval

   Minor Interval

   Unison

   Enharmonic equivalent

   Semitone

   Quality

2. The five common quality classifications for intervals are:

   a.

   b.

   c.

   d.

   e

3. Complete the following:

   a. A perfect interval inverts to a _________________ interval.

   b. A minor interval inverts to a _________________ interval.

   c. A diminished interval inverts to an _________________ interval.

   d. A major interval inverts to a _________________ interval.

   e. An augmented interval inverts to a _________________ interval.

4. Complete the following:

   a. If a perfect interval is increased in size by a half step it becomes _________________.

   b. If a major interval is increased in size by a half step it becomes _________________.

   c. If a minor interval is increased in size by a half step it becomes _________________.

Name:_________________
Date:___________________

Chapter 6: Self-test

1. The five common quality classifications for intervals are:

 a.
 b.
 c.
 d.
 e.

2. Complete the following:

 a. A perfect interval inverts to a ________________ interval.

 b. A minor interval inverts to a ________________ interval.

 c. A diminished interval inverts to an ________________ interval.

 d. A major interval inverts to a ________________ interval.

 e. An augmented interval inverts to a ________________ interval.

3. Complete the following:

 a. If a perfect interval is increased in size by a half step it becomes________________.

 b. If a major interval is increased in size by a half step it becomes________________.

 c. If a minor interval is increased in size by a half step it becomes________________.

 d. If a diminished interval is increased in size by a half step it becomes______________.

 e. If a augmented interval is increased in size by a half step it becomes_______________.

 f. If a perfect interval is decreased in size by a half step it becomes________________.

 g. If a major interval is increased in size by a half step it becomes______.

4. Intervals can be _________________or __________________ depending if the are sounding at the same time or one after the other.

5. Name the following intervals

Name:______________________________
Date:____________________

Chapter 6: Self-test (*Continuation*)

5. Name the following intervals

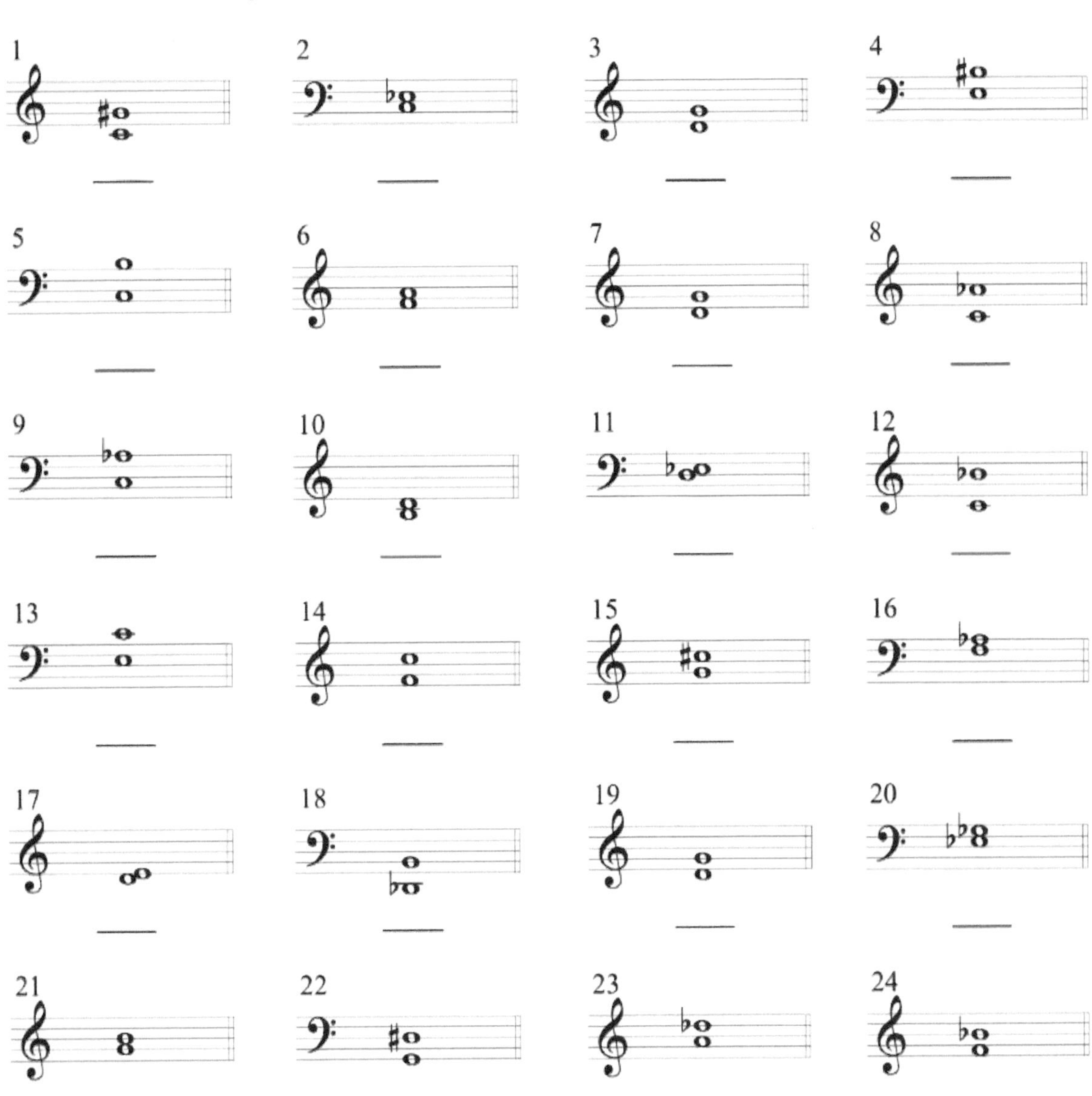

7. Name the following intervals.

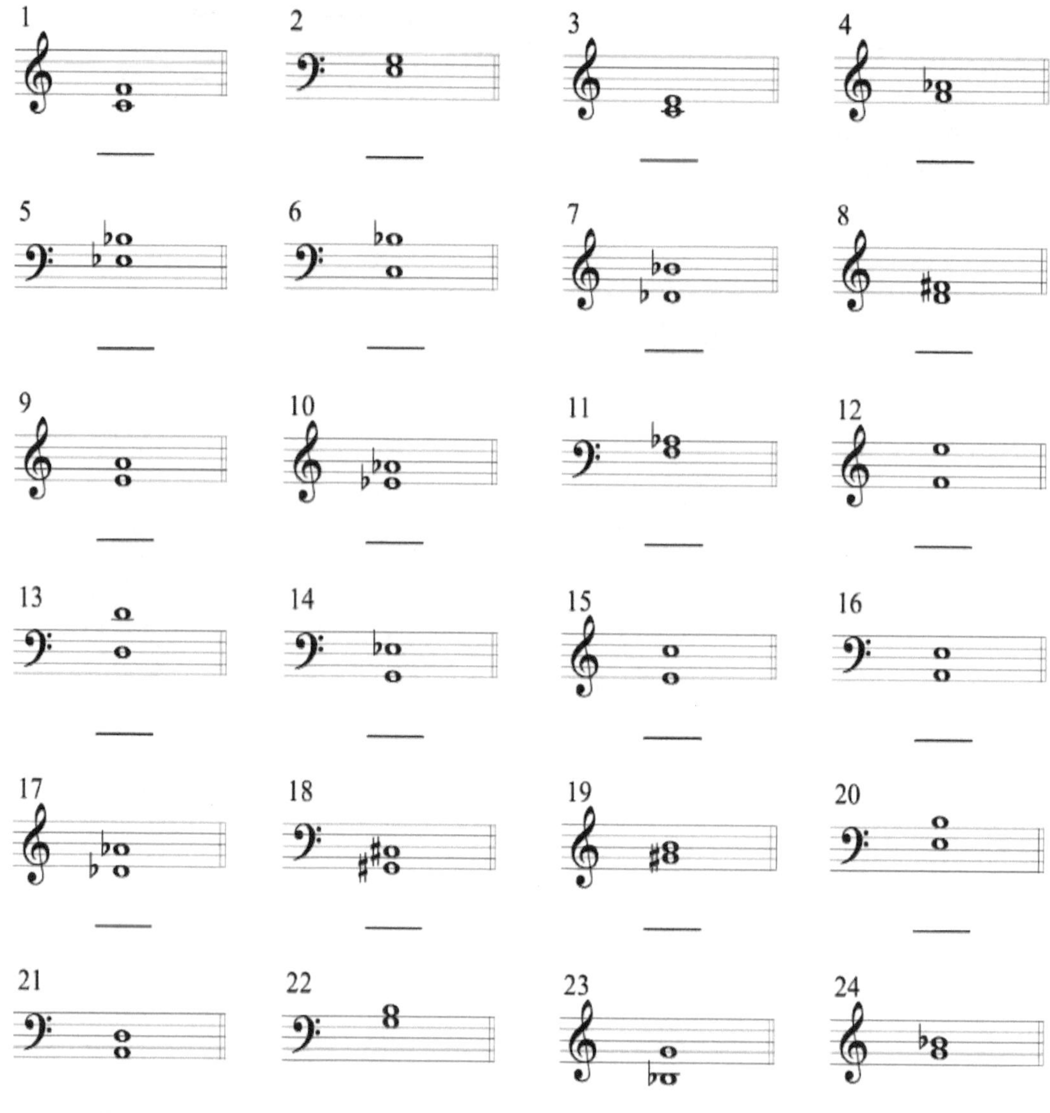

CHAPTER 7

TRIADS

Lesson 24: Triads

Harmony

This course, foundations of music, covers materials basic to a particular tradition in music historically rooted in Western Europe. Other culture's music are of equal importance but are beyond the scope of this introductory course. Arguably the single most unique element in the western European tradition of music is harmony. **Harmony** can be defined as two or more notes sounding at the same time. Chapter 6 introduced intervals which can be studied as either a melodic or harmonic element. More than two notes sounding simultaneously produce a triad or a chord. A complete discourse on all types of chords, chord progressions and chord functions is for a more advanced music course. However, an introduction to triads is appropriate here.

Chord

During the "common practice period" the triad evolved into a ***three-note chord*** constructed of superimposed thirds. It came to be the basic element in harmonic progressions. Triads are built from notes in the major/minor scale system. Triads are their name from the name of the root, that is, the lowest-sounding pitch when the triad is constructed as superimposed thirds.

Triad

The ***triad*** is the basic harmony of tonal music. It consists of three notes: a fifth divided into two thirds. The three notes of a triad can always be written on three consecutive lines or three consecutive spaces. When they are written like that, the lowest note is called the **root**, the middle note is called the **third,** and the highest note is called the **fifth**.

Tertian Sonorities

Four types of triads are found in this system. They are identified by the quality names **major, minor, augmented**, and **diminished.** These names describe the types of sounds generated from the intervals contained in the triads. The intervals contained in the four types of triads are major and/or minor 3rds. Since most harmonies in western music are constructed of thirds, the term **tertian sonorities** came into use. The next example is a triad. Notice that the triad is constructed by "stacking" thirds on top of each other.

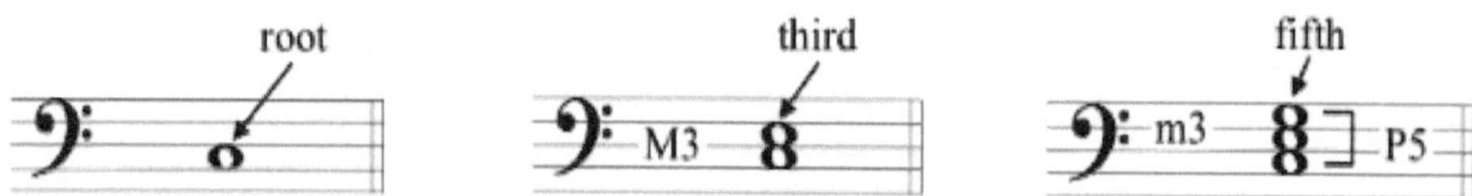

MAJOR TRIAD: When the quality of the third is major and the quality of the fifth is perfect, the triad is major. A major triad may be constructed from any pitch by building these intervals above a given root. The major triad is the first, third, and fifth of any major scale.

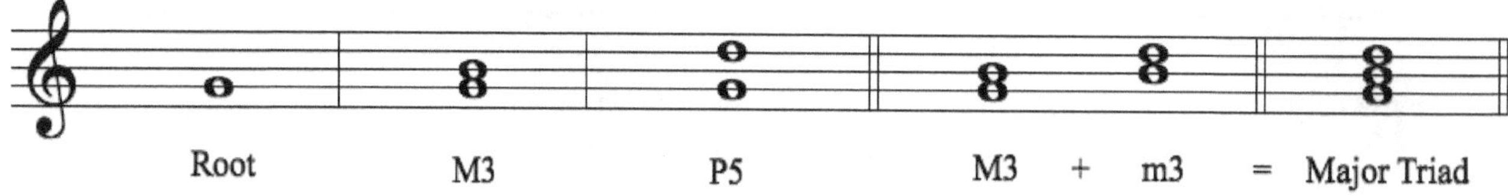

MINOR TRIAD: When the quality of the third is minor and the quality of the fifth is perfect, the triad is minor. A minor triad may be constructed from any pitch by building these intervals above a given root. The minor triad is the first, third, and fifth of any major scale.

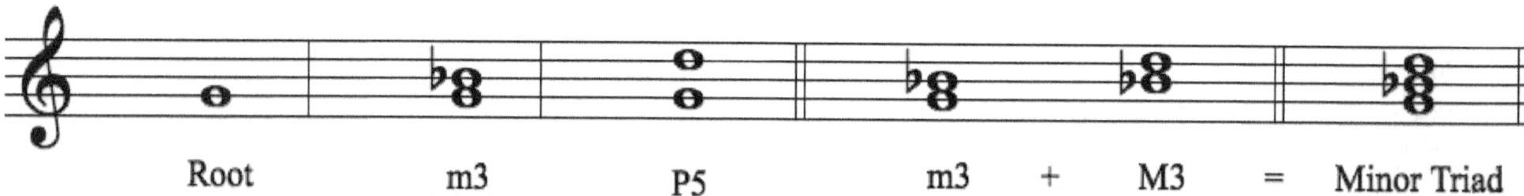

DIMINISHED TRIAD: There are two ways for constructing a diminished triad. (1) When the quality of the third is minor and the quality of the fifth is diminished, the triad is diminished. (2) Another way of thinking about the diminished triad is when the quality of the lower third is minor and the quality of the upper third is minor, the triad is diminished. A diminished triad may be constructed from any pitch by building these intervals above a given root. You can also think about it as a major triad with a lowered third and fifth.

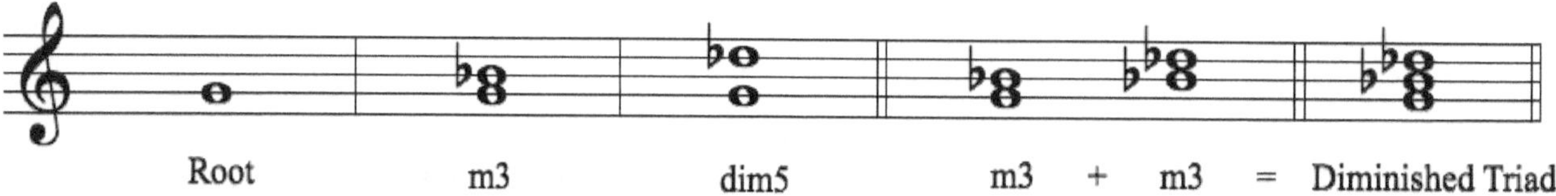

Augmented Triad: There are a few ways for constructing an augmented triad. (1) When the quality of the third is major and the quality of the fifth is augmented, the triad is augmented. (2) Another way of thinking about the augmented triad is when the quality of the lower third is major and the quality of the upper third is major, the triad is augmented. An augmented triad may be constructed from any pitch by building these intervals above a given root. You can also think about it as a major triad with a raised fifth.

Any note can act as the root of a triad. A triad is **named for its root** so, for example a C# major triad is major in quality and has C# as its root,while F minor triad is minor in quality and has F as its root. *(For more information about chord construction see Appendix D)*

Chord Names and Symbols

Each scale degree and its corresponding triad (chord) have a name that indicates their relationship to the tonic, the name of the first scale degree (the name of the main tone of a key signature).

Roman Numerals

Individual pitches can be represented using scale degree numbers that identify their function within a given scale. Similarly, triads are represented by roman numerals that indicate the scale degree on which they are built. For example, a Bb major triad in the key of F major is written as IV to show that it is built on the fourth scale degree in that Key. Uppercase roman numerals are used for major triads; lowercase roman numerals are used for minor triads. Diminished triads are represented by lowercase roman numerals with the addition of a small degree sign “ º .”

In the following example, root-position triads are built on each scale degree of a C major scale. Each triad is named in accordance with two related chord identification systems.

Chord Symbol

1. The letter name of each root is combined with a chord-quality designation to form a ***chord symbol***.

2. Roman numerals associate each scale degree with a chord quality. Chord qualities for each scale degree are consistent in all major scales: I, IV and V are major in all keys; ii, iv, and vi are minor; viiº is diminished.

(For more information about chord names and symbols see Appendix F)

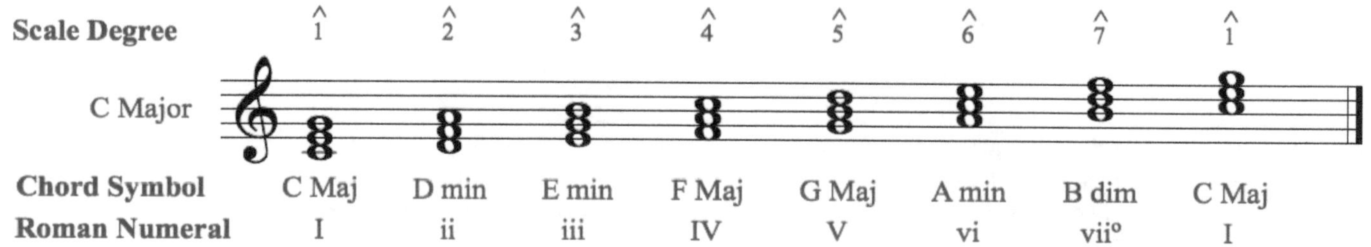

PRIMARY TRIADS

Primary Triads

Secondary Chords

The three most important triads are the ***primary triads*** (those constructed above the I, IV, and V scale degrees of the major of minor scales). Those constructed above the second, third, sixth, and seventh scale degrees are called ***secondary chords***. The primary triads are the three major triads in the diatonic major scale, and they have a particularly close harmonic relationship: the dominant (V) lies a perfect fifth above the tonic, and the subdominant (IV) lies a perfect fifth below the tonic.

The tonic triad (I), constructed on the first scale degree, ranks first in importance. Tonal musical compositions often begin and almost invariably end on the tonic chord. The dominant triad exercises great harmonic influence, especially with the addition of a seventh chord. The dominant chord is second in importance, and the subdominant is third.

Below is a list of some of the primary triads you find in major key signatures. Play these triads on the piano until your hand and ear are thoroughly familiar with them. (*For a complete list of primary triads see* APPENDIX *E*)

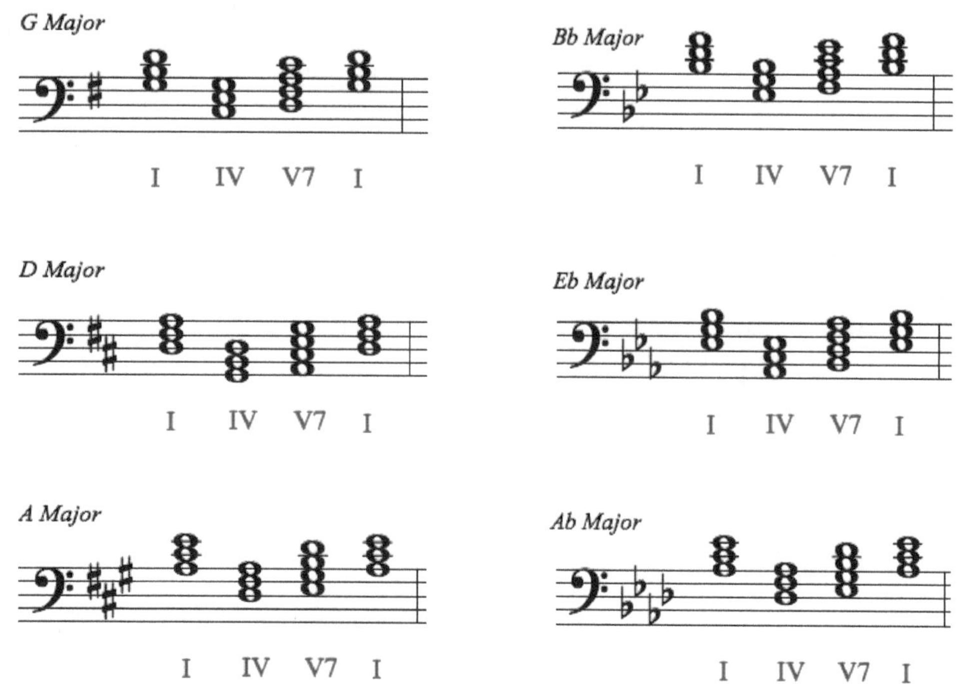

Name: ______________________

Date: ______________________

Lesson 24: Practice Exercises

1. Each of the notes below is the root of a triad. Draw a note a third above each root.

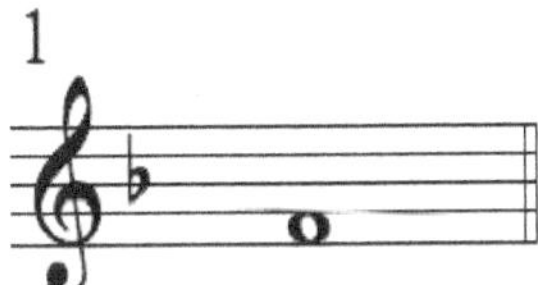

2. Each of the notes below is the root of a triad. Draw a note a fifth above each root.

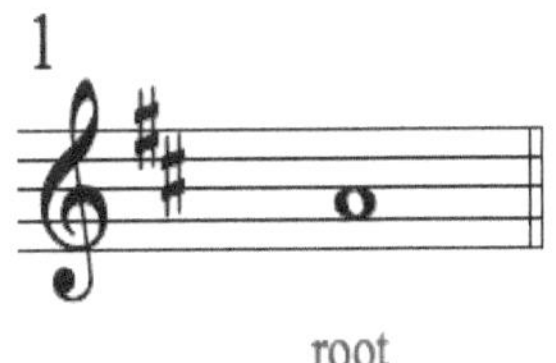

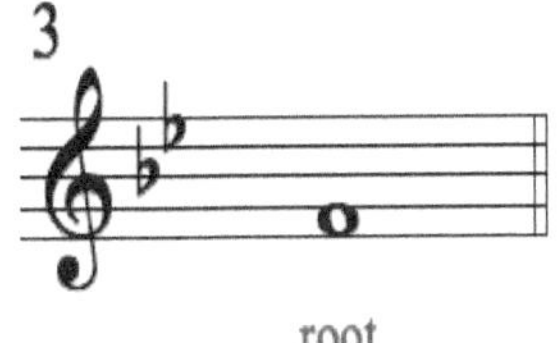

3. Each of the notes below is the root of a triad. Draw the third and fifth above each root to create a root-position triads.

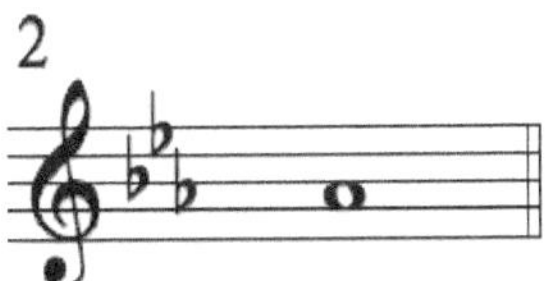

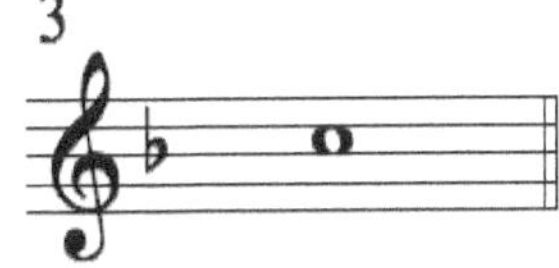

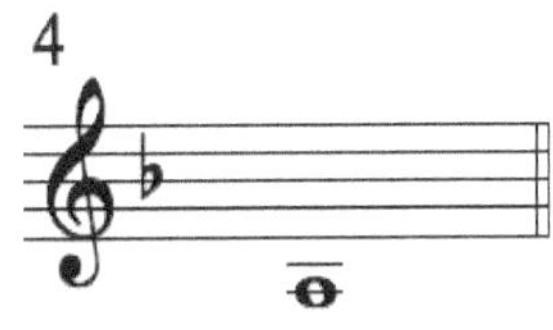

4. Triad position is indicated for each of the notes below. Add notes to create a root-position triads.

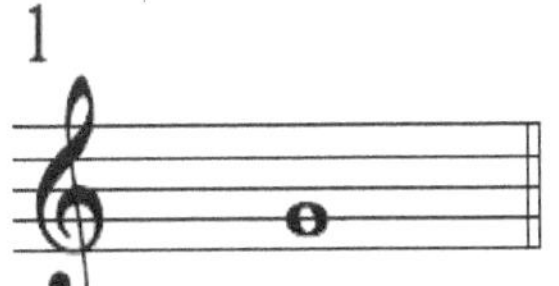

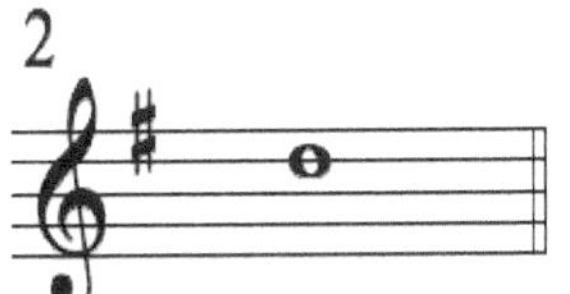

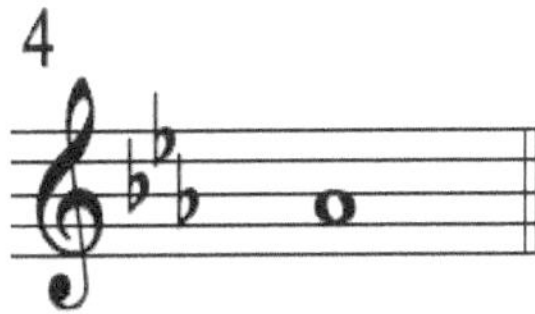

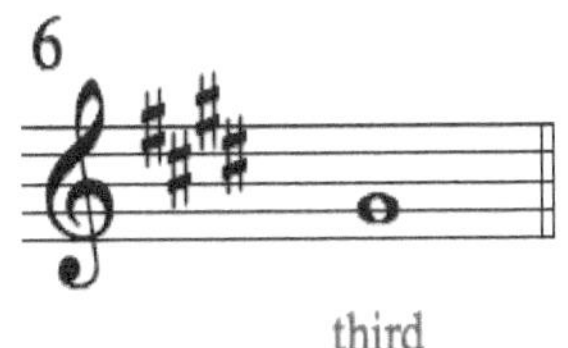

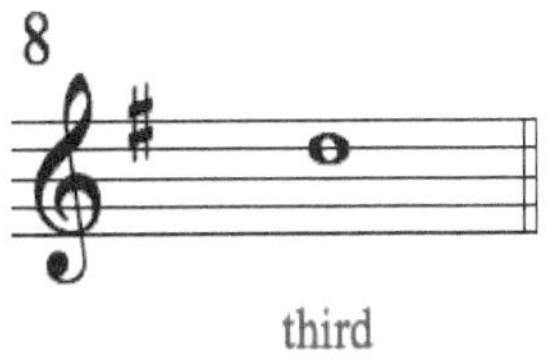

5. Create root-position **major triads** using the provided notes as roots.

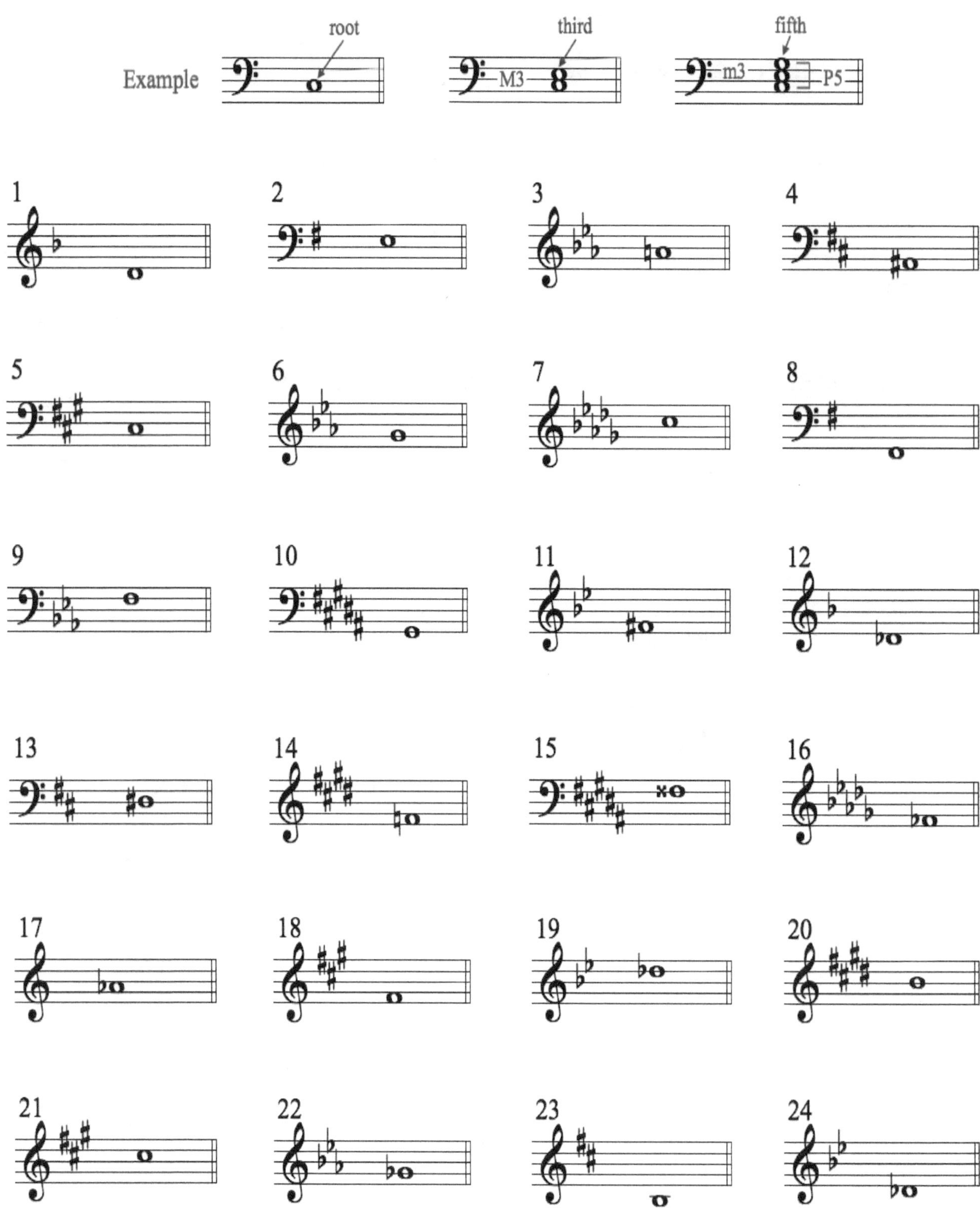

Name: ______________________

Date: ______________________

Lesson 24: Practice Exercises (continuation)

6. Create root-position **minor triads** using the provided notes as roots.

7. Create root-position **diminished triads** using the provided notes as roots.

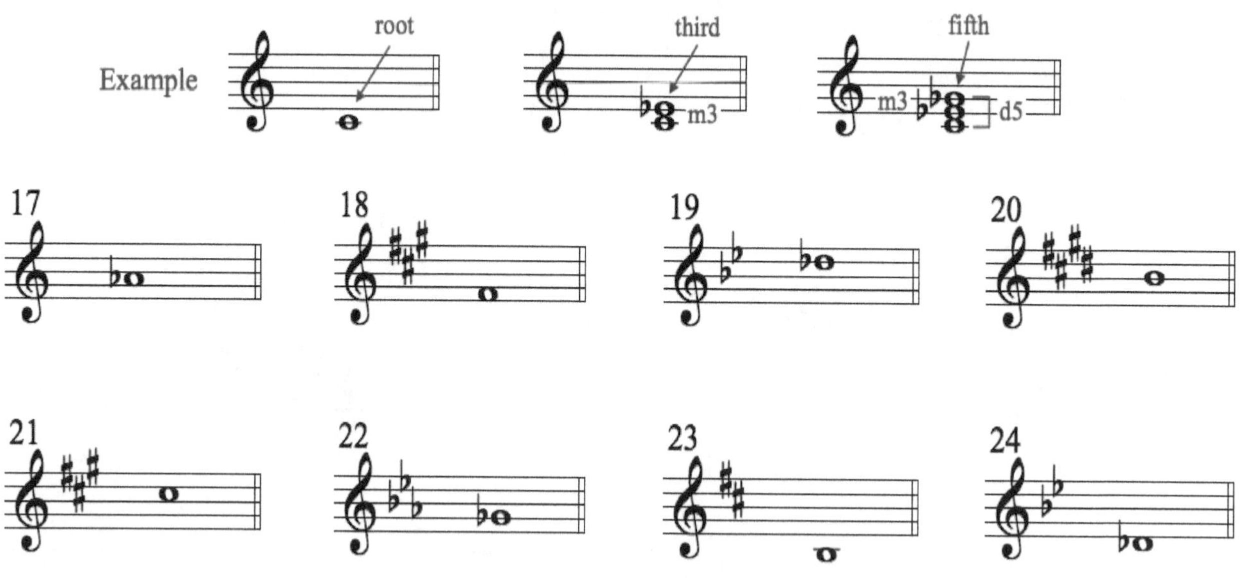

8. Create root-position **augmented triads** using the provided notes as roots.

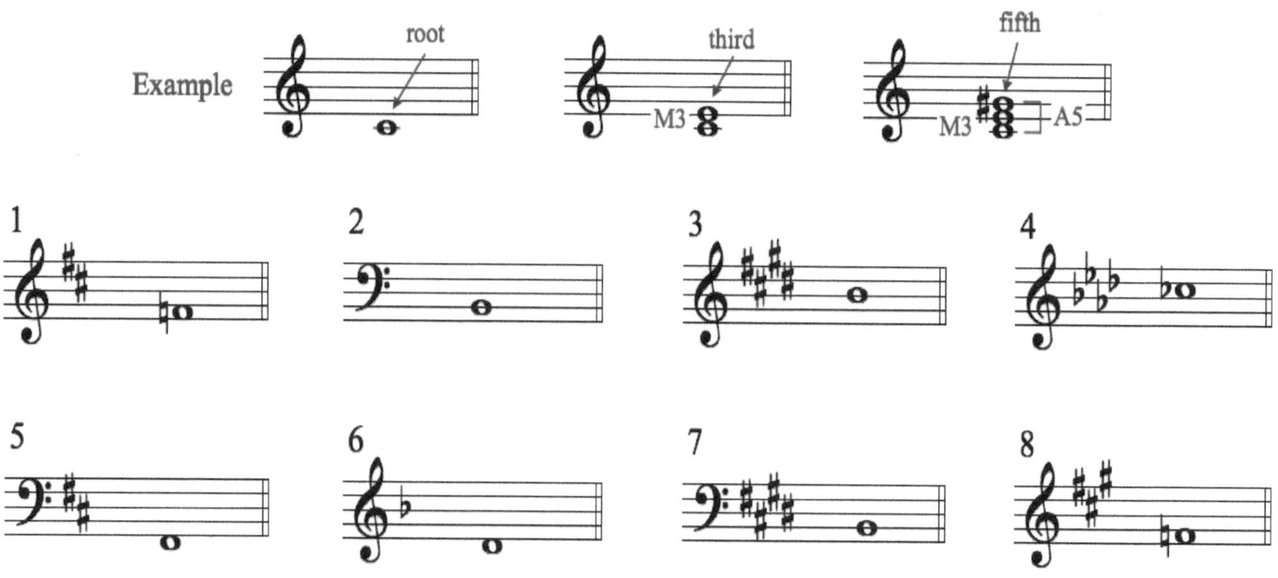

Lesson 25: Triads in major keys

Triads can be built on any note of the major and minor scales. Musicians often identify triads built on scale degrees by the same terms as the pitches of the scale. When triads are constructed on scale degrees, they must conform to the pitches of the scale. That is, if a scale has a Bb, all triads with a B will use a Bb. In the following example you will notice that the major scale produces three major triads, three minor triads, and one diminished triad.

In the example below, root-position triads are built on each scale degree of a C major scale. Each triad is named in accordance with two related chord identification systems.

1. The letter name of each root is combined with a chord-quality designation to form a chord symbol.

2. Roman numerals associate each scale degree with a chord quality. Chord qualities for each scale degree are consistent in all major scales: I, IV and V are major in all keys; ii, iv, and vi are minor; vii° is diminished.

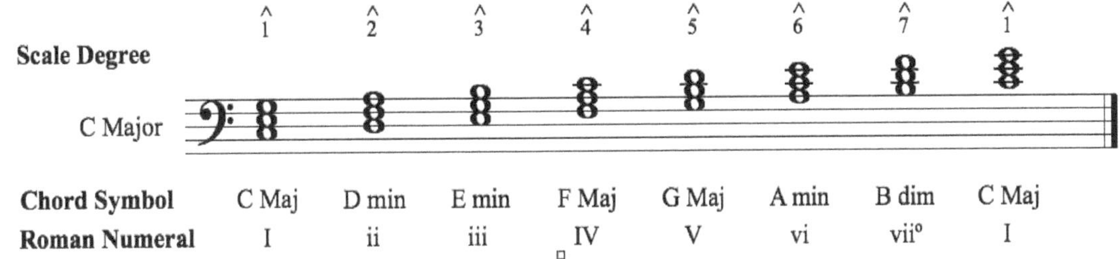

Of the seven triads in a major scale, three are major in **quality** (I, IV, and V), three are minor (i, ii, vi) and one is diminished (vii°). Note that for major triads, the Roman numeral is uppercase, for minor triads is lowercase, and for diminished triads it is a lowercase wit a ° sign.

Lesson 26: Triads in minor keys

As with the major, it is possible to build a triad on each degree of a minor scale. The name of each triad is the name of its root. Roman numerals are used to name triads. The common alteration in minor keys of scale-degree 6 and 7 has the potential to affect the other chords also, but use of a raised 7 to make V and vii° triads is by far the most common. As result, the V and vii° chords are the same in major and minor keys.

Example: D **natural** minor scale

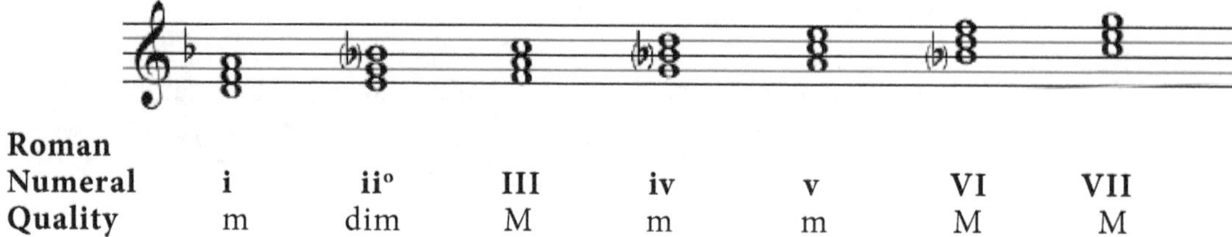

Example: D **harmonic** minor scale

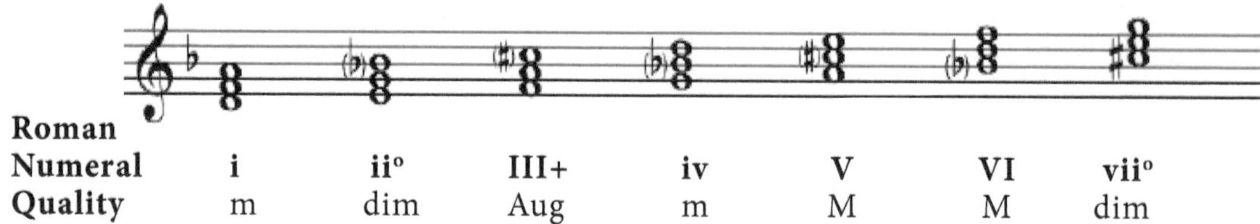

You will notice that in the harmonic minor scale the 3 scale degree is not major, minor, or diminished but augmented. For augmented triads we use the + symbol. Although other alterations borrowed from major are possible, they are a little beyond the scope of this course. Here, we will limit ourselves to the leading-tone alterations discussed thus far.

Triads are one of the primary building blocks of tonal music. If you intend to be a composer or a performer, you will need to know and master them. This mastery includes not only learning to write triads, as we have done in this chapter, but also learning to recognize them in musical situations. In studying triads, two things are important to keep in mind. First, there are four types of triads - major, minor. Diminished, and augmented. And while all triads in root position consist of two superimposed thirds, it is the quality of these thirds that determines the quality of the triad. Second, it is important to remember that while root-position triads are the norm, triads may also be inverted, that is, the third or the fifth of the triad may appear as the lowest sounding note.

STUDY QUESTIONS FOR CHAPTER 7

1. Define the following terms:

    Harmony

    Triad

    Chord

    Tertian Sonorities

    Chord Symbol

    Primary Triads

    Secondary Chords

2. The four types of chords:

    a.
    b.
    c.
    d.

3. A major chord is constructed by a M3 + __________.

4. A minor chord is constructed by a ________ + M3.

5. An augmented chord is constructed by _______________.

6. A diminished chord is constructed by ________________.

7. The _________________________ describes how the triad (or chord) is functioning in the music.

8. How is a “chord” different from a “triad”?

9. What do all triads have in common?

10. What are the primary triads?

Name:____________________________
Date:___________________

Chapter 7: Self-test

1. Write the names of the following chords. (see example)

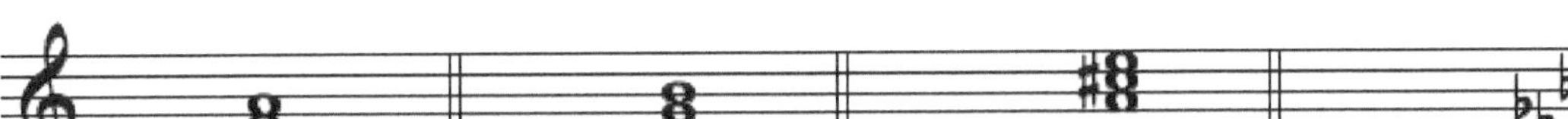

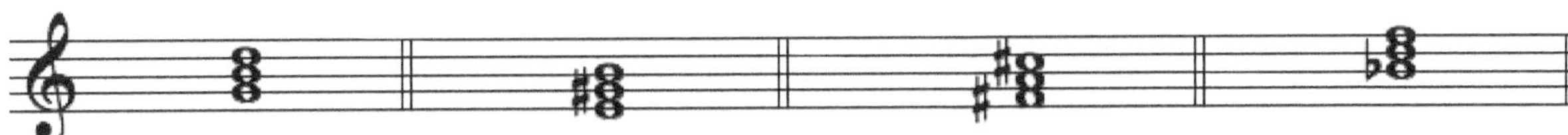

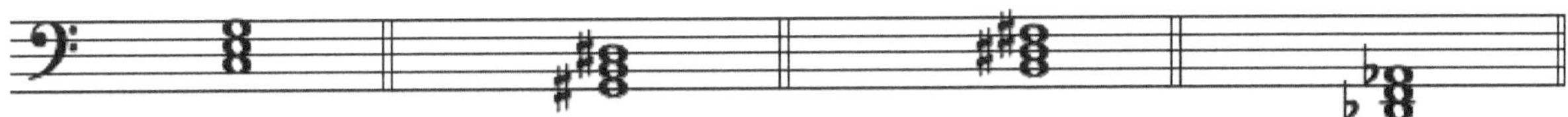

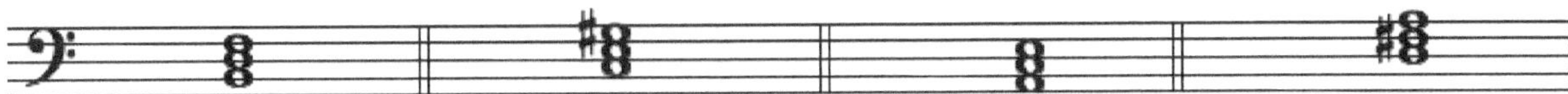

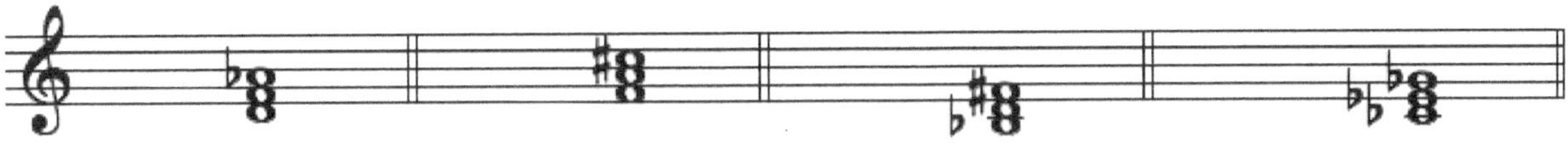

2. Notate the triad, given the root (first note of the chord) and the type.

Symbols: Major = M
Minor = m
Diminished = o
Augmented = +

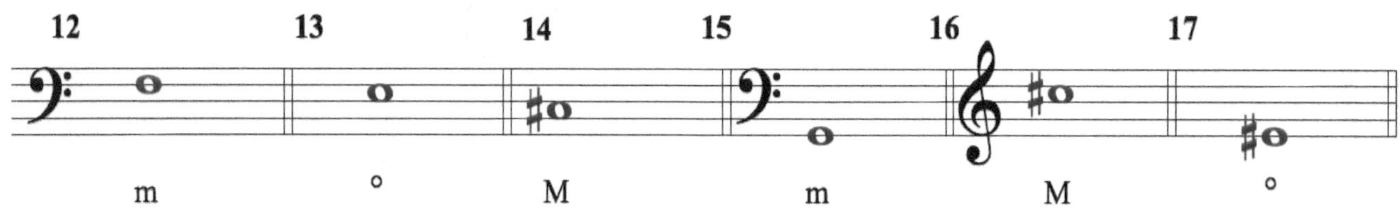

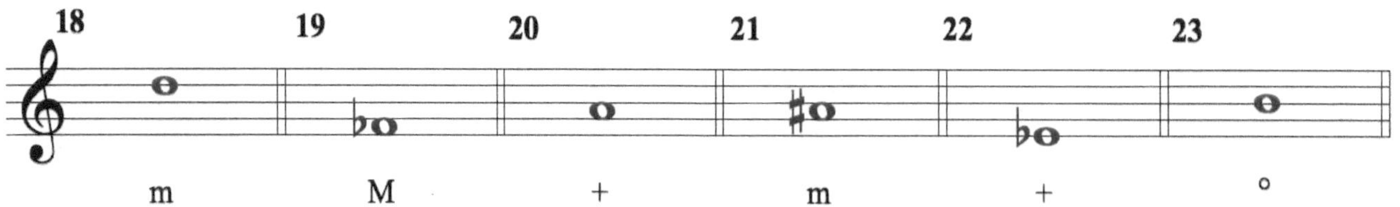

Name:_____________________________
Date:___________________

3. Write the primary triads (I, IV, V) in each of the following major and minor keys. Remember to write the proper key signature in each case. Label each chord with the appropriate roman numeral. (See example)

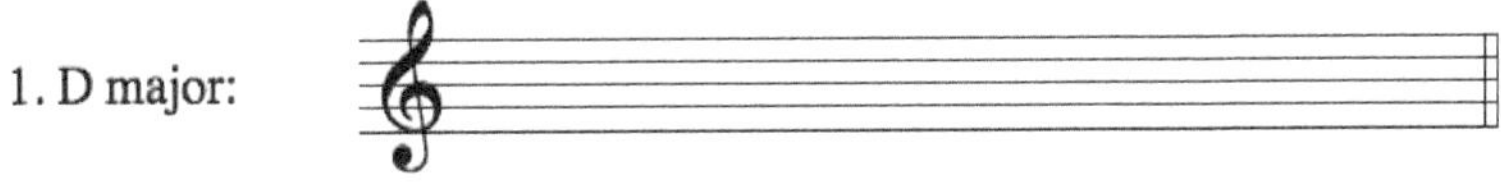

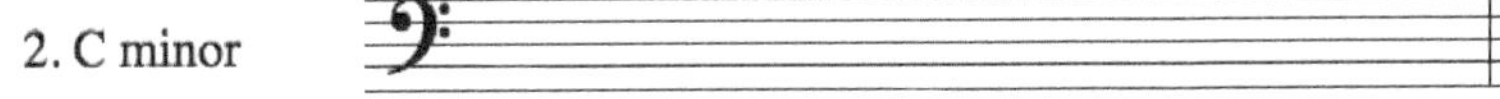

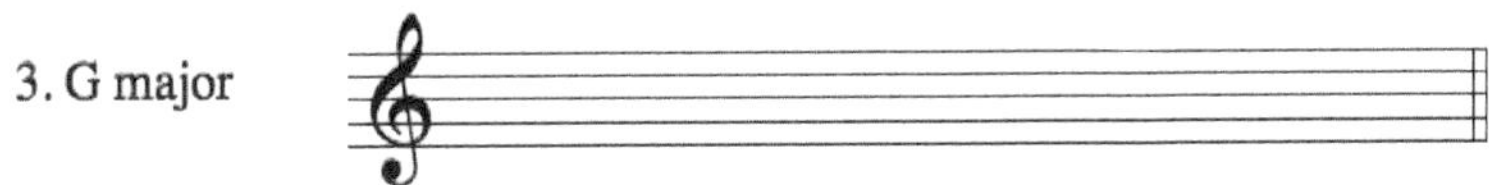

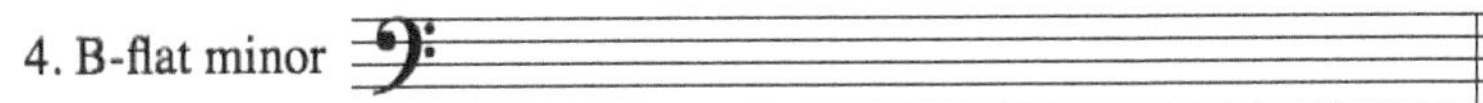

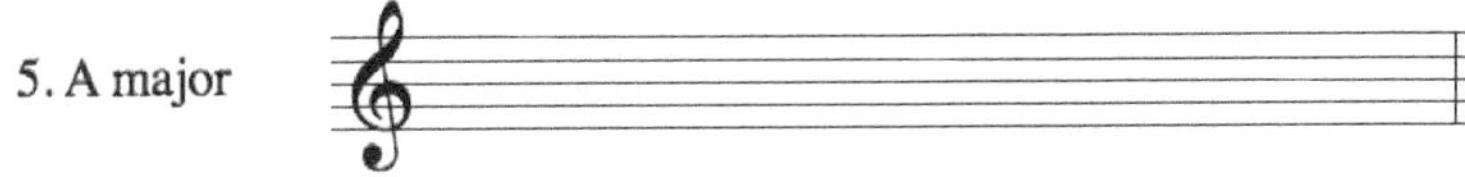

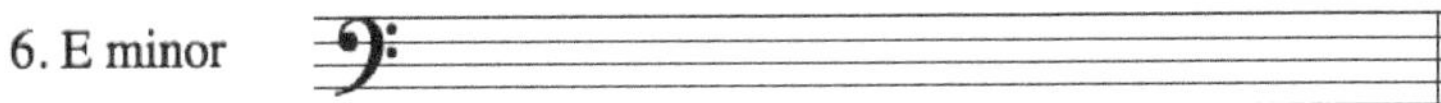

CHAPTER 8

SEVENTH CHORDS

LESSON 27: SEVENTH CHORDS

In this chapter we conclude our studies of the fundamentals of music by exploring four-note (sonorities) chords called ***seventh chords***. Let's examine this new chord.

Seventh Chord

This particular chord looks like a C major triad with an added Bb on top of the triad. Because the additional note spans an interval of a seventh above the root, the entire sonority is known as a **seventh chord**. The new chord tone is known as the seventh; the other three tones are still called root, third, and fifth.

We label seventh chords by their two most audible features: the type of triad (major, minor, diminished) and the type of seventh above the root (major, minor, diminished). There are five important types of seventh chords, though, like the triads types, they are not used with equal frequency. They are listed here and named according to the quality of the triad and the size of the seventh.

Seventh Chord Type	**Symbols**	**Common Name**
Major-minor seventh	7 or Mm7	Dominant seventh
Major-major seventh	maj7 or MM7	Major seventh
Minor-minor seventh	m7 or mm7	Minor seventh
Diminished-minor seventh	half-dim7 or (ø7)	Half-diminished seventh
Diminished-diminished seventh	dim7 or (o7)	(Fully) Diminished seventh

Lesson 28: Musical Characteristics of Seventh Chords

Major-minor Seventh Chord

The ***major-minor seventh chord*** (Mm7) is the most common seventh chord used in tonal music It can be found regularly in music written the early seventeenth century, and it is commonplace in popular music to this day, particularly the blues. The Mm 7 is often called the ***dominant seventh chord*** because it so regularly appears on the dominant scale degree (5).

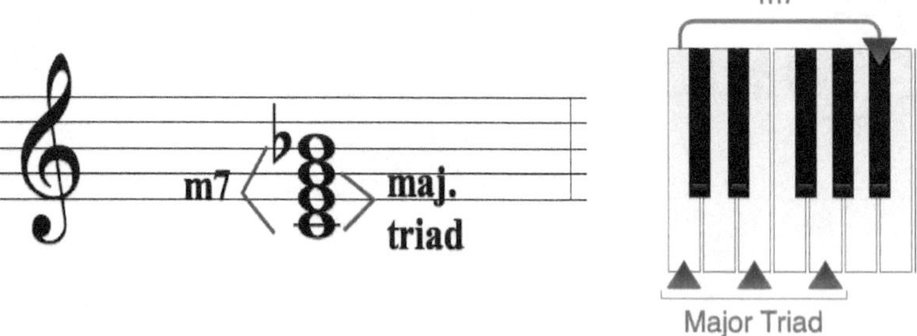

When the quality of the triad is major and the quality of the seventh is minor, the chord is known as major-minor seventh or dominant seventh chord. A major-minor seventh chord may be constructed from any pitch by building these intervals above a given root.

Major-major Seventh Chord

The ***major-seventh chord*** (MM7), with its major seventh, is more strident that the major-minor seventh chord. It appears occasionally in common practice music but more regularly in 20th century popular music and jazz.

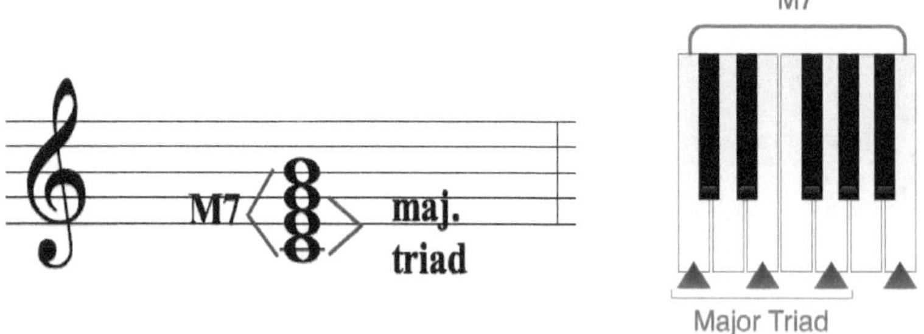

When the quality of the triad is major and the quality of the seventh is major, the chord is known as major-major seventh or major seventh chord. A major seventh chord may be constructed from any pitch by building these intervals above a given root.

Minor-minor Seventh Chord

The minor seventh chord (mm7) is a very soft-sounding chord, because its minor seventh creates a less dissonant sound than that of the major seventh.

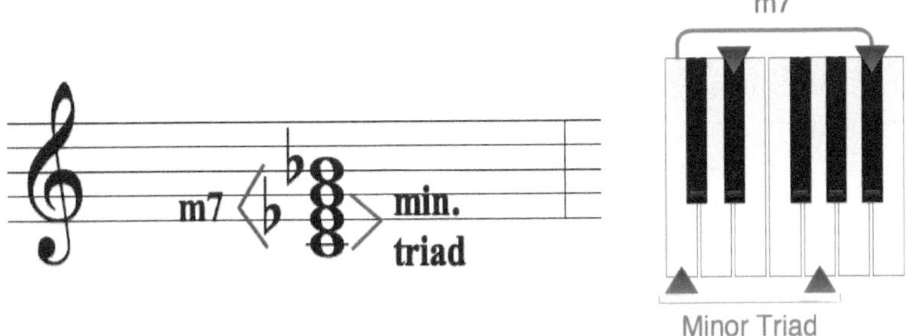

When the quality of the triad is minor and the quality of the seventh is minor, the chord is known as minor-minor seventh or minor seventh chord.

Half-Diminished Seventh Chord

The half-diminished seventh chord (dm7, or ø7) is a mix effect. The dissonant triad is balanced with a less dissonant minor seventh. The chord occurs in both common-practice music and 20th century popular music.

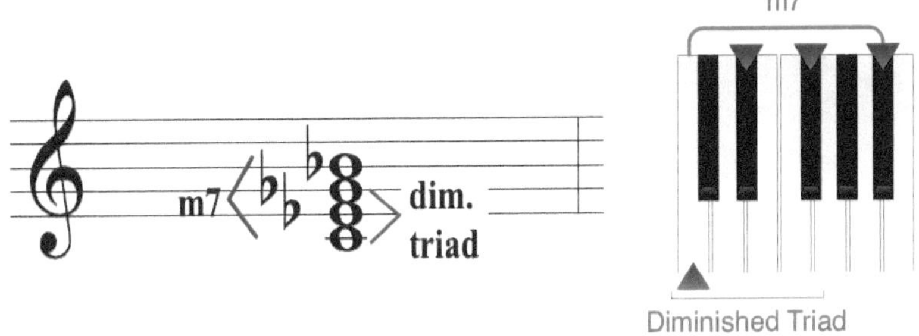

When the quality of the triad is diminished and the quality of the seventh is minor, the chord is known as half-diminished seventh chord.

FULLY DIMINISHED SEVENTH CHORD

The fully diminished chord (dd7 or °7) is the most dissonant of the seventh chords that we will study. It is found in the late 16th century compositions and throughout the 17th and 18th century music. In addition, the fully diminished seventh chord is an asset to silent movie scores, where it often signals trouble, such as the train quickly approaching the maiden tied to the tracks. It is the only seventh chord that contains all the same type of thirds and fifths: three minor thirds and two diminished fifths.

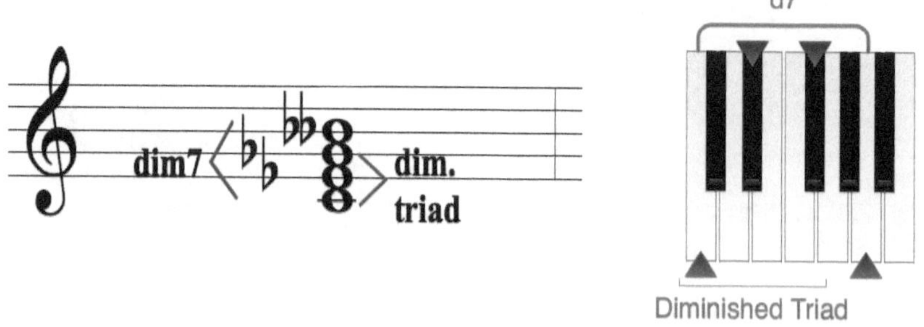

SEVENTH CHORD SUMMARY

Use this chart to reference the five common types of seventh chords. *(For more information about seventh chords see APPENDIX F)*

Seventh Chord =	Triad +	Seventh Interval	Abbreviation
Dominant 7th	Major Triad	Minor	7
Major 7th	Major Triad	Major	M7
Minor 7th	Minor Triad	Minor	m7
Half-diminished 7th	Diminished Triad	Minor	ø7
Diminished 7th	Diminished Triad	Diminished	°7

Name:____________________________

Date:____________________

Lesson 28: Practice Exercises

1. Construct major seventh chords above the following notes:

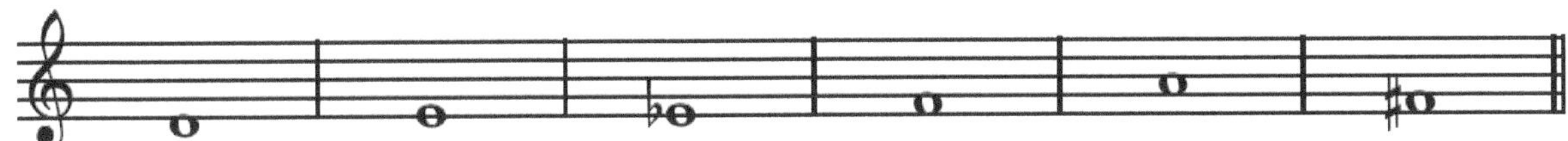

2. Construct major-minor seventh chords above the following notes:

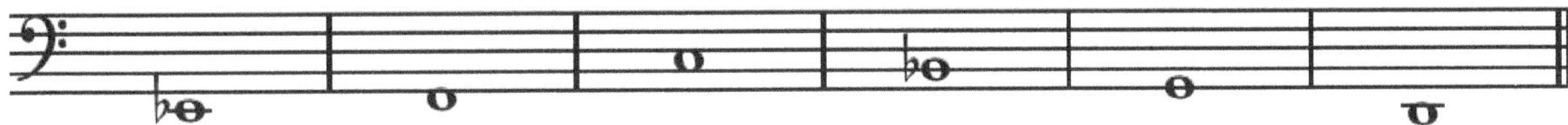

3. Construct major seventh chords above the following notes:

4. Construct half-diminished seventh chords above the following notes:

5. Construct fully diminished seventh chords above the following notes:

Name:____________________________
Date:____________________

Chapter 8: Self-test

1. Identify the following seventh chords:

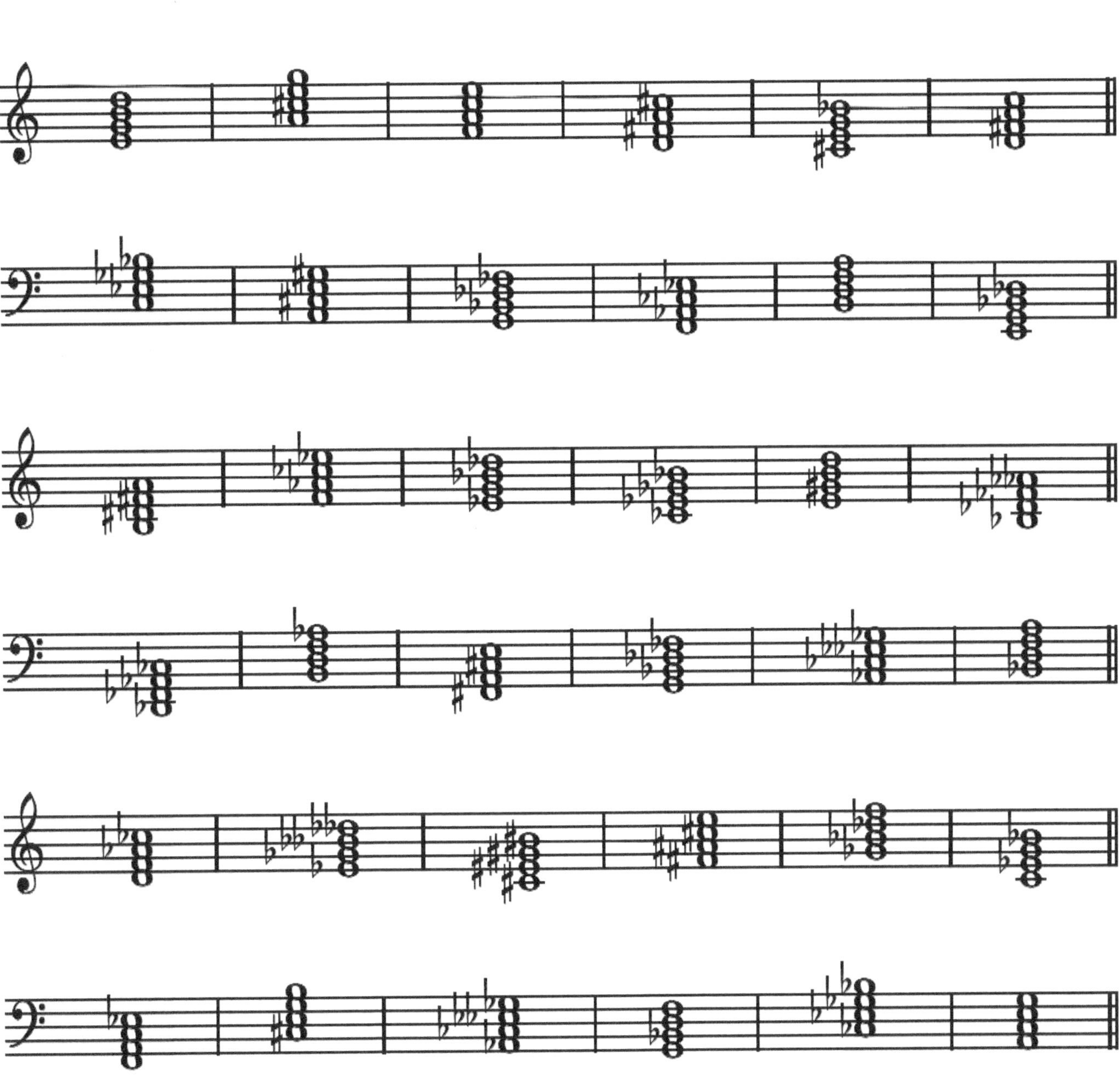

2. Which seventh-chord type have a diminished triad on the bottom?

3. Which ones have a M3 between the 5th and the 7th of the chord?

4. Which ones have a m3 between the 3rd and the 5th of the chord?

5. Which ones contain at least one P5? Which contain two?

6. Which one consists entirely of a stack of minor thirds?

APPENDIX A
A BRIEF GUIDE TO COMMON MUSICAL SYMBOLS AND SIGNS

In this section we will learn more musical symbols. These symbols are used by musicians to help to create certain sound effects while reading the musical score. Let's start with dynamics. The **dynamics** signs indicate how loudly or softly music should be played; each one is very important and should be learned carefully. We use Italian terms to indicate dynamics.

Dynamics Terms and Signs

ppp	*Pianississimo*: Extremely soft
pp	*Pianissimo*: Very soft
p	*Piano:* Soft
mp	*Mezzo Piano*: Moderately soft
mf	*Mezzo forte*: Moderately loud
f	*Forte*: Loud
ff	*Fortissimo*: Very Loud
fff	*Fortississimo*: Extremely Loud

Changes in dynamics may be sudden or gradual:

fp A section of music in which the music should initially be played loudly (forte), then immediately softly (piano)

Crescendo: gradually louder Also abbreviated as *cresc.*

Decrescendo (diminuendo): gradually softer Also abbreviated as *decresc.*

ARTICULATIONS

In music, articulation refers to the direction or performance technique which affects the transition or continuity on single note or between multiple notes or sounds. There are many different kinds of articulation, each having a different effect on how the note is played. Some articulation marks include the slur, phrase mark, staccato, accent, sforzando, and legato. Each articulation is represented by a different symbol placed above or below the note (depending on its position on the staff).

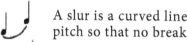

A slur is a curved line that smoothly connects notes of different pitch so that no break is heard between the two notes.

Staccato - play the note very short and detached.

Accent - hit the note harder and louder.

Marcato - Almost a combination of staccato and accent; provides a sharp sound.

Tenuto - Hold the note for its full value.

Sforzando - A sudden, strong accent.

Fermata - Hold the note longer, approximately twice its value, or until conducted to stop.

Repeats

Occasionally, composers want several measures in a composition to repeat immediately. They can indicate this either by writing all of the measures again or by using repeat signs. Repeat signs are two large dots, one above the other, that appear at the beginning and the end of the measures to be repeated. Double bar lines generally accompany the repeat signs at the beginning and the end of the repeated measures in order to call attention to the repeat signs.

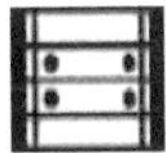

These are the beginning and ending repeat signs. When you reach the second **repeat sign**, go back to the first and repeat the music. These are often accompanied by first, second and even third endings.

D.C.

Da Capo means from the beginning (literally from the head). It is often abbreviated *D.C.* It is a composer or publisher's directive to repeat the previous part of music, often used to save space. In small pieces this might be the same thing as a repeat, but in larger works *D.C.* might occur after one or more repeats of small sections, indicating a return to the very beginning.

D.S.

This is a directional marking. It means '**Dal Signo**'. When you see this in music, you must go to the sign (below). This marking may also be accompanied by 'al coda' or 'al fine'. These mean 'go to the sign, from there go to the coda,' and 'go to the sign, from there go to the end' respectively. Essentially, these are big repeat signs.

𝄋

This is the **sign**. From here you play to the coda, the end or wherever the Dal Signo directs you.

𝄌

This is the **coda sign**. It marks when to go to the special ending, or coda. Usually you won't go to the coda until after a D.S. al coda.

Simile marks. Denote that preceding groups of beats or measures are to be repeated. In the examples here, the first usually means to repeat the previous measure, and the second usually means to repeat the previous two measures.

TEMPO MARKINGS

Composers use the terms *fast* and *slow* as indications of speed, many pieces use Italian terms to assign the tempo. The following is a list of the most important terms and their meaning.

All of these markings are based on a few root words. By adding an -issimo ending the word is amplified/made louder, by adding an -ino ending the word is diminished/made softer, and by adding an -etto ending the word is endeared. The metronome marks are broad approximations.

Note: Metronome markings are a guide only and depending on the time signature and the piece itself, these figures may not be appropriate in every circumstance.
**** **bpm**: *beats per minute ***

Larghissimo — very, very slow (20 bpm and below)
Grave — slow and solemn (20–40 bpm)
Lento — slowly (40–60 bpm)
Largo — broadly (40–60 bpm)
Larghetto — rather broadly (60–66 bpm)
Adagio — slow and stately (literally, "at ease") (66–76 bpm)
Adagietto — rather slow (70–80 bpm)
Andante moderato — a bit slower than andante
Andante — at a walking pace (76–108 bpm)
Andantino — slightly faster than andante
Moderato — moderately (108–120 bpm)
Allegretto — moderately fast (but less so than allegro)
Allegro moderato — moderately quick (112–124 bpm)
Allegro — fast, quickly and bright (120–168 bpm)
Vivace — lively and fast (≈140 bpm) (quicker than allegro)
Vivacissimo — very fast and lively
Allegrissimo — very fast
Presto — very fast (168–200 bpm)
Prestissimo — extremely fast (more than 200bpm)

Additional Terms:

Tempo comodo — at a comfortable (normal) speed
Tempo di valse — speed of a waltz
Tempo di marcia — speed of a march
Tempo giusto — at a consistent speed, at the 'right' speed, in strict tempo
Tempo semplice — simple, regular speed, plainly

Composers may use expressive marks to adjust the tempo:

A tempo — return to the previous tempo after change(s), which also indicates an immediate, not a gradual, tempo change.

Accelerando — speeding up (abbreviation: accel.)

Allargando — growing broader; decreasing tempo, usually near the end of a piece

Calando — going slower (and usually also softer)

Doppio movimento — double speed

Lentando — gradual slowing and softer

Meno mosso — less movement or slower

Mosso — movement, more lively, or quicker, much like più mosso, but not as extreme

Più mosso — more movement or faster

Precipitando — hurrying, going faster/forward

Rallentando — gradual slowing down (abbreviation: rall.)

Ritardando — less gradual slowing down (more sudden decrease in tempo than rallentando; abbreviation: rit. or more specifically, ritard.)

Ritenuto — slightly slower; temporarily holding back.

Rubato — free adjustment of tempo for expressive purposes

Stretto — in faster tempo, often near the conclusion of a section. (Note that in fugal compositions, the term stretto refers to the imitation of the subject in close succession, before the subject is completed, and as such, suitable for the close of the fugue. Used in this context, the term is not necessarily related to tempo.)

Stringendo — pressing on faster (literally "tightening")

APPENDIX B
MAJOR/MINOR SCALE AND ARPEGGIO FINGERING

Major Scale Fingerings

Key Signatures with Sharps:
C has no sharps or flats in its key signature.
RH 123 1234 123 12345
LH 54321 321 4321 321

G has one sharp (F).
RH 123 1234 123 12345
LH 54321 321 4321 321

D has two sharps (F C).
RH 123 1234 123 12345
LH 54321 321 4321 321

A has three sharps (F C G).
RH 123 1234 123 12345
LH 54321 321 4321 321

E has four sharps (F C G D).
RH 123 1234 123 12345
LH 54321 321 4321 321

B has five sharps (F C G D A).
RH 123 1234 123 12345
LH 4321 4321 321 4321

F# has six sharps (F C G D A E). See G♭ major.

C# has seven sharps (F C G D A E B). See D♭ major.

Key Signatures with Flats:
F has one flat (B).
RH 1234 123 1234 1234
LH 54321 321 4321 321

B♭ has two flats (B E).
RH 2 123 1234 123 1234
LH 321 4321 321 4321 2

E♭ has three flats (B E A).
RH 2 1234 123 1234 123
LH 321 4321 321 4321 2

A♭ has four flats (B E A D).
RH 23 123 1234 123 123
LH 321 4321 321 4321 2

D♭ has five flats (B E A D G).
RH 34 1234 123 1234 12
LH 321 4321 321 4321 2

G♭ has six flats (B E A D G C).
RH 234 123 1234 123 12
LH 4321 321 4321 321 2

C♭ has seven flats (B E A D G C F). See B major.

Major Arpeggio Fingerings

Key Signatures with Sharps:
C has no sharps or flats.
RH 123 1235
LH 5421 421

G has one sharp (F).
RH 123 1235
LH 5421 421

D has two sharps (F C).
RH 123 1235
LH 5321 321

A has three sharps (F C G).
RH 123 1235
LH 5321 321

E has four sharps (F C G D).
RH 123 1235
LH 5321 321

B has five sharps (F C G D A).
RH 123 1235
LH 5321 321

F# has six sharps (F C G D A E). See G♭ major.

C# has seven sharps (F C G D A E B). See D♭ major.

Key Signatures with Flats:
F has one flat (B).
RH 123 1235
LH 5421 421

B♭ has two flats (B E).
RH 2 124 124 or RH 23 123 12
LH 21 421 42 LH 321 321 3

E♭ has three flats (B E A).
RH 2 124 124
LH 21 421 42

A♭ has four flats (B E A D).
RH 2 124 124
LH 21 421 42

D♭ has five flats (B E A D G).
RH 2 124 124
LH 21 421 42

G♭ has six flats (B E A D G C).
RH 123 1235
LH 5321 321

C♭ has seven flats (B E A D G C F). See B major.

Harmonic Minor Scale Fingerings

Key Signatures with Sharps:
Am has no sharps or flats except the G# leading tone (LT).
RH 123 1234 123 12345
LH 54321 321 4321 321

Em has one sharp (F) plus a D# LT.
RH 123 1234 123 12345
LH 54321 321 4321 321

Bm has two sharps (F C) plus an A# LT.
RH 123 1234 123 12345
LH 4321 4321 321 4321

F#m has three sharps (F C G) plus an E# LT.
RH 34 123 1234 123 123
LH 4321 321 4321 321 2

C#m has four sharps (F C G D) plus a B# LT.
RH 34 123 1234 123 123
LH 321 4321 321 4321 2

G#m has five sharps (F C G D A) plus an F𝄪 LT.
RH 34 123 1234 123 123
LH 321 4321 321 4321 2

D#m has six sharps (F C G D A E) plus a C𝄪 LT. See E♭ minor.

A#m has seven sharps (F C G D A E B) plus a G𝄪 LT. See B♭ minor.

Key Signatures with Flats:
Dm has one flat (B) plus a C# leading tone.
RH 123 1234 123 12345
LH 54321 321 4321 321

Gm has two flats (B E) plus an F# LT.
RH 123 1234 123 12345
LH 54321 321 4321 321

Cm has three flats (B E A) plus a B♮ LT.
RH 123 1234 123 12345
LH 54321 321 4321 321

Fm has four flats (B E A D) plus an E♮ LT.
RH 1234 123 1234 1234
LH 54321 321 4321 321

B♭m has five flats (B E A D G) plus an A♮ LT.
RH 2 123 1234 123 1234
LH 21 321 4321 321 432

E♭m has six flats (B E A D G C) plus a D♮ LT.
RH 3 1234 123 1234 123
LH 21 4321 321 4321 32

A♭m has seven flats (B E A D G C F) plus a G♮ LT. See G# minor.

Minor Arpeggio Fingerings

Key Signatures with Sharps:
Am has no sharps or flats.
RH 123 1235
LH 5421 421

Em has one sharp (F).
RH 123 1235
LH 5421 421

Bm has two sharps (F C).
RH 123 1235
LH 5421 421

F#m has three sharps (F C G).
RH 2 124 124
LH 21 421 42

C#m has four sharps (F C G D).
RH 2 124 124
LH 21 421 42

G#m has five sharps (F C G D A).
RH 2 124 124
LH 21 421 42

D#m has six sharps (F C G D A E). See E♭ minor.

A#m has seven sharps (F C G D A E B). See B♭ minor.

Key Signatures with Flats:
Dm has one flat (B).
RH 123 1235
LH 5421 421

Gm has two flats (B E).
RH 123 1235
LH 5421 421

Cm has three flats (B E A).
RH 123 1235
LH 5421 421

Fm has four flats (B E A D).
RH 123 1235
LH 5421 421

B♭m has five flats (B E A D G).
RH 23 123 12
LH 321 321 2

E♭m has six flats (B E A D G C).
RH 123 1235
LH 5421 421

A♭m has seven flats (B E A D G C F). See G# minor.

APPENDIX C
INVERSION OF INTERVALS

Intervals can be inverted, which basically means you turn them upside down. The lower note is raised up an octave so that the top note/bottom note relationship is reversed. The figures below show the inversions of intervals.

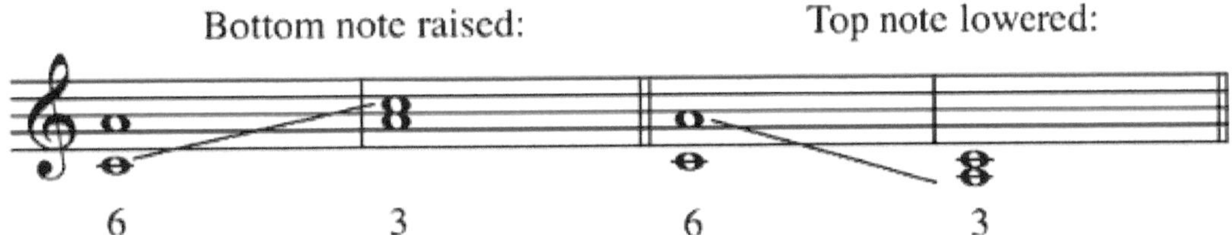

When a sixth is inverted, it becomes a third

Notice the effect of inversion on each of the intervals:

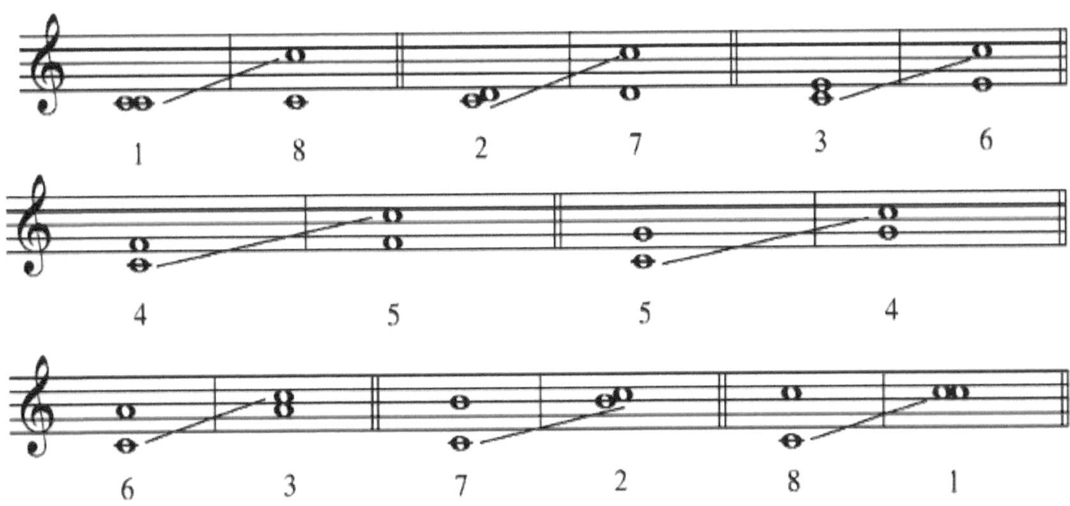

Now that we now how to invert a numerical interval we need to find out what happens to the quality of the interval once inverted.

A Major interval becomes Minor

A Minor interval becomes Major

A Perfect interval remains Perfect An Augmented interval becomes Diminished and a Diminished interval becomes Augmented

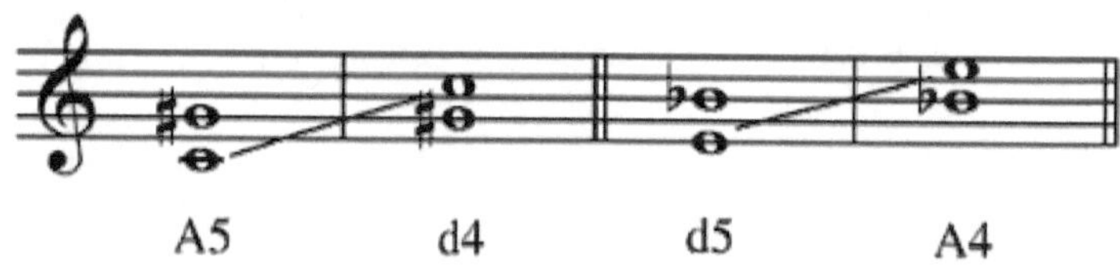

For your own practice, study and play all of the intervals mentioned in Chapter 6 with and with their inversions.

APPENDIX D
CHORD CONSTRUCTION

During the "common practice period" the triad evolved into a three-note chord constructed of superimposed thirds. It came to be the basic element in harmonic progressions. Triads are built from notes in the major/minor scale system. Four types of triads are found in this system: major, minor, augmented and diminished. These names describe the types of sounds generated from the intervals contained in the triads.

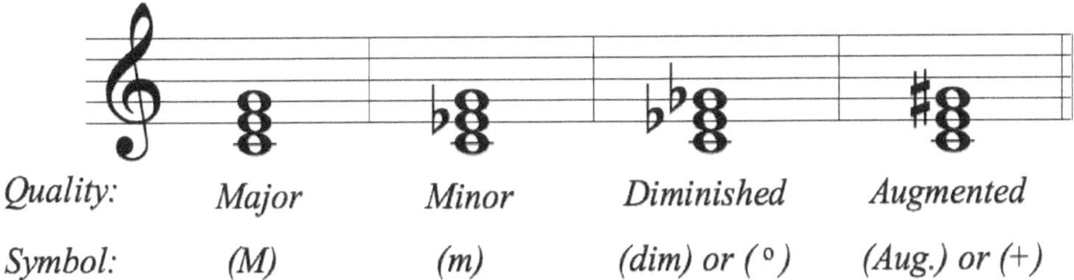

The intervals contained in the four types of triads are **major** and/or **minor** 3rds.

The next example is a triad. Notice that the triad is constructed by "stacking" thirds on top of each other.

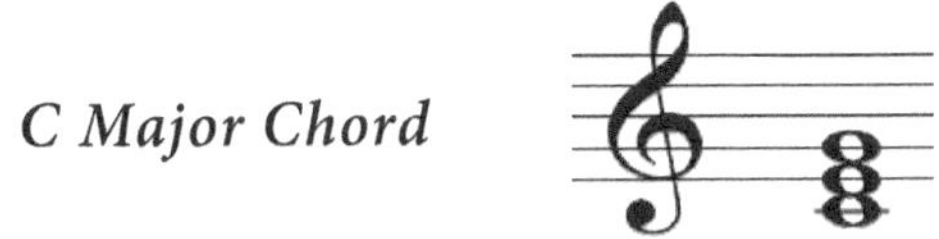

Many chord qualities are not explained in this book. In most cases if you keep stacking more thirds on top of each other you will get more complex sonorities for example:

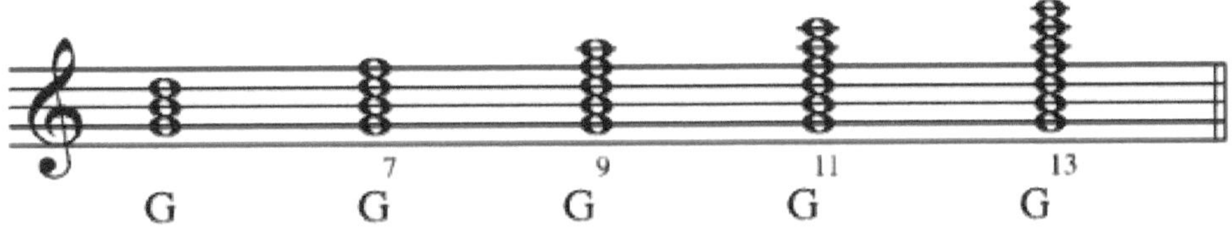

Chords are named for the interval formed between the bottom and the highest note as we see in the example above. The following chart will show you the main theory on how to build a chord.

Triad	**Interval**
Major	M3 + m3
Minor	m3 + M3
Diminished	m3 + m3
Augmented	M3 + M3

A **major chord** is built when stacking a M3 + m3 together:

Root M3 + m3

A **minor chord** is built when stacking a m3 + M3 together:

Root m3 + M3

An **augmented chord** is built when stacking two M3 + M3 together:

A **diminished chord** is built when stacking two m3 + m3 together:

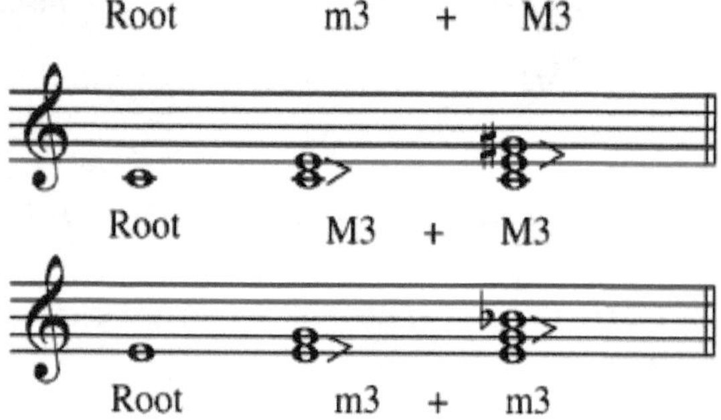

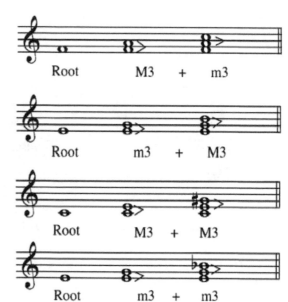

Seventh Chords

The seventh chord consist of four notes: a triad with an added third. There are five types of seventh chords: major-minor, minor-minor, diminished-minor, and diminished-diminished. Each seventh chord has a common name, shown in the following chart. Use the terms recommended by your instructor.

Seventh Chord Type	Symbols	Common Name
Major-minor seventh	7 or Mm7	Dominant seventh
Major-major seventh	maj7 or MM7	Major seventh
Minor-minor seventh	m7 or mm7	Minor seventh
Diminished-minor seventh	dm7 or (ø7)	Half-diminished seventh
Diminished-diminished seventh	dd7 or (°7)	(Fully) Diminished seventh

Dominant seventh

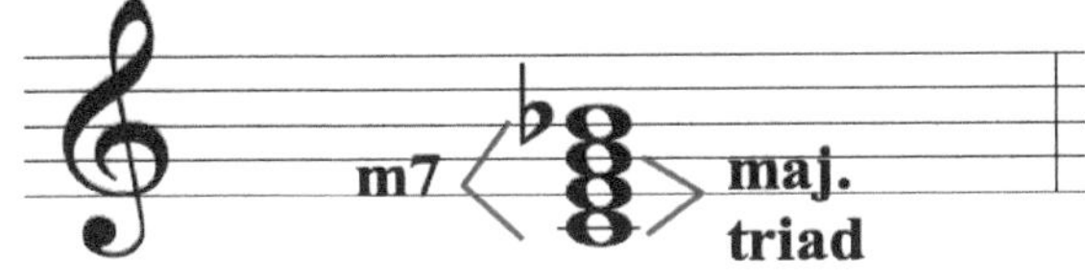

Major seventh

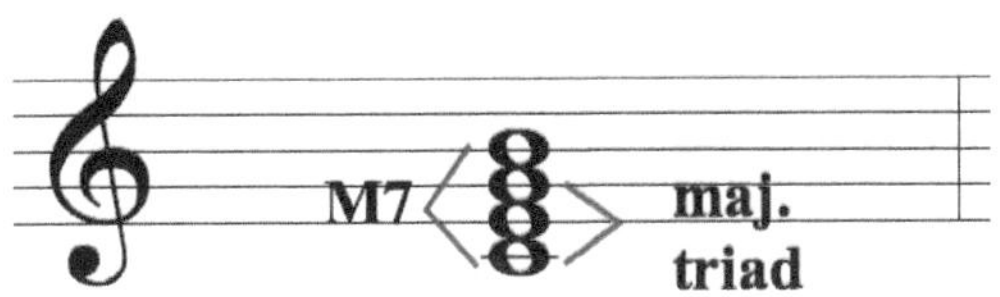

Minor seventh

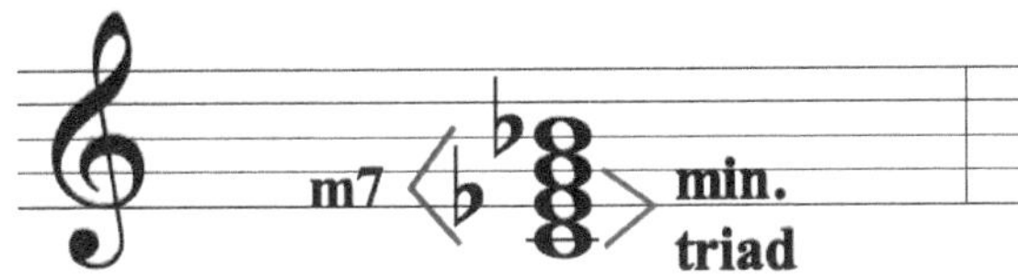

Half-diminished seventh

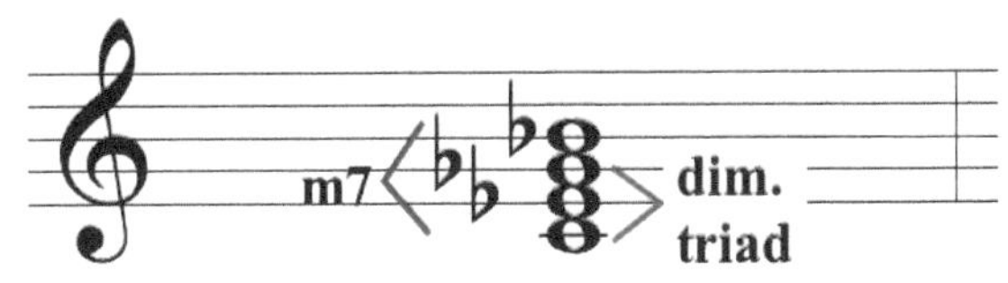

Diminished seventh

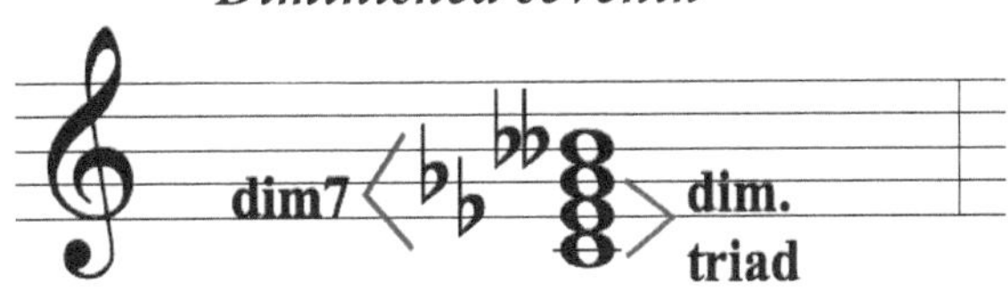

APPENDIX E
PRIMARY CHORDS IN SELECTED MAJOR AND MINOR KEYS

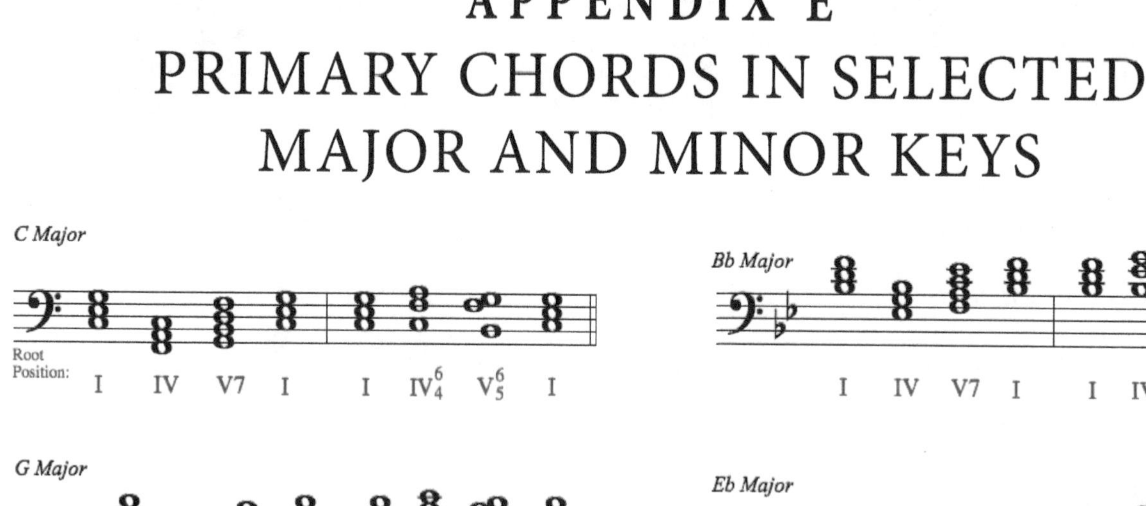

Eb Major

I IV V7 I I IV$^6_4$ V$^6_5$ I

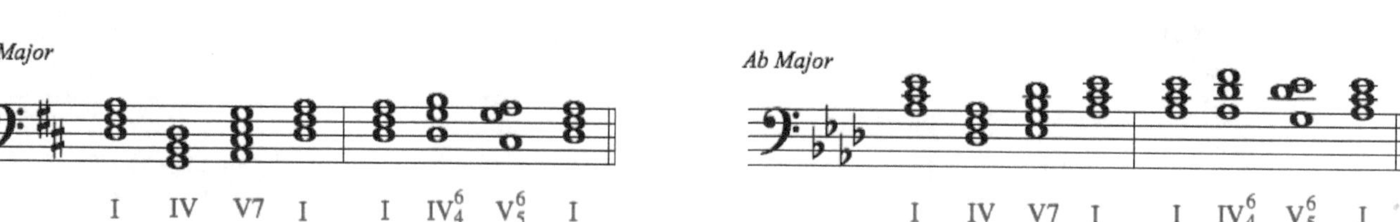

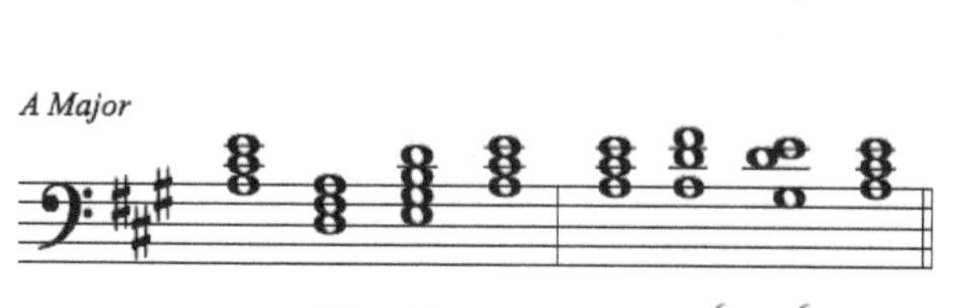

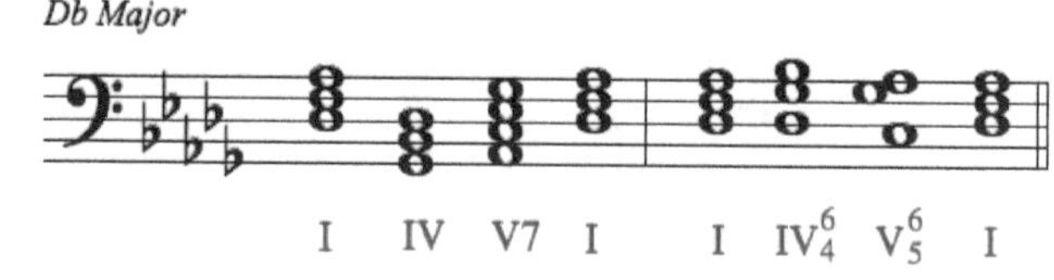

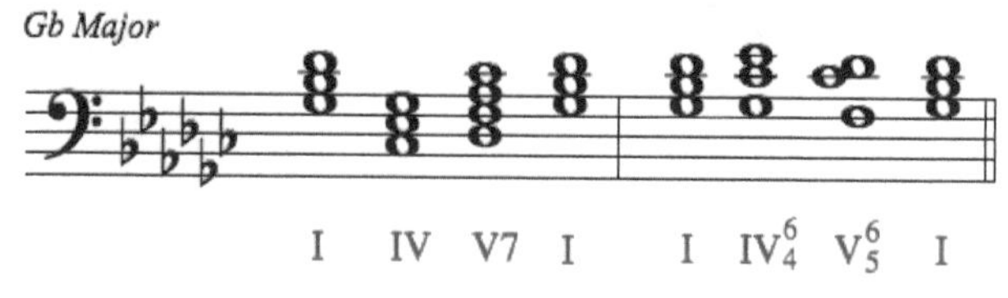

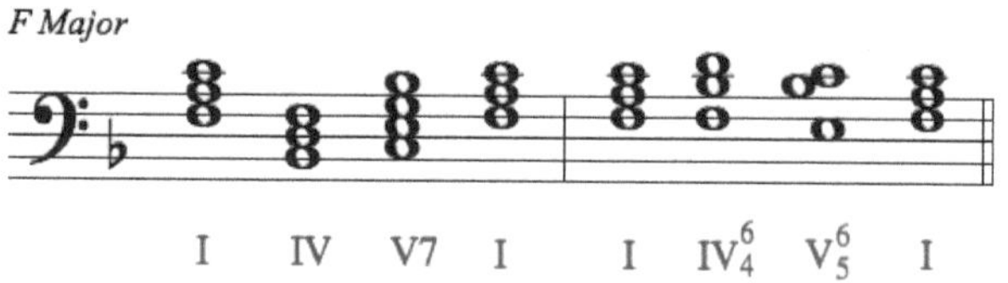

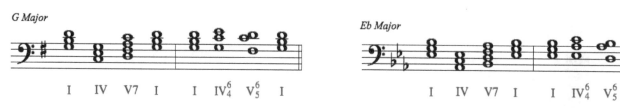

A harmonic minor

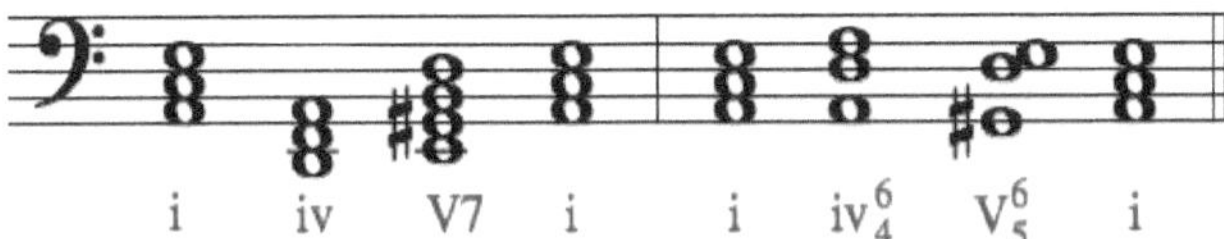

i iv V7 i i iv^6_4 V^6_5 i

B harmonic minor

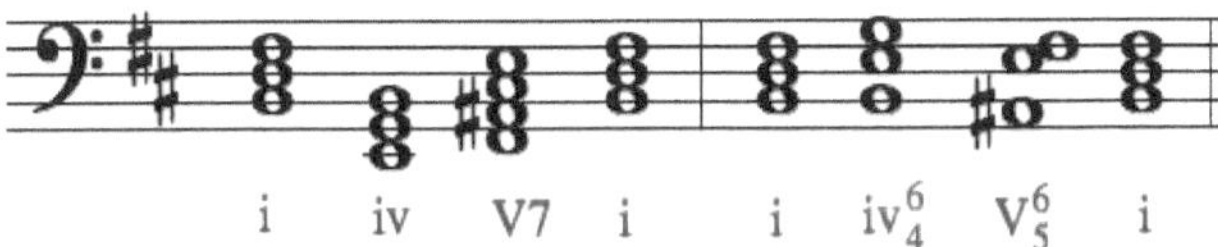

i iv V7 i i iv^6_4 V^6_5 i

C# harmonic minor

i iv V7 i i iv^6_4 V^6_5 i

G harmonic minor

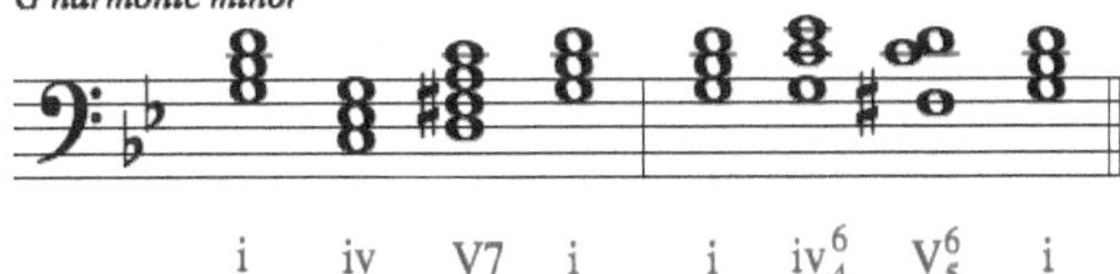

i iv V7 i i iv^6_4 V^6_5 i

F harmonic minor

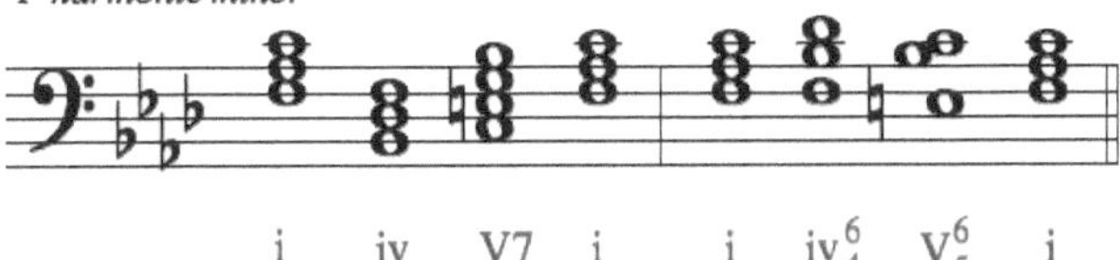

i iv V7 i i iv^6_4 V^6_5 i

E harmonic minor

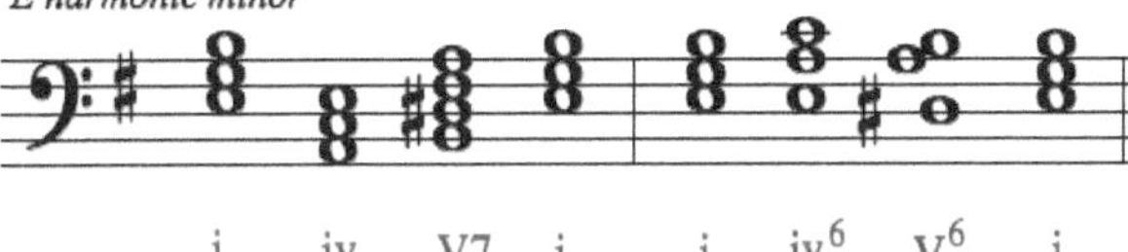

i iv V7 i i iv^6_4 V^6_5 i

F# harmonic minor

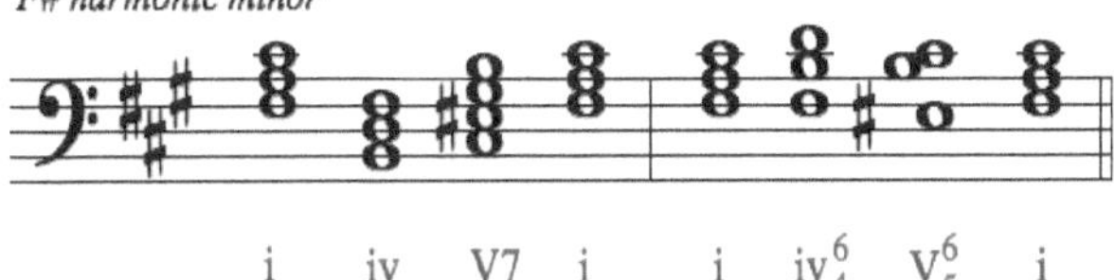

i iv V7 i i iv^6_4 V^6_5 i

D harmonic minor

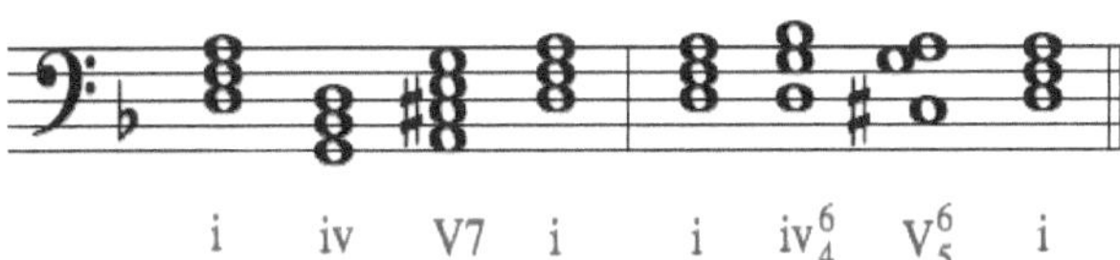

i iv V7 i i iv^6_4 V^6_5 i

C harmonic minor

i iv V7 i i iv^6_4 V^6_5 i

APPENDIX F
SELECTED CHORDS AND CHORD SYMBOLS

KEY FOR CHORD SYMBOLS

1. A capital letter indicates a major triad.
2. A capital letter followed by a lowercase ***m*** indicates a minor triad
3. A capital letter followed by ***dim*** or a small circle (***o***) indicates a diminished triad.
4. A capital letter followed by ***aug*** or a small sign (+) indicates an augmented triad.

APPENDIX G
CIRCLE OF FIFTHS

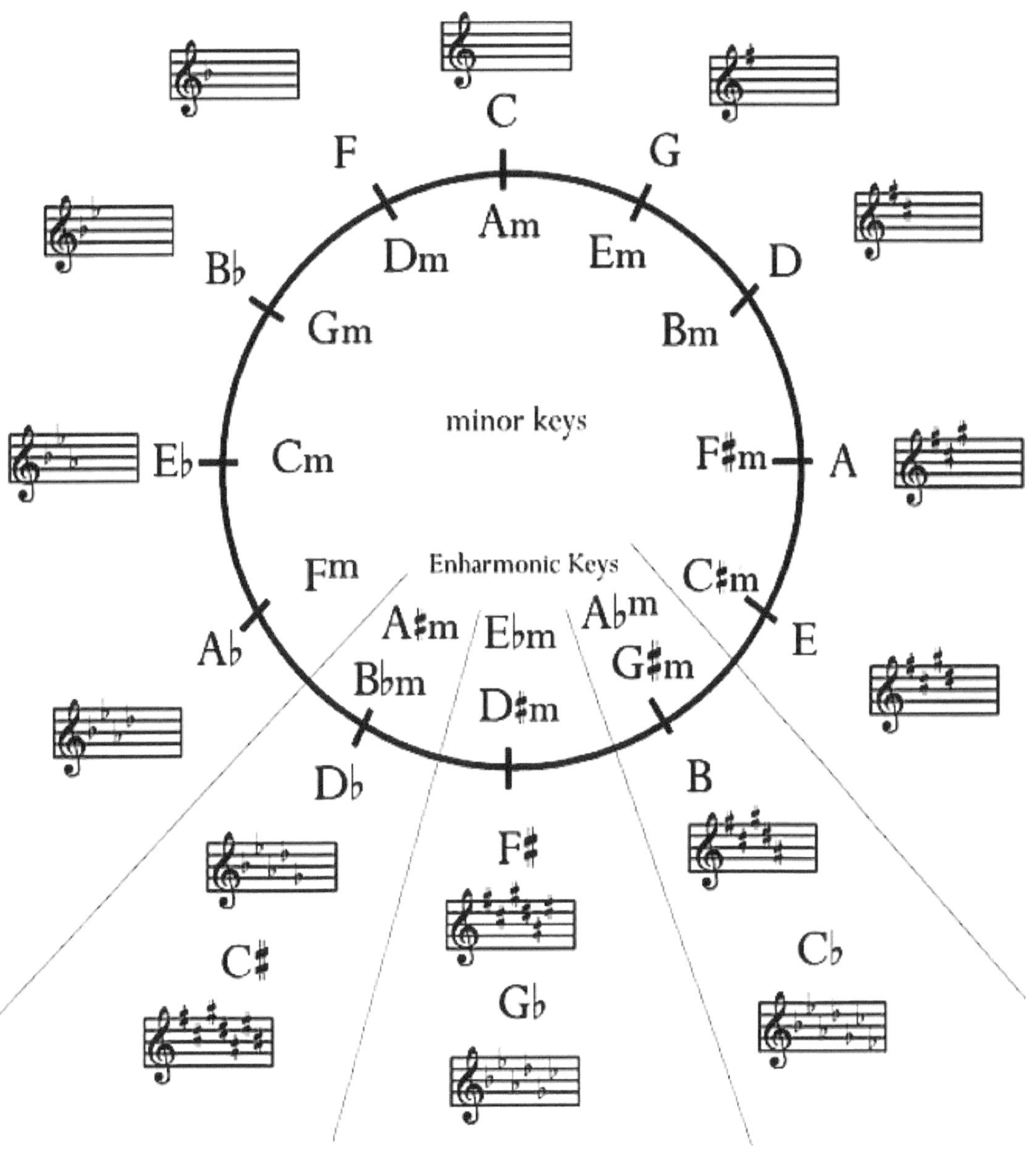

The order for the placement of sharps and flats:							
♯	F	C	G	D	A	E	B
♭	B	E	A	D	G	C	F

APPENDIX H
THE PIANO KEYBOARD

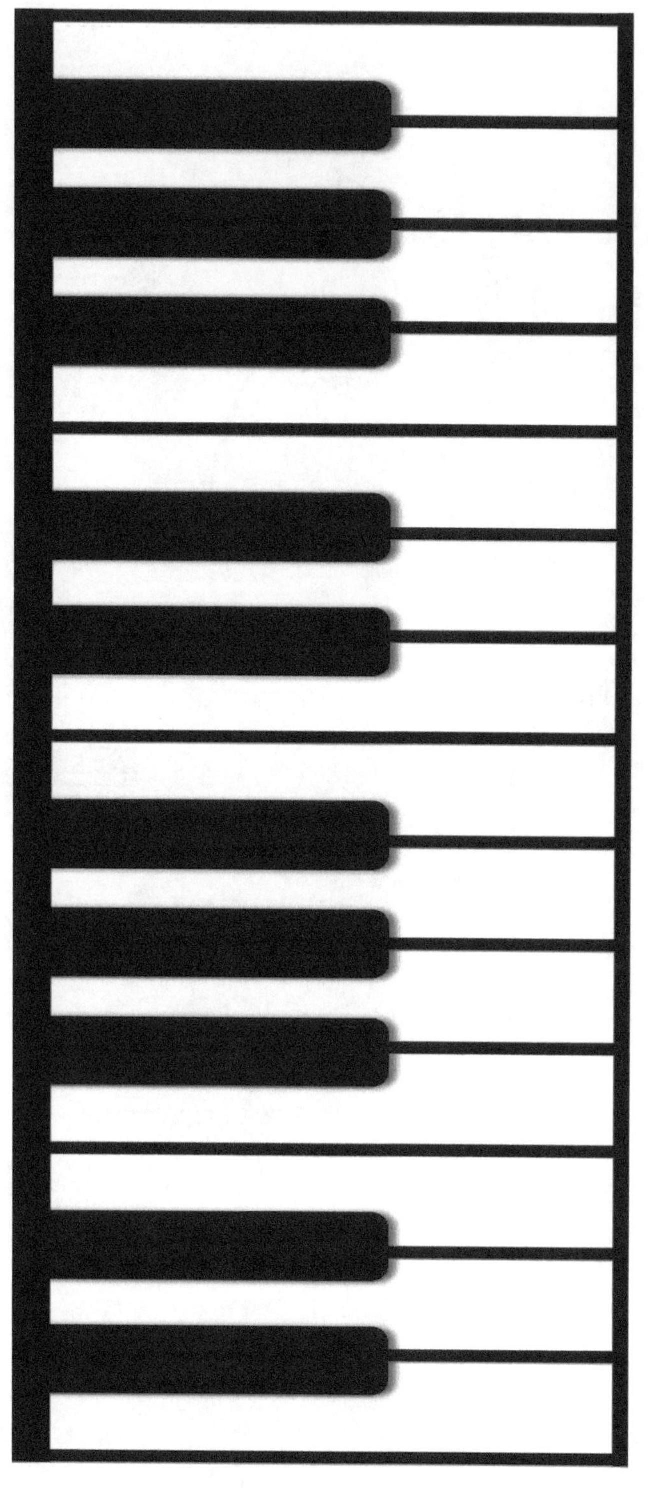

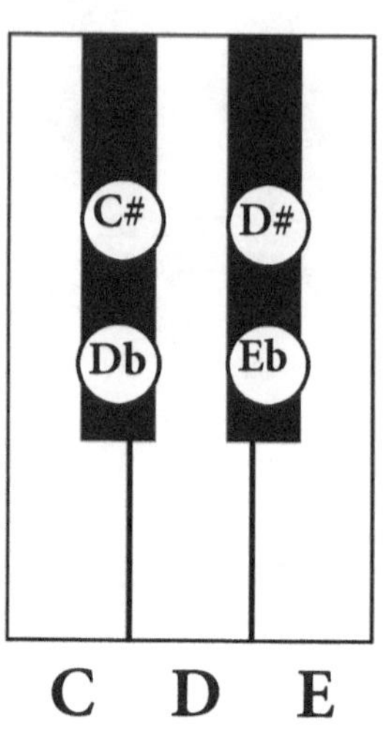

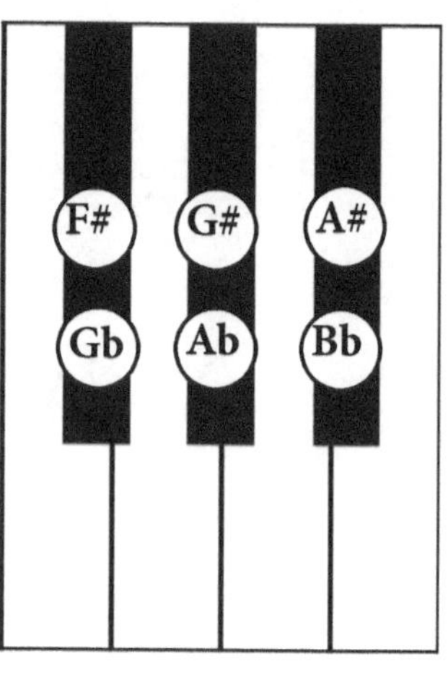

GLOSSARY

a tempo - Return to previous tempo.

Accel., Accelerando - Gradually becoming faster.

Accelerando, accel - Gradually faster.

Accent - placed above a note to indicate stress or emphasis.

Accidental - A sharp, flat, or natural not included in the given key.

Accompaniment - A vocal or instrument part that supports or is background for a solo part.

Adagio - Moderately Slow

Adagio - Slow; slower than andante, faster than largo.

Agitato - Agitated; with excitement.

Al coda - "To the coda."

Al fine - To the end.

Al segno - Return to the sign, Dal segno.

Alla breve - Cut time; meter in which there are two beats in each measure and a half note receives one beat.

Allargando, allarg - Slowing of tempo, usually with increasing volume; most frequently occurs toward the end of a piece.

Allegretto - A little slower than Allegro

Allegretto - Slower than allegro.

Allegro - Fast. Allegro - Quick tempo; cheerful.

Alteration - The raising or lowering of a note by means of an accidental.

Andante - "Walking" Tempo

Andante - Moderate tempo.

Andantino - A little faster than Andante

Andantino - Slightly faster than andante.

Animato - Animated; lively.

Appassionato - Impassioned.

Arpeggio - A term used to describe the pitches of a chord as they are sung or played one after the other, rather than simultaneously.

Articulation - The degree to which notes are separated or connected, such as staccato or legato.

Augmented - The term for a major or perfect interval which has been enlarged by one half-step, e.g. c-g, (an augmented fifth,) or c-d, (an augmented second). Also used for a triad with an augmented fifth, e.g. the augmented tonic triad in C major, C+, c-e-g.

Bar line - The vertical line placed on the staff to divide the music into measures.

Bass clef - The other name for the F clef.

Bis - Repeated twice.

Broken chord - Notes of a chord played in succession rather than simultaneously. Arpeggio.

C clef - A clef usually centered on the first line (soprano clef), third line (alto clef), fourth line (tenor clef), or third space (vocal tenor clef) of the staff. Wherever it is centered, that line or space becomes middle C.

Cadence - A chordal or melodic progression which occurs at the close of a phrase, section, or composition, giving a feeling of repose; a temporary or permanent ending. The most frequently used cadences are perfect, plagal, and deceptive.

Cadenza - a solo passage, often virtuosic, usually near the end of a piece, either written by the composer or improvised by the performer.

Caesura - A sudden silencing of the sound; a pause or break, indicated by the following symbol: //.

Calmo, calmato - Calm.
Chord - A combination of three or more tones sounded simultaneously.

Chromatic - Ascending or descending by half steps.

Chromatic scale - A scale composed of 12 half steps.

Circle of fifths - The succession of keys or chords proceeding by fifths.

Clef - A symbol placed at the beginning of the staff to indicate the pitch of the notes on the staff. The most commonly used clefs in choral music are the G, or treble, clef and the F or bass clef . On the keyboard, all the notes above middle C are said to be in the G clef; all the notes below middle C in the F clef.

Coda - Closing section of a composition. An added ending.

Common time - 4/4 meter.

Composer - A person who creates (composes) music.

Con - With.

Con brio - With spirit; vigorously.

Con calore - With warmth.

Con intensita - With intensity.

Con moto - With motion.

Con spirito - With spirit.

Concert grand piano - The largest of the grand pianos, usually about nine feet long.

Concert pitch - The international tuning pitch -- currently A 440 or 442. The pitch for non-transposing (C) instruments.
Concerto - A piece for a soloist and orchestra.

Conducting - The directing of a group of musicians.

Conductor - The person who directs a group of musicians.

Consonance - Intervallic relationships which produce sounds of repose. Frequently associated with octave, third and sixth intervals; however, fourths and fifths may be sounds of consonance, as in both early and 20th-century music.

Contra - The octave below normal.

Corda, corde - String.

Countermelody - A vocal part which contrasts with the principal melody.

Counterpoint - The technique of combining single melodic lines or parts of equal importance.

Crescendo - gradually become louder

Cue - Indication by the conductor or a spoke word or gesture for a performer to make an entry. Small notes that indicate another performer's part. Music occurrence in a film.

Cut time - 2/2 meter.

Da capo, D. C. - Return to the beginning.

Dal - "From the," "by the."

Dal segno, D. S. - Repeat from the sign . Frequently followed by al Fine.

Damper pedal - On pianos, the pedal that lifts the dampers from the strings.

Decrescendo - Gradually softer. Synonymous with diminuendo.

Degree - One of the eight consecutive tones in a major or minor scale.

Delicato - Delicately.

Di - Of, with.
Diminished - The term for an interval which has been decreased from the major by two half steps and from the perfect by one half step, e.g. c-a, diminished sixth, or c-g, a diminished fifth. Also used for a triad which has a minor third and a diminished fifth, e.g. c, c-e, g.

Diminuendo - gradually become softer

Dirge - A piece that is performed at a funeral or memorial service.

Dissonance - Sounds of unrest, e.g. intervals of seconds and sevenths; the opposite of consonance.

Divisi, div - An indication of divided musical parts.

Dolce - Sweetly.

Dolcissimo - Very sweetly.

Doloroso - Sadly; mournfully.

Dominant - The fifth degree of the major or minor scale. Also, the term for the triad built on the fifth degree, labelled V in harmonic analysis.

Double bar - Two vertical lines placed on the staff to indicate the end of a section or a composition. Also, used with two dots to enclose repeated sections.

Double flat - A symbol for lowering pitch one step.

Double sharp - A symbol for raising pitch one step.

Down beat - The first beat; given by the conductor with a downward stroke.
Duet - A piece for two performers.

Duplet - A group of two notes performed in the time of three of the same kind.

Dynamics - Varying degrees of loud and soft.

E - Italian word meaning "and."

Eighth - Octave.

Eighth note/rest - A note/rest half the length of a quarter note and an eighth of the length of a whole note.

Encore - To repeat a piece or play an additional piece at the end of a performance.

Enharmonic - A term used to describe notes of the same pitch which have different names, e.g. C# and Db, F# and

Gb.
Espressivo - Expressively.

Fermata - Hold; pause .

Festivo, festoso - Festive; merry.

Fifth - The fifth degree of the diatonic scale. Also, the interval formed by a given tone and the fifth tone above or below it, e.g. c up to g, c down to f. Intervals of the fifth may be perfect (corresponding to major), diminished, or augmented.

Fine - The end.

First ending - One or more measures which occur at the end of the stanza or stanzas. It is usually indicated:

Flat - A symbol which lowers the pitch of a note one half step.

Form - The design or structure of a musical composition .

Forte - Loud.

Fortissimo - Very loud.

Fortississimo - fff, Very Very Loud

Fourth - The fourth degree of the diatonic scale. Also, the interval formed by a given tone and the fourth tone above or below it, e.g. c up to f; c down to g. Intervals of the fourth may be perfect, diminished, or augmented.

Full score - An instrumental score in which all the parts for the instruments appear on their own staves in standard instrumental family order.

Fz - Forzando or forzato. Synonomous with sforzando (sf or sfz).

Giocoso - Playful.
Giubilante - Exultant, jubilant.

Glissando - Gliss. The rapid scale achieved by sliding the nail of the thumb or third finger over the white keys of the piano. Glissando is commonly used in playing the harp. For bowed instruments glissando indicates a flowing, unaccented playing of a passage.

Grand piano - A piano with a winglike shape and a horizontal frame, strings, and soundboard.

Grand staff, Great staff - The G and F clef staves together make the grand (great) staff.

Grandioso - Grandiose, majestic.

Grave - Slow, solemn.
Grazia - Grace. Con grazia, with grace.

Grazioso - Graceful.

Grosso, grosse - Great, large.

Half step - The interval from one pitch to the immediately adjacent pitch, ascending or descending, e.g. c-c; e-e; b-c. The smallest interval on the keyboard.

Harmony - The sounding of two or more tones simultaneously; the vertical aspect of music.

Interval - The distance in pitch between two tones.

Key signature - The sharps or flats placed at the beginning of the staff to denote the scale upon which the music is based.

Lamento - Mournful, sad.

Langsam - Slow.

Largamente - Broadly.
Larghetto - Slower than largo.
Largo - Very slow.

Largo, Lento - Slow

Ledger lines - Short lines placed above and below the staff for pitches beyond the range of the staff.

Legato - Smooth, connected.

Leggiero - Light; graceful.

Lento - Slow; slightly faster than largo, slower than adagio.

Liberamento - Freely.
Linear - Melodic; horizontal lines.

Maestoso - Majestically.

Major - The designation for certain intervals and scales. A key based on a major scale is called a major key.

Major chord - A triad composed of a root, major third, and perfect fifth.

Mancando - Fading away

Marcato - Emphasized, heavily accented.

Measure - A group of beats containing a primary accent and one or more secondary accents, indicated by the placement of bar lines on the staff. The space between two bar lines.

Melody - In general, a succession of musical tones. It represents the linear or horizontal aspect of music.

Meno - Less.

Meno mosso - Less motion.

Messa di voce - gradually becoming louder then softer

Meter - The structure of notes in a regular pattern of accented and unaccented beats within a measure, indicated at the beginning of a composition by a meter signature.

Meter signature - The numbers placed at the beginning of a composition to indicate the meter of the music, e.g. . The upper number indicates the beats in a measure; the lower number tells what kind of a note will receive one beat.

Metronome - Invented by Maelzel in 1816, the instrument is used to indicate the exact tempo of a composition. An indication such as M.M. 60 indicates that the pendulum, with a weight at the bottom, makes 60 beats per minute. A slider is moved up and down the pendulum to decrease and increase the tempo. M.M. = 80 means that the time value of a quarter note is the equivalent of one pendulum beat when the slider is set at 80.

Mezzo - Half, Medium

Mezzo forte - Medium loud.

Mezzo piano - Medium soft.

Middle C - The note C in the middle of the Grand staff, and near the middle of the piano.

Minor - The designation for certain intervals and scales. A key based on a minor scale is called a minor key. Misterioso - Mysteriously.

Moderato - Moderate speed.

Molto - Very. Used with other terms, e.g. molto allegro.

Mosso - Rapid. Meno mosso, less rapid. Piu mosso, more rapid.

Moto - Motion. Con moto, with motion.

Music - The organization of sounds with some degree of rhythm, melody, and harmony.

Music theory - The study of how music is put together.

Natural - A musical symbol which cancels a previous sharp or flat.

Non - No; not.

Non troppo - Not too much. Used with other terms, e.g. non troppo allegro, not too fast.

Notation - A term for a system of expressing musical sounds through the use of written characters, called notes.

Note - The symbol which, when placed on a staff with a particular clef sign, indicates pitch.

Octave - The eighth tone above a given pitch, with twice as many vibrations per second, or below a given pitch, with half as many vibrations.

Ossia - "Or." Indicating an alternative passage or version.

Ostinato - A repeated melodic or rhythmic pattern, frequently appearing in the bass line.

Ottava - Octave.

Ottava alta - (8va) An octave higher.

Ottave bassa - (8va or 8vb) An octave lower.

Perfect - A term used to label fourth, fifth, and octave intervals. It corresponds to the major, as given to seconds, thirds, sixths, and sevenths.

Perfect interval - Interval of an octave, fifth, or fourth without alteration.

Perfect pitch - The ability to hear and identify a note without any other musical support.

Pesante - Heavy.

Pianissimo - pp, Very Soft

Pianississimo - Very, very soft; the softest common dynamic marking.

Piano - p, Soft

Pianoforte - "Soft-loud." A keyboard instrument, the full name for the piano, on which sound is produced by hammers striking strings when keys are pressed. It has 88 keys.

Pitch - The highness or lowness of a tone, as determined by the number of vibrations in the sound.

Piu - More. Used with other terms, e.g. piu mosso, more motion.

Pizzicato - "Pinched." On string instruments, plucking the string.

Poco - Little. Used with other terms, e.g. poco accel., also, poco a poco, little by little.

Poco ced., Cedere - A little slower.

Poco piu mosso - A little more motion.

Prestissimo - Very, very fast. The fastest tempo.

Presto - Very Fast

Quarter note/rest - A note/rest one half the length of a half note and one quarter the length of a whole note.

Quartet - A piece for four instruments or voices. Four performers.

Quasi - Almost. Used with other terms, e.g. quasi madrigal, almost or as if a madrigal.

Rallentando, rall - Gradually slower. Synonymous with ritardando.

Range - The full amount of pitches, from low to high, which a singer may perform or instrument produce.

Relative major and minor scales - Major and minor scales which have the same key signature.

Repeat - The repetition of a section or a composition as indicated by particular signs.

Resonance - Reinforcement and intensification of sound by vibrations.

Rest - A symbol used to denote silence.

Rhythm - The term which denotes the organization of sound in time; the temporal quality of sound.

Rinforzando - A reinforced accent.

Risoluto - Resolute.

Rit., Ritardando - Gradually becoming slower

Ritardando, rit - Gradually slower. Synonymous with rallentando.

Ritenuto - Immediate reduction in tempo.

Roman Numeral – a system of labeling chords to show how the function within a key.

Root - The note upon which a triad or chord is built.

Rubato - The term used to denote flexibility of tempo to assist in achieving expressiveness.

Scale - A succession of tones. The scale generally used in Western music is the diatonic scale, consisting of whole and half steps in a specific order.

Scherzo - "Joke." A piece in a lively tempo. A movement of a symphony, sonata, or quartet in quick triple time, replacing the minuet.

Score - The written depiction of all the parts of a musical ensemble with the parts stacked vertically and rhythmically aligned.

Secco - "Dry." Unornamented.

Second - The second degree of the diatonic scale. Also, the interval formed by a given tone and the next tone above or below it, e.g. c up to d, or c down to b. Intervals of the second may be major, diminished, or augmented.

Section - A division of a musical composition.

Semitone - A half step. The smallest interval on the keyboard.

Semplice - Simple.

Sempre - Always. Used with other terms, e.g. sempre staccato.

Senza - Without. Used with other terms, e.g. senza crescendo.

Sequence - The repetition of a melodic pattern on a higher or lower pitch level.

Seventh - The seventh degree of the diatonic scale. Also, the interval formed by a given tone and the seventh tone above or below it, e.g. c up to b, or c down to d. Intervals of the seventh may be major, minor, diminished, or augmented.

Sforzando, Sfz, Sf - Sudden strong accent on a note or chord.

Sharp - A symbol which raises the pitch of a note one-half step.

Sheet music - An individually printed song, most often for voice, piano, guitar,or a combination of the three. Any printed music.

Simile - An indication to continue in the same manner.

Sixteenth note/rest - A note/rest half the length of an eighth note and a sixteenth the length of a whole note.

Sixth - The sixth degree of the diatonic scale. Also, the interval formed by a given tone and the sixth tone above or below it, e.g. c up to a, or c down to e. Intervals of the sixth may be major, minor, diminished, or augmented.

Slur - A curved line placed above or below two or more notes of different pitch to indicate that they are to be performed in legato style.

Smorzando - Fading away.

Suave - Sweet, mild.

Sostenuto - Sustaining of tone or slackening of tempo.

Staccato - Detached sounds, indicated by a dot over or under a note. The opposite of legato.

Staff - The most frequently used staff has five horizontal lines, with four spaces, upon which the notes and other musical symbols are placed.

Subito - Suddenly.

Tempo - The rate of speed in a musical work.

Tempo primo - Return to the original tempo.

Tenor clef - The C clef falling on the fourth line of the staff.

Tenuto, ten - Hold or sustain a note longer than the indicated value, usually not as long a duration as the fermata.

Tertian harmony - A term used to describe music based on chords arranged in intervals of thirds.

Texture - The term used to describe the way in which melodic lines are combined, either with or without accompaniment. Types include monophonic, homophonic, and polyphonic, or contrapuntal.

Theory - The study of how music is put together.

Third - The third degree of the diatonic scale. Also, the interval formed by a given tone and the third tone above or below it, e.g. c up to e, or c down to a. Intervals of the third may be major, minor, diminished, or augmented.

Tie - A curved line over or below two or more notes of the same pitch. The first pitch is sung or played and held for the duration of the notes affected by the tie.

Time signature - Synonymous with meter signature.

Tonality - The term used to describe the organization of the melodic and harmonic elements to give a feeling of a key center or a tonic pitch.

Tone - A note; the basis of music.

Transposition - The process of changing the key of a composition.

Treble clef - The G clef falling on the second line of the staff.

Triad - A chord of three tones arranged in thirds, e.g. the C-major triad c-e-g, root-third-fifth.

Trill, tr - A musical ornament performed by the rapid alternation of a given note with a major or minor second above.

Triple meter - Meter based on three beats, or a multiple of three, in a measure.

Triplet - A group of three notes performed in the time of two of the same kind.

Troppo - Too much. Used with other terms, e.g. allegro non troppo, not too fast.

Tutti - All. A direction for the entire ensemble to sing or play simultaneously.

Un poco - A little.

Una corda - Soft pedal.

Unison - Singing or playing the same notes by all singers or players, either at exactly the same pitch or in a different octave.

Upbeat - One or more notes occurring before the first bar line, as necessitated by the text for the purpose of desirable accent. The unaccented beat of a measure.

Variation - The manipulation of a theme by the use of melodic, rhythmic, and harmonic changes.

Vibrato - Repeated fluctuation of pitch.

Vivace - Lively, brisk, quick, and bright.

Whole note/rest - A note/rest equal to two half notes and four quarter notes.